FROM PRIVATE TO

To Roger –
Whose help made
this book possible –

Amy

FROM PRIVATE TO PUBLIC

A Feminist Exploration of Early Mothering

by

AMY ROSSITER

The
Women's
·Press·

CANADIAN CATALOGUING IN PUBLICATION DATA

Rossiter, Amy B. (Amy Burdick), 1948-
From private to public

Includes bibliographic references.
ISBN 0-88961-128-9

1. Mother and infant 2. Motherhood – Social
aspects 3. Patriarchy. 4. Women – Socialization.
I. Title.

HQ759.R67 1988   306.8′743   C88-094838-8

Copyright © 1988 Amy Rossiter

Cover art: Jody Hewgill
Cover design: Christine Higdon
Editor and copy editor: Susan Berlin
Proofreaders: Kate Forster and Ellen Quigley

Published by
The Women's Press
229 College Street No. 204
Toronto, Ontario M5T 1R4

This book was produced by
the collective effort of members of
The Women's Press
This book was a project of
the Social Issues Group.

The Women's Press gratefully acknowledges
financial support from The Canada Council
and the Ontario Arts Council

Printed and bound in Canada

CONTENTS

Acknowledgments

I would like to express my heartfelt gratitude to the following people who were invaluable during the process of writing this book:

To my children Kate and Ben, who taught me so much of this book.

To my husband Jamie, who made the work possible by giving unstinting loyalty, time, and support in the following ways: emotional, economic, practical, and technical.

To Susan Berlin, a fine editor who became a good friend.

To Roger Simon, who is unusually gifted at offering both challenge and encouragement.

To Sue Malla, who inspired many of the ideas in this book through our stimulating hours of discussion about motherhood.

To Joyce Coombs, who listened patiently and responded helpfully.

To Bluma Litner, with whom I had many productive theoretical discussions, and who provided much-needed boosts to my morale.

To Marilyn Taylor, whose talent for facilitation helped me immeasurably at the beginning.

To Kathy Rockhill, Jeri Wine, and David Hunt, who encouraged me to find and follow my own direction.

And finally to the participants of the study, whose generosity and openness provided the stimulating interactions on which the inquiry is based.

PART
I

INTRODUCTION

For me, to become a mother, despite the delight I took in my relationship with my children, was also to become angry: through motherhood, I learned that I was a woman in patriarchy. This book is part of my ongoing effort to understand the contradictions between motherhood and feminism.

I began the research for the book when my daughter was three and my son was one year old. At that time, I could not have articulated exactly what I wanted to know; but through the process of interviewing new mothers, working with the data, and writing, I gradually began to formulate my questions and to understand the relationship of the data to those questions. In fact, it was only at the end of the research process that I fully understood my central question: how does the way our society organizes mothering help to create the concept "Woman" as it exists in capitalist patriarchy?

I had been a feminist well before I became a mother. Until my children were born, I went along quite nicely – feeling in charge of myself (or so I thought) and setting my own direction, which included the women's movement. For me at that time, feminism meant a commitment to issues of equal rights, rather than an exploration of the complexity of gendered subjectivity.

When my first baby was born, it became less and less possible to ignore how I myself had been formed – was being formed – within a social context. Radical changes – isolation, no longer going to work, being responsible for a new human being, the devaluation of my own needs – seemed to come with the territory of being a mother. With them came the realization that I was inextricably bound up with my social context; that I was no exception to the demands of patriarchy. I could no longer view myself as a person who controlled her own destiny and (parenthetically) believed in the equality of women. This realization started me on the road toward an understanding of how my experiences were put together *out-*

side me, in the interests of capitalist patriarchy, and then made to seem *my choice.*

As a mother with young children, the connections between mothering and patriarchy were clear to me. I stayed home with the kids; consequently, I lived isolation, financial dependency, deprivation of work, and depletion of my energy from constant caretaking. But I *chose* to stay home. It would have been easy to dismiss this choice as the result of my acculturation to the ideology of "the good mother"; but, in fact, that was not the truth. The truth was that my babies and small children were more attached to me and more dependent on me because of our special bodily relationship. I had birthed them. I spent six hours every day nursing them. Nursing soothed and comforted them, so I had the edge on my husband for feeding, soothing, comforting, and in the amount of time I spent with them.

When I read biologistic explanations of mothering it was with absolute terror – because, if those explanations were to be believed, they implied an inevitable triumph of patriarchy through the body. Furthermore, feminist attempts to reconcile a biologically-based preferential infant attachment with a "feminist project" – palliative solutions in the form of "let's make life better for mothers" – completed a picture of despair: making a bad situation better certainly would not transform gender relations. Greater respect for mothering, financial incentives, mom / tot programs were good short-term goals, but they didn't compensate for my knowledge that I was living a life which perpetuated patriarchy. In fact, working toward such goals often felt placatory, like being given a bribe to make patriarchy feel less painful.

So I turned to "social construction" approaches, hoping that mothering could be shown to be socially produced, and therefore open to transformation. I read Nancy Chodorow (1978) and Dorothy Dinnerstein (1976), whose works reject biologism in favour of psychoanalytic approaches to why women mother – essentially a culturalist position. Chodorow, for example, argues that those social arrangements of mothering which make women the sole caretakers of children create relationships which produce girls who not only want to mother, but have the nurturing capacities required to mother successfully. On the other hand, boys' psychological reaction to the necessary separation from the caretaking mother is to push themselves towards public life – where the verification of masculinity can be found.

While this explanation eliminates the biologistic basis for preferential attachment, it doesn't deal with claims regarding the effects of children's special and intense vulnerability to women. After all, I had a one-year-old son who loved me better than anyone else; according to social constructionist theory, he would have to stop this in order to grow up to be a man. I had a three-year-old daughter who also loved me more than anyone else; for her, being in an intense relationship with me was socially permitted.

I was therefore stuck on the horns of a very painful dilemma: I believed that children's attachment to their mothers was based on their physical relationship to the maternal body; yet I understood that same preferential attachment to be implicated in the maintenance of patriarchy.

What made this dilemma so painful was that it precluded feminist action. If I worked toward the goals suggested by biologistic explanations, I was making sole-caretaking by women more tolerable, and thus working in service of the psychological underpinning of patriarchy. On the other hand, if I opted for equal parenting, I denied my body and my baby.

Trying to make sense of all this in the real world, I ended up in ridiculously painful situations: for instance, while my husband was giving an objecting baby a bottle, I would be expressing milk from an overly-full breast into the sink. In my guts, I felt that the fact of uterus and breasts precluded equal attachment – at least in infancy. When I denied my body and baby in favour of an equal parenting solution, it felt bad for my baby and for me.

Sometime near the completion of the research, I read some work by Monique Wittig which seemed to go straight to the heart of my dilemma.

Wittig starts from the position that "... one is not born a woman." For Wittig, "woman" is a *concept construction* created through social relations. Wittig's target is essentially the re-creation of groups of people into categories:

> They [race or sex] appear as though they existed prior to reasoning, belonging to a natural order. But what we believe to be a physical and direct perception is only a sophisticated and mythic construction, an 'imaginary formation' which reinterprets physical features through the network of relationships in which they are perceived. (They are seen *black,* therefore they are black; they are seen *women,* therefore they are women.) But before being seen that way, they first had to be *made* that way. (Wittig, 1979, p. 71)

At first glance, it appears that Wittig denies the body when she claims Woman (like Race) to be a social construction – yet in fact she acknowledges clearly that these are people with breasts, vaginas, black skins. She insists, however, that it is the *concept constructions* which are overlaid on those differences – not the differences themselves – which form the categories of oppression.

I began to understand a way out of my dilemma. I had already learned that mothering as a social form was intricately tied to patriarchy. However, that knowledge was not enough: it is doomed to be entangled on the horns of biologism or culturalism unless one also understands that the construction of mothering is always done *in and through* the concept Woman. The importance of understanding the construction of

14

the concept Mothering is that we can then understand how mothering works to continuously construct the concept Woman.

My contention, then, is that the relationship between mothering and patriarchy can only be understood if we look not only at how women reproduce Mothering, but at how Mothering reproduces Woman. Nancy Chodorow may well have answered the question of why women want to mother; but she neglected to inquire how the enactment of that desire produces Woman.

I am arguing that mothering is a powerful site for enforcing women's constitution as Woman. We can see mothering producing Woman in the countless minute interventions of power in daily life: to be isolated, dependent, "too fat," to have nothing to say, is to be Womaned through mothering. (It should be clearly understood, of course, that mothering is neither a necessary nor an exclusive site for the construction of Woman – being a spinster or a lady plumber produces us as Woman as well.)

The practices of mothering in our society produce a person who is a caretaker, and her function justifies her exclusion from the public sphere in a variety of ways. Perhaps most importantly, in the economic arena, if she works in order to feed her kids, her absence from the home "deprives" them; while if she works because she enjoys it, she is "selfish." Thus, a mother is made Woman every day through ordinary, everyday practices. These practices have been overlaid on maternal-infant attachment for so long that we have come to understand that attachment, based in biology, as necessitating a *particular form* of mothering called "staying at home." We have lost the actual history of women's separation from the workplace, while the social arrangements of mothering are made to seem the "natural and normal" outcome of attachment.

If we can deconstruct the ways in which our mothering

arrangements produce Woman, we can begin to *refuse the assumption that preferential attachment of infants to mothers dictates a particular kind of social arrangement of mothering.* When we can do this we will be free to acknowledge early preferential attachment as of course related to the needs of the body, without fear that we need accept patriarchy as an inevitable outcome of that attachment, of those needs. We will be able to act, as feminists, with the political purpose of disconnecting Woman from women with attached babies rather than with the hopeless goal of denying the reality of the attachment.

It was only in retrospect, however, that it became clear to me that these questions formed a political project. At the beginning of the research, I was aware only of my own experience of a contradiction between feminism and mothering. The central perception with which I began my work, therefore, was the desire to understand how our natural, normal, daily lives as mothers reproduced patriarchy. This question guided my decisions about how to conduct the research.

I felt very critical of much traditional research, on the grounds that its inherently political character was often obscured in order to fortify the "scientific" stance on which its claim to authority was based. The issue of authority is an important one for women: if research reflects an understanding of our culture, then it is clear that such understanding should articulate women's experience within patriarchy. But women most often find themselves described in social science in ways that fit male images of who they are – and these images, in turn, are crucial in directing women to accept the demands of capitalist patriarchy.

For me, Marx's discussion of ideological inversion – the creation of an abstraction based on a fact and the subsequent representation of that fact as based on the abstraction – was connected to the issue of regulation. I felt that the process was critical in producing the cultural images which form our subjective selves. It was clear to me that images of "mothers," when produced by experts, come to define mothering – that is, to lay claim to all that can be said about mothering, to become final statements of how mothers *naturally are*. This process leaves mothers attempting to relate their experiences to such images, rather than themselves making images which conform to their own concrete experiences.

I felt, also, that the ideology of individualism, as it attributes emotions, actions, and motivations to mothers *as individuals,* creates abstractions about mothers with the goal of achieving social control, rather than of exploring the real experience of mothers. William Ray Arney, critiquing the "scientific" basis of bonding theory by exposing its political and cultural roots, concludes that

> ... the scientists' knowledge is accorded a privileged status and is used to prevent women's knowledge from being heard and considered. (Arney, 1980, p. 566)

Individualistic ideologies in the form of biologism shape beliefs that the consequence of women's reproductive capacity is "naturally" the way families are organized. Mothers need to be at home with their children because of instincts and hormones; without access to knowledge of the historical and social creation of the *forms* of mothering, political purpose is lost.

Understanding the social construction of mothering is essential to an ability to resist "knowledge" about mothers – knowledge created by abstractions, which controls women through individualism and biologism. An approach which defies such abstractions must necessarily begin with the concrete; it must begin with the practices which make up daily life. This conviction necessarily informed my decisions about method.

THE METHOD

The need to see and address the concrete in my subjects' lives came from my desire to change the way women are represented in our culture. Images of mothering, created by men who are located in the ruling apparatus, have helped to structure women's concepts of mothering. We are led to believe, for example, that our culture's organization of mothering derives from nature. When this "fact" becomes part of our common-sense knowledge, we tend to overlook the organization of mothering through history, through the material world, and through language. Overlooking these constitutive processes enables us to overlook the ways in which we create a culture built on relations of domination.

Oppression exists because we do it every day. Oppression can only occur through our concrete actions. If we are to understand the historical, linguistic, and material practices which produce mothering as a process of patriarchy, then we must look at the sites in which that process is carried out. It is only in the ordinary sites of daily life that we can observe the operation of power as it works to maintain relations of domination. Our task, then, is to analyze power as it is made visible in sites of contradiction between common-sense knowledge and knowledge of socially constructed practices of oppression.

Yet if I am shaped by patriarchy's understandings about the "natural and normal," how can I begin an inquiry? How can I deconstruct how I am made?

This inquiry began with a set of contradictions generated from my dual position as reproducer of patriarchy through mothering, and as a feminist in opposition to patriarchy. The existence of these contradictions impelled me to search for a new form of discourse which would allow me to speak about those contradictions.

There were several understandings – concepts which felt

true to me – which underpinned the need to find a new discourse. Those understandings were the starting points which allowed me to begin to "look outside" the taken-for-granted. Those understandings helped me focus on, be interested in, things which initially had only obscure or partial meaning to me.

One such understanding was feminism's discovery that women's reality is not represented in culture. Women's voices are excluded from dominant representations of "life": since culture has been made by men, women have been unable to find conceptual structures which describe their reality. In areas of the dominant culture in which women have been represented, bits and pieces of women's experience have been lifted out of the context of women's lives, and a version explaining those pieces has been constructed in the interests of the ruling apparatus; those versions have then been re-absorbed by women as both natural and ideal. The pieces of womens' actual experience that don't fit into the "official" versions of reality become sources of shame or discomfort, fit only for burial in our ignorance.

Nevertheless there were pieces of my experience that stuck out of ideological versions like sore thumbs. The pieces that stuck out, although they didn't form a pattern or a concept, pointed to two assumptions which underscored my attempts at looking outside my contradictions. The first assumption was that Something could be found in Nothing – since apparently mothering was made up of doing Nothing. "No, I'm not working now"; "Dr. Ross delivered the baby"; "I didn't do anything today." Yet I knew that all of that Nothingness was in fact Everything: that is, the reproduction of the next generation, physically and emotionally. Always, when I looked out, I stubbornly believed there was Something in all that Nothing.

Secondly, my own experiences taught me that it wasn't me, with my knowledge of myself and my babies, that organized my life. What I did as a mother came from outside, came from a place that was different from the inner reason of my experience. For instance, following the birth of each of my children, I lay awake, too excited to sleep and yearning to see the baby – but it had been taken away so that I could sleep. Again, when my children were small, even though I hated isolation, I was alone all day. I didn't go to public events for fear of causing a disruption, although my babies rarely cried. These situations presented themselves to me as "natural and normal," the way my life should go; yet the organization of that "normalcy" always seemed to take place outside me, beyond my grasp. Part of looking outside, then, was looking at where and why the experiences of mothers were put together as they were.

These ideas formed the basis of my "positive paranoia" (Mary Daly, 1978) regarding the experiences of mothering. The work of the research, then, would be to use the state of mothering as a "dis-ease" which could stir contradiction toward new discourse, rather than as a "disease" which would lead to shame and madness.

I felt that in order to understand the organization of mothering experiences, it would be necessary for me to turn to the histories of other women who were in the process of beginning mothering. Having access to such histories would help to make my own experiences more conscious and visible.

I selected five women for interviews; I chose them because each was, in a number of ways, quite different from me; they came from different ethnic backgrounds and from different classes. Of the five sets of interviews, three were used to generate accounts of first-time mothering.

I came to the inquiry with the aim of looking for Something in Nothing, with the aim of hearing silence, and with a belief that Mothering is not natural and given. That was my part in the dialogue; that was the lens through which I looked out. Only the subject could tell me what *she* did not know, because of the specific way in which she was embedded in "... historical processes and the development of social relations which organize, shape and determine [her] directly experienced world" (Smith, 1981, p. 17). As the nature of ideology shapes me, too, as an "overlooker" of my *own* historical processes, it is only the subject who can teach me what neither of us knows.

To see my research as stemming from a "double subject" became crucial for me at the point at which I had to account for my selection – from among all the subjects' experiences – of those experiences which *taught me*. I took from those experiences what I needed to know: sites which could be explained through the discourses of subjectivity, patriarchy, social construction of knowledge, etc. The sites I chose to look at were actual, specific events, behaviours, or actions. Thus, while the subject would agree with me that she had spoken to me about being given an anaesthetic during childbirth, or that she hadn't gone out for six weeks, or that she was afraid she would be thrown out of shopping malls if she breastfed there, she had in fact told me about a great many other things as well. Out of all the experiences she told me about, I chose certain events to settle on and reflect about. And so, interviews reflected "territory shared." Data were grounded on the subjects' actual experience; yet that actual experience was organized through *my* meanings, the *subject's* meanings, our *shared* meanings.

This is really why I don't claim that the accounts in this inquiry are representations of the subjects' reality. Rather, the accounts are texts that were co-produced by myself and the subjects. I am not concerned with being able to verify the truth of "my" version of an account; I am concerned with establishing a means of judging the *quality* of the accounts, with an understanding that the goal of the account is to provide a text that is useful to both the inquirer and the subject in the process of naming their different realities.

A major criterion of an adequate account is that the subject and I must agree that the specific events as set forth in the text are accurately described. This is important because the subject must be able to recognize herself in the inquiry. The text must provide a coherent unfolding of the everyday life of the subject. I have tried to put forth a version of that everyday life which is close enough to the subject's experience to let her see herself in it, yet is far enough away, through interpretation, to let her make new knowledge out of her own experience.

An adequate account, from my point of view, must serve what I believe is the ultimate goal: facilitating the naming of one's own experience. The subjects and I encountered the texts from the perspectives of our different areas of ignorance and knowledge. While it was critical for us to have a common base in the concrete events of the text, we had to be able to differ openly in our understanding of those events; if we were to do this, my stake in the texts had to be clear.

For example, the subject and I would agree that her obstetrician had pulled out her placenta – but I would place that event in a discourse about power and the objectification of women's bodies during birth, while the subject would see it only in terms of the damage it might have done to her body. We differ. But I am able to say that I see it like that because I am a feminist, because I want to understand how women's oppression is done. The subject can say that it means something different to her, a difference that is based in her reality, on what is important to *her.*

In order to be adequate, the text must also provide the grounds for consideration of my own experience. My framework for developing the texts breaks with the ideology of individualism by focusing on the material, historical and discursive practices which organize early mothering; consequently, the accounts must enable me to understand the specific from the perspective of this framework.

THE INTERVIEW

As a method of data collection in social science research, traditional interviewing has increasingly come under attack. The
usual form of researcher/subject relationship has been characterized as a relationship of inequality, where the researcher's
power comes from the ability to determine content, posses-
sion of extra "knowledge," and control of methods.

Critics of such traditional interviews identify two general
sources of discomfort within the model: one is that the understanding of human experience is severely constrained by the
model – indeed, the true goals of science are violated by it; the
other is that traditional research relationships are exploitative
and manipulative, and that this exploitation does damage to
both researcher and subject.

Much feminist criticism has demonstrated the implicitly
political nature of research methods, and how a research relationship which excludes the personal can only reproduce cultural bias – because the subject can participate only according
to what is "allowed" by the researcher, who is obviously
located in his/her own biases.

Indeed, Ann Oakley (1981b), in what is probably the most
comprehensive article on interviewing women, explicitly
defines standard interviewing as a masculine paradigm. She
sees the norm of leaving out emotions and feelings as typical
of male culture. She finds that the "... motif of successful interviewing is to be 'friendly' but not too friendly ..." (p. 33) and,
in contrast, sums up her model for feminist interviewing as
follows:

> ... when a feminist interviews women: 1) the use of pre-
> scribed interviewing practice is morally indefensible; 2)
> general and irreconcilable contradictions at the heart of
> the textbook paradigm are exposed; and 3) it becomes
> clear that, in most cases, the goal of finding out about

people through interviewing is best achieved when the relationship between interviewer and interviewee is non-hierarchical and when the interviewer is prepared to invest his or her personal identity in the relationship. (Oakley, 1981b p. 41)

My interviewing practices didn't conform completely to Oakley's model, particularly with reference to the issue of *control of the relationship.* Oakley claims that interviewing women demands the establishment of an intimate non-hierarchical relationship, whereas I found that in carrying out my interviews I did not have the kind of control needed to allow me to say what kind of relationship would *evolve.* The relationships that developed between the subjects and myself did so out of the various kinds of needs the subjects brought to the relationship, as well as out of my needs as a researcher and as a person. Each relationship was specific to the two unique people involved, and could not have been determined in advance by one person as "going to be intimate and non-hierarchical." That is why first interviews, for me, were always filled with the fear of not knowing what I was getting into, of unease about making a start in a new relationship.

In the first "official" interview of the study, for instance, as I approached the subject's flat, I was anxiously thinking about what I was going to ask, whether the subject would like me, whether I would like her. As we headed up the stairs, however, she began to ask me about the signs of early labour, and even in my haze of anxiety it dawned on me that she was trying to tell me that she thought she was in labour. After we had established that she was, indeed, in early labour I made a few feeble attempts to tell her about the study and "begin interviewing," but that soon went out the window as our relationship was quickly shaped by our respective needs and viewpoints. I became the experienced one, the person who had been through it, who could give information, support, confidence. That particular subject became, under those very specific circumstances, a person whom I worked to take care of, whom I wanted to support – and in fact, those aspects of our relationship were maintained throughout the succeeding seven months: I always felt like mothering her, and she always saw me as an experienced mother. We had a history of sharing an exciting moment – one that could not have been predicted – and that fact helped to "shape" all our interviews.

I was in a class once in which a student expressed amazement that a subject, when interviewed by two different interviewers, had given each of them dissimilar material; the subject was virtually accused of lying or at least of hiding the truth. I believe, however, that people shape their speech in accordance with the audience and that good interviewing results not from attempts to pre-define relationships, but from an understanding of how each participant in a particular relationship unfolds as an audience to the other.

"Putting oneself into the interview" is often presented as a feminist cure for the ethical problems of traditional interviewing. I think such a "cure" is a red herring which only draws attention away from the real ethical issues of interviewing. I would like to suggest that a feminist interview is not characterized by "putting oneself in fully," but rather by the *intention of the interviewer*. To my mind there are two crucial notions within the concept of intention: the notion of discovering women's experience and the notion of women speaking for themselves. Clearly, these notions identify intention as *political* intention.

If those intentions define feminist interviewing – if we are to discover women's experience through hearing women speak for themselves – then the work of interviewing clearly resides in the activity of listening, rather than in "putting oneself in fully." Perhaps this confusion has arisen because, in our dichotomized Western thinking, listening is defined in "female" terms as passive, uninvolved, non-contributing – as not "putting ourselves in"; whereas in reality listening is the real work of interviewing.

It is therefore important, in developing method in feminist interviewing, to understand listening as doing: listening so that we can hear, make sense of and understand the language of women's experience. Listening is as active a task as talking.

In this study, the primary method of the interview was listening. The act of listening included a constant interrogation of my mental image of the subject's experience, usually to find out what was missing in my image, what was incomplete, how what she was saying was not meant for me.

From questioning the images, other questions arose. For example, if the subject mentioned she was tired "... for no good reason ..." my interest would be twigged at once, because of my desire to see the Something in Nothing. The statement "I've been tired lately for no good reason," might normally be overlooked, just one of those things, the way life is, just sort of "natural and normal." But in an interview where my interest was focused on Something in Nothing, I tried to develop an image of being "tired for no reason." No image came to mind – how could one be tired for no reason? Questions were formed in order to establish a meaningful image. What did she mean by "tired"? What did she do about being tired? Was she sleeping at night? Questions pushed at the meaning of being "tired for no reason." I began to see that *her* "being tired for no reason" was *my* idea of being depressed. I checked it out with the subject, and we agreed on a meaning. This example captures what for me is the essence of the work of listening.

I did not share my own experiences or talk about myself in the interviews – I felt that to talk about myself during the interviews would have pulled me away from the work of listening, since I could not have done both at the same time. How then do I account for the times when I *did* speak about my experiences? I think that many times I used my own experiences to try to enlarge the *conceptual space* in which events could be talked about. Dale Spender says,

> Many women have tried to articulate positive meanings of female outside the 'private' realm and have found that there is no readily available conceptual space to accommodate them.... They may begin to doubt the authenticity of those meanings, to 'lose conviction,' as Tillie Olsen puts it, because self-generated meanings can become vague, shadowy, and elusive when they have no outlet.... (Spender, 1980, p. 82)

Thus I often spoke about my experiences if I felt that a meaning was there but that the subject did not quite have a language for expressing it. Speaking from my own experience produced one of two outcomes: either the subject's own language and meaning emerged; or it became clear that I was wrong, that there had been no unexpressed meaning.

The development of intimacy was not a goal of the interviewing method. For me, it was important to be clear about why I was there: I was *not* there to meet my needs for intimacy; I didn't want to talk about my issues, as I would expect to in an intimate relationship. I was interviewing in order to develop as full a picture as possible of the subjects' experiences. Although this study originated in my own contradictions, and its adequacy depended partly on my ability to address those contradictions, that ability would come into play during analysis of the accounts, not during interviewing.

By its nature, an interview is problematic because it is the result of a relationship. To do in-depth, open interviewing requires that the interviewer maintain flexible personal boundaries in order to permit images of others' experiences to develop. It requires that the interviewer be empathic and have the ability to partially suspend her own meanings. But that very flexibility of boundaries sometimes causes problems: it can become difficult to distinguish one's own experience from the other person's. For example, at one point I had a problem with my own understanding of the difficulty one mother had in leaving her baby. I identified with her pain and felt that I really understood her process of dealing with it, because I had had a similar experience with my own children. However, when that particular mother got a job and went to work without a qualm, I realized that she was different from me, that there was a piece of her that I didn't understand. I don't think there are any easy answers to this dilemma of incorporation and differentiation. I ended up trying to consciously maintain flexible boundaries as a useful tension whenever I reached an awareness of their existence.

Another constant source of tension in the interview process came from the fact that I was both an experienced mother and a social worker with rescue tendencies. Usually, I felt great relief that my job was to listen and make sense of the subjects' difficulties, without the need to intervene; but there were times when I could make no clear distinctions between myself as Interviewer, as Sister/Mother, and as Rescuer. One such occasion arose when I arrived at a subject's home to find her very depressed and tearful about her constant isolation. I was torn between finding out more about the depression (Interviewer), helping her think about community resources (Rescuer), and telling her to walk to the drugstore and have a cup of coffee while I babysat (Sister / Mother). I ended up doing some combination of all three, rather incoherently, with doubts about whether I was "doing research." Again, I have no easy answers to this problem, but I feel it is important to document the complex nature of what is so blandly called an interview.

I would like to conclude this chapter with a discussion of how I handled the interview data and generated the accounts. This was a curious process marked both by tedious, routine and repetitive method, and by a creative, intuitive process that in some ways was outside my conscious control.

To be faced with approximately 2,500 pages of typed interview transcripts was daunting, to say the least. To make myself stay in the room with such a monstrous pile of raw data required sheer will power and many episodes of compulsive eating. My first approach was to read a set of transcripts several times, making notes and reviewing field notes. However, when I tried to write about the interviews, no order, no logic seemed evident. The problem with this process was that I was trying to find a Something whose name I did not know. Before I could write, the data had to teach me, and I had difficulty finding a method which allowed for my instruction by this mass of pages.

Finally, I started with the first page of transcript of the first subject I wanted to work with. (I had chosen Maria because her accounts reflected both similarities to and differences from my own experiences, and I felt that this would facilitate my being taught by her.) I took every statement made by the subject (except chitchat about where we would sit, did I take sugar in my coffee etc.) and tried to "place" it within a general category; I created about forty such categories. I physically cut each statement from the transcript and pasted it on a sheet of paper labelled with the appropriate category title.

I ended up with files varying in length from one to eight or even ten sheets of paper. If a statement seemed to belong to two or more categories, I noted this next to the paste-up. I could then begin to "learn" my material by categories: I could read everything the subject had said that fell into the category of "separation" for example; or "husband," "birth," "body," etc.

This tedious cutting and pasting procedure was long and boring, but proved essential in the process of separating myself from the subject's experience. It forced me to acknowledge what each subject had said, line by line, and prevented me from focusing on only those parts of what she had said that I already had meanings for. It was this part of the process that generated the surprises and the contradictions which forced me to suspend my own meanings in favour of what the subject was actually saying about herself. This was how the data taught me the accounts.

After I had organized the categories in what I thought was the best compromise between faithfulness to reality and the need for coherence, I began to write. As I did so, the unconscious connections which had been forming during my immersion in the data began to emerge into consciousness. The most valuable part of the research process, for me, was learning to have confidence that the connections were there and would come to consciousness if given time and opportunity.

Getting up from my desk, wandering around the house in a fog of data, staring mindlessly into the refrigerator was at first frightening as well as fattening. But usually the inchoate fascination with the data, fed by attempts to really "know" it, produced – at a level that was out of conscious control – a clearer understanding of why I was fascinated, of how the data entered into the larger picture I was piecing together.

CHAPTER ONE

THE WOMEN IN THE STUDY

MARIA, TINA, AND NATALIE are the women whose experiences of early motherhood are the focus of this book. I worked with them over a period of approximately seven months; with each of them, the first interview took place shortly before the birth of the child, and interviews terminated when the babies were six months old. I met with each woman eight times.

MARIA

Maria and her husband Tony live in a lower-middle-class / working-class Italian neighbourhood in Toronto. Their apartment is on the third floor of a low-rise building which is clean but not fancy: there are no buzzers, intercoms or elevators; the hallways are somewhat shabby, with patterned indoor-outdoor carpeting on the floor and gold-flecked wall paper. The sounds of TVs and the afternoon soaps filter through the varnished and crackly doors into the hall.

On my first visit, Maria seemed to me to be a warm person – she had a pleasant face and a friendly manner. I was immediate reassured – I knew I was going to like her. It was going to be all right. Her apartment was tidy and clean – a small two-bedroom, with a new dinette set beside the kitchen, a brown plush sofa, and walls decorated with wedding pictures. The apartment felt calm.

We talked about the study. Actually, my profession was of more interest to Maria than the study itself. She wanted to know if I had my B.A., and when I explained that I had done my M.S.W. some years ago she was very impressed. Education meant a great deal to her. She agreed to participate in the study, saying it would be a good opportunity to talk about the impending new experiences.

Until she stopped working well along in her pregnancy, Maria had been a child-care worker. Trained in a community college, she had her child-care certificate. Her husband Tony, a certified mechanic, had recently set up a partnership, and now owned and operated a service station.

BIOGRAPHICAL DATA

Maria is a 23 year-old Canadian-Portuguese woman. She came to Canada as an infant; she was the oldest of three children. Maria's family lives in Toronto; her father is a cook and her mother does not work outside the home. Neither of her parents speak English. Maria's two siblings and her grandmother live with Maria's parents.

Maria was educated in the separate school system and went to a Catholic girls' high school. In discussing her childhood, she mostly provided negative comments. She described the difficulties of being the eldest child – and a girl – in a family which maintained its Portuguese identity and wanted her to remain untainted by Canadian ways. Her father was the authority in the family, making all decisions about what Maria could or could not do – and Maria's mother backed up the authority of the father. Maria expressed resentment about having had to "break the ice." For example, she described her desire, as a teenager, to have a bike. Her father refused to let her have one because it would take her out in public, where boys could see her. She had never stopped wanting the bike, and was profoundly hurt when, long after Maria had married and was out of the house, her younger sister got a bike for her birthday.

Throughout the interviews, Maria's mother came across almost as a shadow figure. All through high school Maria was aware of her friends' "free" relationships with their mothers, and she yearned for closer emotional ties to her own mother; she longed to be able to talk to her mother and to be understood. She never achieved that closeness: her mother always held her off, unable to respond with the emotional intimacy her daughter needed. Maria remembers herself as clumsy, a "klutz," inadequate.

At the end of Grade 12, Maria experienced a crisis which still has implications for her life. Her parents valued education, and Maria had believed that somehow through education she could become worthy of their affection. She had always planned to go to university in order to become a teacher – this was her cherished image of making good. Then she met Tony. He held out the possibility of a relationship in which she would feel loved, a relationship which offered a way out of an unhappy home. But she saw marriage and university as irreconcilable, presenting an either/or choice. Tony offered her the sense of personal approval that she longed for, while university held out the prospect of becoming worthy. She had a "nervous breakdown," which gave rise to fears – which still plagued her at the time of the interviews – that she really was crazy.

After the seven months of "official" interviews, I saw Maria for counselling in the agency where I was employed; the interviews had raised issues which she felt she needed to explore further. At that time, I asked her to write about an area she had had difficulty speaking about in the interviews: her "nervous breakdown." She produced the following chronology:

Had a nervous breakdown before grade 12 end. Had to make the decision to go to college or university. The letting go of my dream – the denial of my whole saved up entire life – future goal – to prove who I was show them all what I could do but also have the sense of career.

love – very worthy course

[Tony] made me feel very good, worthwhile, respect as person, help me to stand up, feel freer, breathe easier, (a sense of humour)

very, very nervous, fidget, greasy hair, look awful, no appetite, state of depression, screaming – tension – study of exams

walk – Queen's Park

don't know what to do

talk to Guidance Counsellor

Mother doesn't see anything

Tony helped me out – tried to push him away but he really loved. stayed – so that convinced me – I pushed everything else aside – and denied all that – didn't need to prove myself anymore. To be loved was more important than to be my own person all of the sudden.

The last line of this statement reflects what for Maria was an ongoing dichotomy: to be loved or to be her own person.

Maria became engaged to Tony and did a child-care course at George Brown College. She married Tony and worked in a daycare centre until the birth of her daughter. For Maria, work was clearly a source of self-esteem. She spoke of her work with a sense of professional accomplishment – clearly taking it and herself seriously, enjoying it and experiencing it as a source of positive self-respect.

THE RESEARCH RELATIONSHIP

Maria experienced herself as torn between two identities: her "Canadian" and "Portuguese" selves. She saw herself as located in a Portuguese world – a world which she perceived as inhibiting and restricting her development as a person. Within her was a discourse called "Canadian," which contained all the spaces she wanted to claim for herself. For Maria, the term "Canadian" embodied meanings of freedom and independence; "Portuguese," on the other hand, stood for restriction and authority. The following table shows the issues about which Maria felt caught between her Portuguese and Canadian selves – usually while struggling to move to the Canadian side:

Portuguese	*Canadian*
no bikes	bikes
superstition	science
mother as authority	mother as nurturing friend
children must obey	children as people
women have no needs	women as people
ignorance	education
work	leisure
husband as breadwinner	husband as companion

As our relationship developed, Maria increasingly came to see me as a representative from the "Canadian" side of her struggles. I was North American, middle class, also a mother, educated, married, and I represented values to which she aspired. Those values had to do with respecting her needs, seeing her baby as a person, being sympathetic to her attempts to get out of the house, or being excited during her discussions about going back to school.

In an unspoken, unacknowledged process, I became a kind of mentor to Maria: someone who came from a place that attracted her, but from which she was still excluded. This left me wanting to support her attempts to reach for her own space – and also feeling guilty about not ever having had to reach for mine.

After the formal interviews had been completed, I invited Maria to my house for lunch. I wanted to acknowledge the reality of a relationship that had gone beyond researcher-subject limitations. It was a necessary but not entirely comfortable occasion. We both, I think (I am speculating here about Maria's point of view), felt the pain of wanting an egalitarian relationship within the terrible constraints of my already having what she still struggled so hard to get: status as a person, education, autonomy and freedom to raise one's children the way one thought best. In such circumstances, my own struggles could not be visible; hence genuine intimacy was precluded.

Some months later, I called to ask Maria to read the analysis, and to give me her comments and reactions. I found it very difficult to ask her to read the account; I was very anxious about whether I had the right to present her with my interpretation, which might seem like an imposition of my framework on her reality. I thought she might feel that I had withheld my "real" views for use in interpreting, and had thereby betrayed the relationship. In short, I was terrified about the ethics of what I was doing. I gave her the analysis and asked her to call me when she had read it.

When she phoned me back, I expected the worst. I was tremendously relieved that she wasn't furious with me, and in fact had felt positive about the account. Later, when we got together to talk about it, it seemed that most of the meaning which she took from the account was relief that I hadn't thought she was crazy. She was relieved that I saw her episodes of depression as tied to a concrete reality, which made her feelings legitimate; this was a major validation for her and the source of her real interest in the account.

It is this experience which made me aware of a difficulty in planning the interview process: we simply can't know what a subject needs in her own process of naming, but nevertheless we are responsible for providing accounts which contain space for the subject's interests as well as those of the researcher.

Wherever Maria and I differed in interpretation of the accounts, Maria provided her own rationale; usually we ended with a mutual acceptance of difference stemming from different viewpoints. For instance, when she read my interpretation of the removal of her placenta by the obstetrician, Maria said, "I know that's what happened, but I think you feel a lot angrier about it than I do."

My major concern in handling these differences was with respect to my interpretation of Maria's interaction with Tony. I was afraid she would see the account as a pigeon-holing of her husband as selfish and cruel. She laughed about that, saying he was who he was, a Portuguese man with particular expectations. She also mentioned positive things about him, things that hadn't emerged during the formal interviews; in fact, I saw some of those things myself while having dinner with Maria and Tony some time later.

One outcome of her relief that I – with my status as an educated Canadian – hadn't found her crazy was that Maria asked to spend some time with me at the family service agency where I was working part-time. Since by that time it was clear to me that Maria's fears of craziness stemmed from her "nervous breakdown" – a function of her marriage / career dilemma (read Portuguese / Canadian dilemma) – I saw the time we spent together in counselling as an extension of the mentoring relationship of the interviews.

The experience with Maria gave me a somewhat different view of the "adequacy of account" issue. From Maria's point of view, adequacy rested on the alleviation of her self-blame about craziness, on the recognition of the rationality of craziness. Adequacy rests on destroying the ideology which captures individuals within a rhetoric of shame and blame, destroying the possibilities of uncovering "revolutionary moments." The revolutionary moments which are important to *me* in Maria's account are not necessarily important to *her.* The important moment for her is the recognition, upon seeing herself reflected in the text, that she is not a person to be ashamed of.

TINA

Tina and her husband Ernesto (Ernie) live in a large, bright, airy house in a downtown, working-class mixed ethnic neighbourhood. They bought the house and totally renovated it: it is modern, comfortable and inviting.

Tina herself fits with the house. She is open and warm, with a bright, mobile face; I felt connected to her immediately. In the first interview she expressed interest in the research and asked quite penetrating questions about it. She was excited by the topic and felt the study would offer her a chance to discuss and reflect on the upcoming new experiences of motherhood.

In the first interview we talked about many things: yoga and its application to birth, distrust of doctors, going back to work after being at home with babies, her mother, etc. Tina went from topic to topic with great ease, sometimes leaving me behind with her high-speed leaps of thought.

Tina and Ernie are both teachers in the separate school system – Tina teaches primary school English and Ernie is a high-school social guidance teacher. Tina speaks fluent Italian and English, and the house seems filled with language: I spoke English with Tina and heard Italian used on the phone, with visitors, and with the baby. There was an inherent excitement to this interchange of languages.

BIOGRAPHICAL DATA

Tina is thirty-two years old. She was born in Toronto, the second child of an Italian immigrant family. Tina's father had been a carpenter in Italy, but with insufficient capital to start his own business in Canada, he got a job here as a cabinet maker. Tina's mother was pregnant with Tina when the family moved to Canada; a third child, Tina's sister, was born here some years later.

Tina's mother, who did not work outside the home, always longed to go back to Italy. There, she had lived in a small town surrounded by relatives and friends; in Canada, she had no social supports and didn't know the language. When she became pregnant with her fourth child, her husband sent her back to Italy, and a baby boy was born there. However, Tina's mother no longer "fit in" in Italy, and when her own mother – Tina's grandmother – died, she returned to Canada. She then became pregnant with her fifth child.

Soon after the birth of that baby, when Tina was twelve, Tina's mother went mad. As the oldest daughter, Tina assumed active care of her mother, dealing with medications, doctors, etc. The care of the fifth baby – another boy – fell to Tina as well. In the three years of her mother's madness, Tina recalls hours spent rocking the youngest child.

For Tina, school was a haven from the storms of family life. At home, her father was strict and authoritarian: he saw himself as the bulwark against permissive Canadian culture. "Normal" Canadian teenage social life was strictly prohibited.

Tina recalls her father as an extremely negative, bitter man to whom being happy and being right were inherently contradictory concepts. He chose being right. Tina sees much of her adolescence as having been one long revolt against him. Where he told her not to trust, she trusted; and his belief that there was nothing in life worth exploring influenced her need to seek out value in the world. To be like her father was, says

Tina, like death. At fourteen, in order to buy her own clothes so as not to be subject to his authority, she got a job by lying about her age. The experience of working was wonderful for her: she met different people and became part of the world she wanted to explore. She used to lie to her father about having to work extra hours just to walk along Yorkville Avenue and watch the people.

Her mother was her silent support. Never once did her mother take her father's side in the battles of adolescence; her message to Tina was, "Do what you feel." Tina sees her mother as open-minded and supportive, but trapped by circumstance and conditioning. As an example of the differences between her parents, Tina described their feelings about their house. It was a "standard" house, with a living room, kitchen and dining room; the design did not permit any flow between kitchen and dining room during family dinners. Tina's mother wanted to knock down the dividing walls to create a better space, but her father would never consider such nonconformity.

Tina and her older brother were close friends. When he went to university, he would come home to tell her about his world. He then transferred to another university, ostensibly because the subjects of interest to him weren't available in Toronto – but really that was an excuse to leave home. He took Tina to the new university on weekends, introducing her to art, music and literature. Tina and her older brother supported each other in the rejection of paternal authority as a constraint on curiosity and exploration.

Tina went to university and studied English. After graduating, she got a job as a primary-school English teacher. At the age of twenty she married Ernie – also of Italian background, also a teacher. She went back to school part-time and did her fourth year specialist certificate.

The couple began to have difficulties, particularly in the area of sexuality. Ernie began to have affairs, while Tina felt sexually unresponsive. At the age of 25, Tina went into psychotherapy and began to deal with the negation of sexuality with which she had been raised. When she was 27 she left Ernie. During this time she saw other people and arrived at some level of resolution about her body and sexuality. In the meantime, Ernie entered therapy and began to deal with the "macho" attitudes with which *he* was raised. After two years of separation, Tina and Ernie got back together; they both described their relationship as having improved immeasurably. They decided to begin a family.

At the time of the first interview, Tina was planning to take a maternity leave of three months, go back to work for the month of June and then take the summer holiday, which would let her be with the baby until September.

THE RESEARCH RELATIONSHIP

My sense of the relationship between Tina and myself was that we worked very much as colleagues. In contrast to both Maria and Natalie, who saw me as invested with things they did not have (Canadian-ness, class position, education, or access to the "right" answers) Tina and I, although we came from radically different class and ethnic backgrounds, were able to work collegially. Tina did not need me to join in her struggles for identity, as Maria and Natalie did; she had claimed her identity through the conflicts and struggles of late adolescence and early adulthood.

I think this left us with a sense of mutual goal: understanding the construction of mothering. Tina took the study seriously and never forgot that we were working toward conceptualizing her experience. We attempted to work out problems of meaning together. We saw ourselves as having a similar "location," and trying to work toward understanding that location in terms of motherhood; from that position, differ-

ences in background could be treated as *resources* for understanding differences in our current experience.

When I gave the account to Tina for comment, it was with
the same sense of dread as when I gave Maria her account.
Had my interpretations violated the nature of the relationship?
Did I have the right? Would the interpretation open up hurt,
would it wound? Yet Tina's reaction was to treat the account as
our work, and her first response was annoyance at sugges-
tions for improvement that had been pencilled in the margins
by an academic colleague. She felt protective of the work. Our
discussion of the account took place in a rather comical setting: we met at my house, and Tina defended me from my colleague as four children, busy setting up a lemonade stand on
the first muddy day of spring, trooped in and out. I defended
my colleague from Tina, trying to show her that the nature of
the colleague's comments were intended to protect Tina's
experience from interpretation.

In the process of reviewing the account with Tina, however, it became clear to me that the version which I had constructed from the viewpoint of my own interests was a version
that was usable by Tina as well. The sections that Tina most
valued were those which explained the personal as political;
of particular interest to her were the conflicts between Ernie
and herself, as interpreted through the lens of social construction rather than individualism. I think Tina and I have a shared
sense of the moments in the account which indicate where
change might be instigated.

NATALIE

Natalie and her husband Jim live in a bungalow in a suburban
development in east Toronto. It is a neat and tidy house with
new-looking furnishings and ruffled starched curtains. Natalie
was thirty-one at the time of the interviews.

Jim asked to sit in on the first interview so he could get an idea of what was involved in the study. I ended up explaining the study primarily to him, as Natalie seemed already to have made up her mind to participate – and once having done so, she didn't seem interested in the details. Jim, however, listened with curiosity. The two seemed very different: Natalie was forthright, somewhat brusque, and unambiguous, while Jim was quiet, soft-spoken and gentle.

My field notes reflect Natalie's characteristic need to feel in control. In that first interview, this became apparent in discussions about her job – she was a probation officer. She spoke of her clients as being lazy and manipulative; of good mothers as not using disposable diapers; of there being only three circumstances in which babies would cry; and of not having many friends and not wanting to. All her statements reflected a judgemental quality which seemed to be underlain by a fear of uncertainty. Her harshness disturbed me, and I wondered how successful I would be at interviewing her. Yet there was also a part of her that was warm and hospitable, and her caustic remarks were often tempered with wit. I was unsure about what kind of relationship would develop between us.

BIOGRAPHICAL DATA

Natalie was born in Saskatchewan, but spent most of her childhood in a small community east of Toronto. Her parents were Lithuanian immigrants.

Natalie spoke of her mother as being her best friend, which (she said) was why she had no need for other close friends. She spoke with respect of her mother's hardships and struggles. Her mother had been married to an older man at the age of eighteen, a marriage arranged by Natalie's grandmother as a way of ensuring her daughter's safety: the man had some money, and would be able to get his wife out of Lithuania. At nineteen, Natalie's mother had a baby, who died; at around the same time, her husband also died.

Natalie's mother had been in a Displaced Persons' camp in Germany, where she met Natalie's father and became pregnant with Natalie's older sister. Her mother and father were married in a civil ceremony; her mother never regarded the marriage as binding because it was not carried out as a rite of the church.

Following marital difficulties caused by her husband's sexual infidelities, Natalie's mother asked her own father – Natalie's grandfather – who had managed to immigrate to Canada, to sponsor her to come to Canada. When permission to immigrate came through, and without telling her husband, Natalie's mother left Germany for Saskatchewan. Upon finding out her whereabouts, her husband, claiming his moral right as father of her child, induced Natalie's mother to sponsor his immigration to Canada.

The couple's early years in Canada were marked by poverty. They lived apart on and off in those years – Natalie's mother staying in Saskatchewan (with the now three small children) while Natalie's father looked for work in Ontario. Eventually, his job situation stabilized, and the whole family moved to Ontario.

Natalie was brought up to respect obedience and "right and wrong." Police, laws, schools and church were "right" and were institutions to be respected. Her father was the family authority, who had next to no nurturing relationship with his children, but who meted out discipline and punishment. A belt was the threatened punishment – and according to Natalie, it had only had to be used a few times. Natalie claims as well that being brought up in a close-knit Lithuanian community also exacted obedience: many members of the community, not just family members, kept track of the children and brought them into line if they misbehaved.

Natalie went to a community college for two and a half years and then took a job as a probation officer. She detested the job, which she nevertheless held for approximately ten

years; she never felt sufficiently career-oriented to do anything else. In her early twenties, she married a man who
turned out to be a compulsive gambler and a drinker. Racked
by guilt at the thought of leaving him, feeling like a failure and
a social outcast, Natalie ended up in hospital with a "nervous
breakdown." During her hospitalization she made the decision to leave her husband, and did so – with guilt, but no
regrets.

Then came what Natalie called her "swinging singles"
period. She frequented downtown singles bars with the aim
of attracting men. Her whole identity, she felt, was linked to
being a married woman and having children, and she
believed that fate had destroyed the possibility of her achieving that identity. Then, just as she was adjusting to single life,
she met Jim.

Jim was the son of a minister, and he was a constable in the
R.C.M.P. – a position highly respected by Natalie. Natalie and
Jim had a goal in common: to be married and to have children.
After a short courtship, they married, and Natalie's intention
was to get pregnant as soon as possible and be able to quit her
job. She saw this as the beginning of what she was made to do
in life: to be a mother.

THE RESEARCH RELATIONSHIP

My relationship with Natalie was very complex. My initial
fears about responding negatively to her harsh judgemental
manner was soon a non-issue. It became obvious to me that,
while she often displayed characteristics that were authoritarian, controlling, harsh and judgemental, the origin of those
characteristics was clearly Natalie's own uncertainty, her negative judgement of herself, her fear of being out of control,
and her vulnerability.

Natalie lived out an incredible number of contradictions; a

few examples will show the intensity of the conflicts she had to deal with:

- Natalie prohibited a three-year-old visitor from eating attractive snack food because it was for the adults; but she spent literally all day walking her baby around the house to keep her amused.
- she believed that babies only cried when wet, hungry or tired; but she panicked when she heard her baby whimper.
- she believed that she was naturally cut out to be a mother; but having a new baby was a source of tremendous trauma for her.

These contradictions were only a few of the many that Natalie lived with; the chaos of her conflicts gave rise to an overriding sense of panic about being out of control. The severity of her conflicts structured my relationship with Natalie.

In her attempts to regain control, Natalie marshalled her investment in authority. I was an authority: I was a social worker, I was a mother, and I was a mental health professional. To Natalie, that meant I had the answers. A particular structure to the interviews evolved as a result: before the tape recorder was turned on, Natalie would ask me questions. When her agenda had been completed, she would tell me that she had gotten what she needed and I could go ahead now and ask *my* questions. It was clearly a *quid pro quo* arrangement, one in which our separate purposes were markedly different from one another.

Handling her questions was not easy for me. Giving point-blank answers to questions such as "Should I let her cry?" or "Do you think she's getting spoiled?" would have undermined the possibility of her naming her own experience. She wanted definite answers that I felt uncomfortable giving, because my answers couldn't possibly fit her experience. Unstated questions regarding my competence filled the air as I hedged on straightforward answers. My values and beliefs held me to the assumption that the only useful answers could come from her – but at that time Natalie had no ability to locate "herself." Despite the doubts my "hedging" raised, Natalie continued to see me as having the answers. Often, if we had discussed an issue or problem at one interview, at our next meeting Natalie would say, "I did what you told me to do last time." I would not be able to recall having told her to do anything.

Because Natalie conceived me to be something I felt I was not, I usually had a sense of feeling false, of feeling not myself. I was in a double bind: I believed that I had the responsibility of treating her as the expert on her own needs; yet those needs were for *me* to be the expert, and thus to act as an obstacle to her own naming process. Had I been working as her therapist, I would have stepped outside the authority paradigms and begun to work on her need to invest me with authority. But as researcher, I couldn't do this, and I remained in the contradiction of believing in her as the speaker of her needs, while she insisted that she needed me to be her speaker.

Overall, I was left with a sense of awe at the power the difficult issues of control and authority had had in shaping Natalie's investments in discourses – and at the same time, a tremendous sense of respect for the stamina and grit with which she got through traumatic times. Her sense of "doing it because you have to" probably saved her from madness.

Those experiences with Natalie influenced my later decision not to give her the account. This was a very difficult decision, on two grounds: ethically, I felt obligated to give her back something useful to her; and in practical terms, I knew that in part, the adequacy of the account rested on her agreement with my descriptions of concrete events. Yet I felt that Natalie had been so insistent on constructing me as an authority that she would have had no way of finding her own version in the account. She would have had no way of differing from me in my interpretations; thus to have given her the account would have constituted an attack on her fragile sense of autonomy and of being in control.

As well, I didn't feel that Natalie either needed or wanted the account. I am aware of the danger of such a one-sided judgement, but I make it in the belief that it is grounded in the data. Natalie's primary interest in the interviews was in how they met her own perceived needs. Her life was simply too filled with trauma for her to be concerned about my interests in the study. She never expressed any desire to see the account, and was indifferent to the process – except for her occasional worries that she wasn't really giving me what I needed during interviews.

Natalie was surviving by virtue of her stamina alone, her sheer determination to withstand bad times. She did not work through conflicts in a way that would have made the account usable to her. Part of the reason for not giving her the account was precisely in order to respect her approach and her own process as different from mine. I felt that the only reason to give her the account would be if she were to use it within the context of working with a therapist.

Interestingly enough, Natalie called me several months ago for "my advice" regarding a severe marital crisis with Jim. I referred her to a therapist and mentioned the account to the therapist, telling her that with Natalie's permission it could be made available. Natalie and Jim did not maintain contact with the therapist, and the issue didn't re-surface; but I still hold this out as a possibility for a productive and ethical use of the account.

THE TAPE RECORDER

I would like to conclude this chapter by mentioning the effect of the "third party" to the interviews: the tape recorder. The tape recorder was a kind of patriarchal presence, which gave rise to two categories of talk: what could be said in its presence, and what could not.

Generally speaking, the first twenty minutes of each interview (approximately) was not taped, and that was usually the time we talked about "trivia" – the Somethings that seemed Nothing. Here, "mothertalk" – discussions of feeding problems, rashes, crying, sleeping habits and development – took place. These conversations were generally very valuable to me, as they contained material about the subjects' assumptions, beliefs and values as manifested in their actions. However, if I turned on the tape recorder, this talk would inevitably stop, in order to get on with talk about the "important" things: the interview itself. Consequently, keeping track of this "trivial" material often proved difficult for me; when I went to write up field notes, the "trivia" – which is so much a part of my life – was difficult to recall as figure, when it is normally ground.

Certain forms of humour were also triggers to turn off the tape recorder. Dorothy Hobson (1978) says,

> There is no need for them to explain why they laugh, or indeed why I laugh with them at certain points, because the laughter is a form of non-verbal communication which is understood by both of us. It 'works' against a background of tacit (consensual) knowledge, of common sense about women, which is constantly evoked in the exchanges, on the basis of which the statements 'make sense.' (p. 82)

I think the need to turn off the tape recorder during moments of laughter occurred at times of shared knowledge between two members of a muted group. This shared knowledge, expressed through laughter, is highly political: it acknowledges an implicit solidarity, and is thus too charged to be voiced in the patriarchal presence of the tape recorder.

There were also moments when I shut off the tape recorder because the relationship demanded that the situation be redefined. For example, I shut off the tape recorder when a subject was depressed and crying, because the depth of her feelings demanded the context of a relationship, not the context of an interview. Turning off the tape recorder signalled a redefinition of the context from interview to relationship. The presence of the tape recorder would have implied valuing the research over the needs of the woman – so that shutting it off meant that for that moment the relationship took precedence over the research. In the long run, I don't think this affected the data, as I could later record any missed material in field notes; and, in any case, I feel that the relationship between myself and the subject was likely to be a much more important factor in generating meaningful data than the existence of an exact recording of our conversation.

CHAPTER TWO

MARIA

MY FIRST TAPED INTERVIEW with Maria took place twelve days after the birth of her baby girl. The apartment seemed a different place from the one I had seen at our first meeting. It was messy; the kitchen was filled with dirty dishes and it was stiflingly hot. Maria was dressed in shorts and a shirt, while the baby had on a shirt and diapers and was wrapped in a blanket. Maria's face was haggard; she had circles under her eyes, and she was clearly exhausted.

As we talked, Maria breastfed the baby, looking as though this were her tenth rather than her first baby. She handled the baby with a sense of ease, somehow putting across the impression that she felt secure about the learning in which she was engaged. Her attachment to the baby was obvious: throughout the interview she kissed the baby, talked to her, cuddled her. In this and all subsequent interviews, the tapes were interlarded with bits of "dialogue" between Maria and the baby. All the interviews were also interrupted by Maria drawing my attention to details of the baby's development and maturation: we spent time watching the baby follow a mobile figure in a circle, or watching her discover her hands. Maria maintained a keen interest in her baby's development all through the seven post-partum interviews. She watched for changes and anticipated stages of development eagerly. Part of her enjoyment stemmed from the knowledge about babies she had gained through her daycare training and experience.

As well, Maria's baby was the most reactive baby in the study: at ten days, she tracked objects with obvious enjoyment, and she showed an early and very strong preference for Maria. She seemed to seek out stimulation. As we consider Maria's post-partum experience, we should bear in mind that Maria's baby was a strong-willed, demanding, active baby, who required a great deal of stimulation, who slept little, and who was very attached to her mother.

I have divided Maria's account into three sections in order to present a coherent account. This presentation is not intended to imply that Maria's lived experience had occurred in stages, but is rather a rough chronological organization intended to facilitate the narration of her experience. The first section deals with the birth of the baby, and Maria's mediation of that experience; the second section involves Maria's developing relationship with the baby; while the third focuses on her reaction to isolation.

BIRTH

This section focuses on an examination of what Maria learned as a result of a situation in which her body worked in an entirely new way. Labour, birth and lactation are powerful bodily experiences, which a woman is compelled to conceptualize in some way.

After the birth, Maria expressed her feelings about her body by describing herself as too fat, or as being an undesirable shape. Most of her comments on her body centred on her concern that she no longer looked as she had before her pregnancy. In the second interview, for instance, she expressed concern about her "huge tummy," asking me when it would go away. Her concern was based primarily on how she would look to others: she was worried about whether she would look good at social functions (weddings), and whether she

would look good during the summer in shorts or bathing
suits. She worried about how her appearance affected her
husband: she believed he had a right to see her looking good
and that it was her responsibility to work toward the goal of
getting back her figure by exercising. She experienced pressure from her husband to achieve that goal – a pressure she
thought was appropriate:

> I was looking at a picture and I thought, gee, am I ever
> going to have that waistline again? ... People keep com-
> menting, you know, 'Oh you really got wider – you have
> your tummy still.' My husband says, 'when do you think
> you're going to be losing it?'

For Maria, the major issue regarding her body following
childbirth was how to make it look pleasing to others, as it had
before pregnancy. The meaning of the birth was positive in
the sense that it had resulted in her having a baby – but the
process had left her body looking not as good as she thought
it should. Maria held to the opinion that in order to be acceptable to her husband, her friends and herself, she should be a
specific shape. The comparison between that ideal shape and
the reality of her post-partum and lactating body inevitably
led to a negative judgement on the state of her body. Maria's
response to her body not measuring up to an ideal was not to
re-shape the ideal, but to work at re-shaping herself. She did
this with a sense of futility, however, saying,

> I think I'll lose my tummy if I work on it. I'll lose my
> tummy but the rest is going to stay – like I just got wider,
> you know, my hips, my legs, everything, you know. So if
> I could at least lose my tummy, that would help.

How do we account for the failure of such central events as
pregnancy, birth and lactation to have an impact on Maria's

conception of her body? Maria's account of the birth of her child and the immediate post-partum period gives us insight into this question. Here, three categories overlap: Maria's involvement with medical procedures, her interaction with her husband, and her interaction with hospital personnel.

Maria had several expectations of the birth itself. She wanted to be alert and "present" for the delivery; she wanted to feel the baby as it was born; she wanted her husband to be with her at the birth; and she wanted to hold the baby immediately after delivery. These expectations were derived primarily from the reading she had done, and through her pre-natal classes. However, Maria claimed she was "no nature freak," meaning that she did not identify with strong advocates of natural childbirth. She also had no "political" beliefs about women's experience of childbirth.

Maria's labour and delivery were long and complicated. She began labouring on a Tuesday morning and, after a painful labour, delivered her baby on Thursday night. She had not wanted epidural anaesthesia, because it would prevent her from feeling the baby's birth; however, during the second day of labour, after learning from her doctor that the labour was still progressing slowly, she decided to have an epidural.

> I wanted to be sort of awake and present at the birth, right? And I was so scared of being drugged and all of a sudden the contractions speeding up ... I just kept asking, 'Are you sure it's going to wear off?'

She had the epidural, which allowed her to sleep for the first time in two days and nights. She felt relaxed for the first time since the start of labour because she was out of pain. Her description of the labour in hospital was as follows:

> When I woke up from that top-up [anaesthesia re-administered] – I had two top-ups – when I woke up

from that top-up, he decided to break my water. That was the first thing he did. The first step he did, he broke my water. That speeded it up a little because I was on a monitor. Oh yeah, so as soon as I went on the epidural, they put me on a monitor since I couldn't feel the contractions, so I had two belts – one for the contractions and one for her heartbeat – so I was getting monitored from then on and that's when he put the I.V. into me too. One I.V. was for – I think it was for the epidural – or was it the monitor. Gee, I can't remember what the other she put in was for. I know I had two I.V.'s stuck in my hand and all that. That was the first time I had had an I.V. too. Well this was a first for everything – first time in hospital, first anaesthesia, first I.V., first everything.

This quote offers us three important insights. First, Maria's description is never given in terms of what she did, but always what medical personnel did to her. Second, she describes the impact of technological devices, not the functioning of her body. Third, the "firsts" that remain for her are the medical procedures, rather than the experience of labour itself; the experience of her labour no longer lay within her body, but was recalled as an experience of medical procedures.

As she looked back on the actual moment of birth, Maria said,

Oh it was great – it wasn't like the birth experience that I really wanted – to feel her come out. Like they pulled her out – I felt them pull her out.

Again, we see the transfer of activity from Maria to medical personnel, leaving her with the feeling that the process was not her accomplishment. In telling me about the events immediately following the birth, Maria described how her expectations were disappointed:

Well, I was disappointed. Like we had planned with my doctor that they would deliver her right onto my tummy and they didn't do that. They just took her right away.

I wanted to see her the way she came out. She came to me all wrapped up. I wanted to unwrap her and look at her, but the delivery room was quite cold.... And, as much as I wanted to feed her, I didn't want her to be cold, so I didn't.

I wanted to wait until the cord stopped pulsating, but it was cut right away.

And Maria described the delivery of the placenta:

The same with the afterbirth; I thought that you were supposed to let the uterus contract the afterbirth out itself, and this doctor went right in and pulled it out. And I asked the doctor [her general practitioner] how come he did that and you could see in his face, he says, 'Look, I'm sorry. It's just his way. I wouldn't have done that.' He says, 'I would have waited a bit.' That was kind of very funny, kind of annoying. Yes. He just went right in and just tugged it right out. Right after she was born, like they were cleaning her up and he just took it out.

The physical and social functions of Maria's body were taken over by hospital personnel and procedures. Her baby was taken away following birth, to be returned clean and wrapped – Maria had no opportunity to explore the baby, feel her, or feed her immediately after the birth. She did not experience her own body's work of delivering the placenta, because the doctor pulled it out rather than waiting for contractions to occur.

In attempting to account for the absence of change in Maria's post-partum perceptions of her body, it is important to understand that she did not experience much of the activity of labour and delivery; medical procedures took over. It is also important to note that the takeover of those functions produced a particular relationship between Maria and medical personnel: Maria became the passive body to be acted on, while doctors and nurses became the actors. Medical personnel had the expertise in procedures which implemented the delivery of the baby. Thus, much of the basic new data which might have stimulated changes in Maria's relationship to her body were either radically altered by technology, or were obliterated through the effects of anaesthesia.

The other major element which helped to produce Maria's post-partum sense of her body was Maria's interaction with her husband. In carrying out the eight interviews with Maria, I became aware of a particular process which I found to be a cornerstone of Maria's interaction with Tony. I have called the process "forgoing," and it occurs when Maria does not attend to her own experience because she is focusing on another's needs. Maria's forgoing of her own experience while attending to Tony is seen many times in her account of the hospital stay.

In Maria's first reference to her husband, for example, she described her need for him to come home from work because of her advancing labour. The description ends with her need for him transformed into a statement about how much time he had to take off from work. She said,

Wednesday, during the day, I called him and he came home because they were eight minutes apart. I ended up being home all day. Wednesday and Thursday and Friday he took off from work.

This is a good example of Maria's difficulty in focusing on her own needs: she shifted instead to the problem her needs created for Tony.

Continuing with the description of her labour, Maria said,

> ... By Wednesday night – by about one o'clock – I was in tears, I think. Like with the contractions – just the backache. I think if it wasn't for the backache I could have handled it better and – like my husband was up with me till that point, and finally he conked out and went to bed – and here I was all alone with the contractions, and that was the worst part.

Maria said this with full acceptance. She did not think about waking Tony up; she wanted him to sleep, to get rest, and she withstood being alone and in pain so he could sleep. However, there is a complication here: my speculation is that part of the reason she wanted him to sleep was so that later she wouldn't have to worry about his not having had enough rest. So the process of forgoing can work in two ways: first, it organized Maria's attention away from her own experience; and second, it functioned to save her future worry – at the cost of forgoing her experience in the present.

Maria's next reference to her husband concerned their arrival at the hospital. They both thought then that the birth must be imminent, because Maria had laboured so long. However, after an examination, the doctor told Maria she was only five centimetres dilated – very slow progress for such a long labour. I asked her how she felt at that point, and she said,

> Frustrated, you know. My husband, he said, 'Oh how long is it going to be?' And he was really tired and the nurses were feeling so sorry for him and he had bags under his eyes. And I think it was really hard on him just to stand there and sort of watch me through this, you know.

Maria could not describe her own experience in any detail

because she was busy attending to Tony. Her experience was structured through the process of forgoing, and thus data which might have had the potential to restructure her postpartum concept of her body became ground, rather than figure, in her experience.

After a long labour and a series of alternations between pain and anaesthesia, the staff assured Maria that the birth would occur within an hour. Maria started to feel the urge to push. She was excited. Her husband said, "Okay, you have your epidural and it'll be another hour yet. I'm going to lie down a little bit." Maria said,

> So he went to the waiting room and the urge to push was getting stronger and stronger and finally I was 10 centimetres dilated, and I just felt like hooray. I felt like screaming, 'Go get my husband, go get my husband.'

Here, at the moment when she was readying herself for the actual birth, she had to think about getting her husband into the delivery room.

It is interesting that Maria continued to sustain the belief that her husband was her chief support during delivery. She continued to believe this despite evidence from her own experience that it was she who supported him. For example, she laughingly described the moment where she was being wheeled into the delivery room, and Tony became frightened and didn't want to go in. Her doctor took him by the arm and escorted him in, telling him he would be fine. Nurses gave him instructions to hold Maria's leg; Maria herself told him repeatedly not to worry.

> I saw her, and I said, 'It's a girl.' That's when my husband wanted to look. Like he was trying not to look. He was looking at me and he thought he'd be real queasy. But when I was saying all this I kept looking, saying, 'Oh

look, there's the shoulders, oh look.' Then, when I said 'It's a girl,' he tried to look in the mirror but in the position he got himself in he couldn't see so he regretted he didn't see anything; he didn't look in the mirror, but he looked at her right away. Like she was out and I looked at her and I was just screaming, not screaming, 'It's a girl!!!' and I just looked at him – I knew he really wanted a boy but all I could say was 'It's a girl,' and he was smiling too and he goes, 'Oh great!'

From this description, it is apparent that Maria remained conscious of her husband's needs even through the moment of delivery. She was worried that he couldn't see, she described the emergence of the shoulder to him and finally she worried about his disappointment at having a girl. Again, a significant moment in her experience was filtered through concern for her husband's needs.

The process of forgoing is complex, because it is double-edged. It is both the root of empathy and compassion, and a mainstay of oppression. It is erroneous to assume that forgoing is never in Maria's interests; we see many examples, in Maria's relationship both with Tony and with the baby, in which Maria's satisfaction in meeting the other's need is greater than the satisfaction of attending to herself. The oppressive aspect of forgoing comes into play when Maria's own experience and needs are habitually obscured. When that happens, she loses the data about herself which might lead to change. Also, she is the only person in the family who has the ability and the motivation to forgo – so that reciprocity in need-meeting is not achieved.

The third element which helps us understand Maria's experience emerged when statements about Maria's needs were pulled from the data. These statements showed a process with two aspects: one was Maria's inability to be assertive about her needs, and the other was hospital personnel's assumption of expertise as a way of maintaining control.

A number of factors influenced Maria's inability to assert the importance of her needs. Of primary importance is that, as a woman, she equated valuing her own needs with being a bad girl – selfish, greedy, demanding and visible – so that the stage was set before her encounters at the hospital for her needs to be poorly – if at all – made known to others. In combination with the physically overwhelming nature of labour and delivery, this meant that Maria's statements about her needs were ineffective in achieving what she wanted. For example, during labour, Maria asked for a hot water bottle. She had already had one earlier in her labour, and it brought her some pain relief. The nurse, however, denied her request, saying Maria might burn herself. Maria accepted this. We see her making weak requests: "Oh, do I have to be up in stirrups?" We also see needs that were not expressed at all: "I wanted to wait till the cord stopped pulsating, but they went ahead and cut it." Throughout the account it is clear that Maria's ability to state her needs dwindled as her stated needs were ignored. In describing the day after delivery, she said,

> I asked her right then if she [the baby] could stay rooming in and she said 'Let's wait till your I.V. comes out because you can't walk around yet.' So I said, 'Okay,' so I thought well next time she comes – she said she would bring her for the 9:00 feeding, so I thought I'd ask at 9:00. I asked her, and what was the excuse then? Something else ...

Maria's difficulty in making assertive statements was matched by the hospital personnel's assumption that their expertise gave them power over her body. It is important to note that the intervention of medical experts did not stop at medical matters, but extended to all features of Maria's stay in hospital. Most of Maria's desires during delivery were "managed" away by hospital staff, on the assumption that they knew what was "good for her." The area in which staff knew what was good for Maria increasingly subsumed the entire decision-making process:

> One nurse, she had brought her [the baby] in, and she said this is just for you to see her, just for a visit, so I thought, okay, fine, so I didn't even try to feed her. I just held her and was with her. Then a different nurse came back to pick her up and it was about half an hour later or even more, and she said, 'Did she eat?' and I thought, well, the other nurse said it was just for a visit. I thought I wasn't supposed to feed her – she was sleeping anyways, right? And she said 'Well, wake her up and feed her,' so I said fine, so I did.

This is a good example of the interactions between Maria and hospital personnel, in that it shows Maria relinquishing control in the face of an expert's knowledge. The chief reason such a relinquishment of control could occur was that Maria felt so vulnerable. In reflecting on the delivery she said, "Now I can feel more angry, but at the time I was just worried about her. I wanted her to be okay." This sense of vulnerability pervaded the hospital stay and eroded Maria's sense of competence. When describing her discharge, Maria said,

> She didn't give me a wheelchair, so I remember asking her and she said, 'Oh, you seem to be okay.' But down the elevator and walking down the hall I started to get dizzy, so she went and got a wheelchair.

Here, the nurse made the assessment of how Maria felt, and Maria acceded to the assessment and erased her knowledge that she needed a wheelchair. Thus Maria was sent home divested of even the competence to determine whether her body should sit or stand.

These three elements in Maria's account help us to understand how it happened that the experience of giving birth for the first time did not lead Maria to make new knowledge about her body. Medical procedures eliminated data from which she might have made new concepts; at key points, Maria's focus of attention was on her husband and consequently she didn't fully attend to her own experience; finally, medical personnel assumed total expertise "over" Maria, demolishing her sense of personal competence, particularly with regard to her own body.

How did Maria herself mediate the hospital experience? Let us look at her reflections on labour and delivery:

MARIA Well, all the things I wanted to have, I didn't have, and all of the things I didn't want to have I had. Like I had forceps, I had the epidural, I had – he broke my water – and all that stuff I had. So the last time you saw me I was still kind of going over that, but, I think, you know, it doesn't bother me anymore. If it had to be it had to be. I just hope the next time will be better.
AMY So when you look back on it, is it positive or negative?
MARIA I think positive. Just that, you know, just that there's a little resentment about, like, her not being on my tummy and seeing her all messed up ...
AMY What part is positive?
MARIA Just that she did come through okay and I didn't have to have a C-section and she just came through it.

In the sixth interview, after the passage of a fair amount of time, I asked Maria again to reflect on the birth. She said,

I feel really okay now – like I still – I'll always feel, you know, I wish it had been that they took her out and put her right on my tummy, and I'm – it's too bad to go through the epidural and all that, but it's not like, what do you say, because I'm not a regretter or anything – I had to go through it.

Maria's reaction to the birth was one of some disappointment and a sense of fatalistic acceptance. Overall she was happy with the staff. However, there was one thing she didn't accept – Maria was clearly disturbed that the placenta had been pulled out, rather than being left for her to deliver. Yet there was no way for her to be angry about it, because she had no way to make a pattern or to make sense of her feeling of invasion. It was interesting to note that by the fourth interview, while Maria was discussing her "big tummy," she had formulated a concept that allowed her to be angry with the doctor. She said,

I keep thinking it was the doctor who pulled out my afterbirth and he shouldn't have. He should have let it come out naturally.... I hope he didn't screw up anything.... I keep thinking that if I had contracted it out myself – the first contractions are supposed to be good to contract the tummy....

Here she stated that the doctor was wrong and she said it with anger. Her rationale was that the manual extraction of the afterbirth was responsible for her muscles sagging. This rationale suggests two things: that Maria needed some way to account for her anger about the afterbirth extraction, and that there wasn't any discourse available to her which directly legitimated her anger.

Maria's stated preferences for a particular kind of birth procedure were not met. She gave rather than received support during the delivery. Her sense of competence was usurped by hospital personnel. Yet her reaction to the experience was that it was positive – a little disappointing, but acceptable. Nothing about the experience changed her pre-pregnancy feelings about her body – she remained constant to the goal of transforming her body into the ideal form.

MARIA'S DEVELOPING
RELATIONSHIP TO THE BABY

The popular and academic literature on new mothers has long characterized the immediate post-partum period as one filled with anxiety, tension, and fear and laden with crises to be overcome by the developmentally normal. However, data from Maria's account shows a much more complex and rich experience. Indeed, her data suggest that basic processes of the post-partum period have yet to be adequately conceptualized.

Maria was able to provide a particularly thorough account of what actually happens in the first few weeks of mothering. From her detailed descriptions of her everyday world, I generated the concept of "containment": the incorporation of a baby into a mother's boundaries. The baby's needs became Maria's needs – she experienced the baby's needs as her own, and meeting those needs took precedence over meeting her own needs as a separate individual.

A crucial element of containment is that it is inherently contradictory: one cannot truly contain a separate person within one's own boundaries. That is, the baby was included within Maria's boundaries, thus transforming the baby's needs into Maria's needs; yet in order for Maria to recognize the baby's needs, she had to see her as a *separate* person. The tension or anxiety of early motherhood, which has appeared to many observers to be a function of inexperience, is really the product of living with fundamentally unstable personal boundaries within which one contains a separate person.

Containment is best understood not as an abstraction, but by observing actions in everyday life. There are five categories of action which make up the process of containment as given in Maria's account. They are: listening, changing one's rhythm, working at different levels simultaneously, experiencing uncertainty, and coping with physical exhaustion.

LISTENING

Throughout the interviews we see Maria's listening as an intense activity which takes place in interaction with the baby. Forgoing, which we saw operating during her experience of birth, is a requirement of containment; in fact, it is conceptually difficult to separate containment from forgoing because in many instances they appear to be interchangeable. However, by using the concept of containment to describe Maria's relationship with the baby, I am trying to emphasize Maria's feeling that the baby's needs have a higher priority than her own precisely because the baby is inside her boundaries, is part of her own identity.

Listening involves a constant "tuning in" to the baby's needs, preferences, dislikes, and responses. Listening is the way Maria constructs the baby as a separate, unique person. This activity allows her to understand the world from the baby's point of view. By listening to the baby's uniqueness, by seeing the baby's separateness, Maria develops a sense of intimacy with the baby, because she comes to understand the world from the baby's perspective.

Listening shapes behaviour through constant trial and error learning. The following quotations illustrate the trial and error work of listening:

> I was popping the breast into her mouth all the time. Just this week I've noticed I only give it to her when she's

really hungry now because she really does, you can see
her mouth, she's just searching. So now I'm noticing her
different cries. Her hunger cry is much stronger and her
other cry I can see is not hunger, so I'm sorting it out.

Oh she loves her breakfast – sometimes she can't decide
whether she wants to eat or sleep. She'll be eating and
then she'll drop off to sleep. What I found was happening at first was, when she would drop off to sleep, I
thought, oh, she's finished, so I'd take her away and put
her down, and she'd wake up in a few minutes because
she wasn't finished because, when she doesn't want it
she closes her lips, and you can't get it in there.

Now I'll change her position, and she'll go back to sleep
like she did now. Whereas before I'd pick her up, and
she'd be cranky because she was still wanting to sleep,
and I'd be talking to her and showing her bells and
stimulating her, and she didn't want that. She wanted to
shut that out so she'd be cranky.

The work of listening and the work of trial and error are
clearly learning processes. The character of this kind of interaction has often been subsumed under the concept of "natural instinct." To believe this is to deny the struggle to learn
which we see in Maria's account. It is to deny the effort and
sense of agency in Maria's work as she experienced it:

If I walk around and rock her I find that's the best way so
far. I had to learn that. I've had to learn which way for
burping. I've had to learn which way she burps easier.
I've learned that she likes being on her tummy and that it
calms her down, too. She really likes the light, like the
bright coloured objects.

CHANGING ONE'S RHYTHM

An excerpt from Maria's written description of one day's activities gives the sense of how her rhythm changes to mesh with the baby's rhythm. Here, the baby is three months old:

5:30. She woke up. I changed her and fed her. She falls back to sleep and so do I.

8:00. She wakes up. I change her and play with her a little. She is happy and smiling.

8:20. I feed her.

9:00-9:30. She sits in her chair, on the kitchen table. She is 'gumming' some toys while I have breakfast and tidy up.

10:00-10:30. She starts fussing. I change her and try to rock her to sleep, but it doesn't work. She is searching for the breast, so I give her some (just one side).

11:00. She is crying. I try to rock her to sleep, but again rocking alone doesn't work, so I feed her the other side.

11:30. She is asleep again. I write this and begin rinsing another load of diapers.

11:40-12:10. She is awake again, and I attempt to put her back to sleep – but she refuses and is wide awake. I notice that she is wet right through, so I go change her and give up fighting her to sleep.

12:10-1:00. She sits in her chair in the bathroom as I rinse out her diapers. She is very quiet because she is so sleepy, so I don't even talk to her and she listens to the sound of running water. Then I notice that she has poohed right through, so I change her again.

1:00-2:00. I carry her with me in her chair as I go up and down three times to the laundry [three floors down]. Her chair sits on top of the dryer, and she falls asleep from noise and vibrations. So I carry her upstairs gently leaving two loads of laundry in the dryer and one load in the washer.

2:00. I let her sleep right in the chair, and I come to lie down on the couch. I'm quite tired from all the stair climbing. I get one short phone call from Tony, and I'm thinking about what to have for lunch when I hear her cry!

2:10. I take her out of the chair and begin to rock her – but she is searching, so I come back out to the couch, and I feed her. I myself am falling asleep while nursing her so for the second side I transfer to the bed and nurse her lying down.

2:45. She is finished eating and asleep, so I just leave her on my bed and close my eyes. I would love to take a little nap, but I know my clothes should be ready now, and my stomach is growling.

3:10. I get up and go get the clothes downstairs, leaving her asleep. Then I make and eat lunch. I'm starving and also exhausted. I come and lay on the couch and write this. Believe it or not I hear her crying.

4:00. She is up and takes a temper fit on me. She doesn't.... [Maria doesn't finish – the baby is too demanding and she is too tired.]

All this is a good example of forgoing as part of containment. Maria can be starving or exhausted, but her priority is the baby's contentment. Eating or resting won't be satisfying for her unless the baby is contented as well.

WORKING AT DIFFERENT LEVELS

The third category which makes up the process of containment is working simultaneously on different levels. This involves thinking or doing several things, often unrelated, at the same time. Many times carrying out the interviews was itself an example of this: the baby had to be fed, changed, amused or put to sleep while Maria focused at the same time on the interview. My field notes from the third post-partum interview demonstrate this:

> The tape was interrupted by an unsuccessful attempt to put her down. She cried and we picked her up again. I walked her and she fussed. Maria immediately took her from me. While she was up, Maria was distracted – she put her down in the crib to play and came back, sat down, and had a hard time answering a question, saying, 'Why am I so blank today?' But the reality was she didn't know how long she could concentrate for – would the baby cry just as she was talking? Half her mind was on the fact that the mobile in the crib would stay on for only a few minutes, then she would have to get up and create another solution.

The baby's needs were always a part of Maria's awareness, no matter what she was doing:

> If I'm washing the dishes then the chair goes on the table – if I'm making the bed I take her.... Oh, no, not to go to the bathroom, but if I'm cleaning the bathroom or something, I can take the chair and set it right in the hall.

Finally, she described moments of near panic during which everything converged, everything needed her attention at once:

> I needed to fry my dinner and I needed to give her a bath and I needed to tend to her. Luckily Tony had just called and I said I don't know whether to cook dinner or give her a bath and he said 'Oh, don't worry, give her a bath,' and I thought, 'Oh, thank you.'

UNCERTAINTY

The fourth category in the containment process is dealing with uncertainty. There were many points during the day when Maria had to live without answers. The reality of being responsible for an infant is that there are many situations in which one doesn't know how to meet the baby's need – or even what the need is. Maria said,

> When she's colicky, then you're tired because you worry – and you don't know what's wrong, and you try this, and try that, and she's still crying, and you walk back and forth, and finally she's getting a few minutes' sleep, and you try to do something, and she wakes up again. Those are the days when you don't even bother with the dishes or anything – just sit down and rest when she's asleep.
>
> ... last week every time she cried ... I think I was popping the breast, but I wasn't too worried about it because I kept thinking I might not have milk because my mother didn't have enough milk to breastfeed, so I kept on thinking, oh, I don't have any milk....
>
> I'm still trying to work out her bath.... I haven't figured out when to give her her bath – sort of whenever she's in a good mood I give it to her.

EXHAUSTION

Finally, we see that forgoing is a process of containment that often occurs in connection with physical exhaustion. Maria forgoes rest and regular meals in the service of the baby's needs:

> She's getting up and I'm up an hour or two during the night and that's getting tiring, that's getting tiring.

or

> She always wakes up for lunch time; she always inter-
> rupts my lunch. I always eat a cold lunch and for dinner
> she's usually up.

Maria compared the physical exhaustion of caring for a
baby at home with her experience as a daycare worker, saying,

> Working in a daycare centre I thought, oh, it would be
> easy – just one at home – after having all these little
> babies, but no, tougher, because it's twenty-four hours a
> day, no lunches, no breaks, etc.

Housework also accounts for part of being physically
exhausted. Maria described her preoccupation with housework, which she hated:

> When I was at work, right? you would come home, like I
> wouldn't mind just having the cooking, dishes and the
> bed – that would be the daily thing, but then I would just
> clean the house like on Saturdays, you know? But now it
> seems the whole day there's something to do, then laun-
> dry, this and that ...

Housework becomes automatically tied to being a mother
(Oakley, 1974). Housework becomes an extension of baby-
work. Sheila Rowbotham (1973) says: "Housework devours
itself, there is a kind of cyclical rhythm of endeavour and col-
lapse – into exhaustion. There is a particular kind of exhaustion in work which half preoccupies you – fatigue" (p. 72).
  Maria's worst image of herself as a mother hinges on being
too tired to interact with the baby:

I think the exhaustion gets to you because then you don't have as much energy to cope with her and just sort of feeding her and hoping she'd go back to sleep but before, you know, you always have time for a little kiss.

Maria's best image of herself as a mother came from the times when she was able to keep the baby's needs uppermost while still getting the housework done. She did not articulate the fact that this ideal is impossible to achieve because it is a contradiction: keeping the baby's needs uppermost creates more mess and disorder, which in turn creates more housework. Trying to live up to this impossible ideal produces physical exhaustion.

Identifying this contradiction is very difficult in view of the images of homes that are held up as ideal. Rosalind Coward talks about the magazine-display houses, which mirror perfection and simultaneously obliterate any sense of labour attached to achieving such perfection. Babies create messes of diapers, equipment, toys, etc., yet the ideal homemaker has a perfect home that requires no labour, for labour and elegance are mutually exclusive. Every time Maria acknowledged the tedious labour of housework she had to acknowledge herself as outside the ideal. She mediated this as her own inadequacy – as not being a good enough homemaker. Rosalind Coward says,

> It is usually important to women that they feel all right about where they live. But the creative aspects in women's wish to determine their environment have been submitted to a visual ideal whose main statement is the absence of the work they do, and the absence of conflict about that work. (Coward, 1984, p. 71)

Paradoxically, the process of containment is coincident with the process of separation. Leaving the baby was a big step for Maria, a step that was necessarily painful. We have seen the enormous energy she invested in the process of containment. To invest this energy and at the same time learn to leave the baby was a contradiction that Maria found difficult to handle.

Maria described separating as being painful both for her and for the baby. "I've been with her twenty-four hours a day now and I think I'll be uncomfortable." Maria described planning to go to a store to buy a new dress; she envisioned herself dashing in, trying it on, and getting home as fast as possible in order not to leave the baby for too long. The pain she described was the pain she experienced when thinking of the baby's anxiety at not being "contained": at not being cared for by the one who knew the intimate details of comforting and soothing. She described the knowledge that she was the one who was able to perform these tasks by saying,

> Yesterday she was crying.... When I picked her up it just took a few minutes and she calmed down, and I think she's used to a certain way of me holding her. I think of that, too – maybe she'll start to notice the difference too [if Maria weren't there]. I guess that would be anxious for her and she'd cry.

Yet Maria sees a need to push herself to go out:

> I'll just have to go – I know my first time, no matter how long I've waited will be like this, so I'll just have to go through it and the second time will be better.

Two realities made the separation particularly difficult. One was that Maria had a baby who attached preferentially to her very early. My field notes describe the baby's obvious preference for Maria over me at six weeks. She was clearly more easily comforted by Maria. For the first five months she showed acute distress at being without Maria.

The second reality was that Maria was the only person who engaged in the containment process with the baby. Maria believed that an infant's first experience with other people would profoundly affect her emotional well-being as she developed. Consequently, Maria saw the entire responsibility for the infant's experience of the world as resting with her:

> She's trusting more, I think. She doesn't like it on her back, so when I put her on her tummy (in the bath) she's quiet. She'll stay in the water a little bit on her tummy, so I started turning her, and I'd turn her to her side – she was okay on her side – but then when I turned her onto her back she'd go frantic again, so I kept turning her slowly, so then yesterday she was okay on her back. I started her off on her tummy, then I'd turn her onto her side, she's okay, and then I turned her slowly to her back and she stayed. She was okay and I thought, oh, I saw a progress of trust through the bath.

> She likes having her tummy against you and she obviously gets very anxious if you just leave her in her crib. And you see tears coming down her cheeks sometimes. It's just that I think she'll outgrow it. Like once she's not colicky anymore she won't need it as much and I think she'll settle down to sleep on her own.

We see very clearly that the intimate knowledge of responses required to soothe the baby were known only to Maria; there was no one else who knew the baby, or who felt responsible for the baby's development. She was the only one. Maria's husband saw the baby as Maria's work, not his:

Even with Tony, he'll have a hard time because he likes her and everything but he can't stand her crying. He makes me more nervous, he drives me more nuts than she does. 'What's the matter? Do something. Do this. Do that.' And I say, 'Tony, it's okay.' And sometimes he'll try to calm her like for five minutes, and if he can't he'll pass her to me; he won't take her. I don't know what he'll do leaving her alone with him so I'm very apprehensive about leaving her.

Maria's ability to leave the baby was curtailed by her distrust of her husband's ability to handle the baby. She didn't trust him to meet the baby's needs. Maria tried to facilitate the relationship between Tony and the baby by making bathtime at night; she hoped that being able to participate in the bath would help Tony's relationship with the baby. However, Tony worked late, and usually missed the bath because the baby got too tired. "I think he's seen two of her baths and she was still crying at that time and he hasn't seen her since."
Maria tried to get him to be involved with the baby:

Well, you see, he's never had very many babies at all. He hasn't been around babies so he's afraid to carry her and like even when he picks her up he's still quite careful, you know. He's much better, but – so he says when she's older don't worry; I say, 'No. You've got to start now or else you'll never get into it.'

Well, I'm starting to put pressure on him. Yes. Like I want him to try, you know. Like don't pass her over like a hot potato all the time. Yes. I want him to try and – the only thing he hasn't gotten into and I'm putting pressure on is that he hasn't changed one diaper on her, and I said, 'Listen here, you better change her diaper, right?'

But in the long run, her efforts are not significant. Tony works twelve to fourteen hours a day, six, sometimes seven days a week, and he doesn't see the baby. And both of them see a baby as the mother's job:

You see, I'm used to the idea that the mother mostly takes care of them, right? But I want him to be able to do everything in case I have a really bad day or I'm sick or something.

And so, in a situation in which Maria and Tony and the baby live as an independent unit, and in which the baby is the project for only one person, the trust in another adult that Maria needed to be able to leave the baby was never built:

When I went to get my unemployment he stayed in the car with her for about an hour. He nearly went crazy and he said he was about to throw her out the window. He couldn't park. He kept driving around the block and she kept screaming and screaming, and he said, 'Never again.'

Thus, the pain of separating is generated from the inherently unstable nature of containment and separation, and is then exacerbated by the social forms of mothering. The social organization of mothering puts forth Maria as the baby's sole caretaker, and this model is continually reproduced when there is nobody else who has "learned" the baby. Consequently, Maria's separations are ambivalent occasions. On the one hand, she is glad to be out; on the other, she feels guilty at leaving the baby:

I guess there's a certain guiltiness – already I'm feeling guilty about leaving her to cry with someone else and I know I won't be there to soothe or pick her up.

But once I was outside the fresh air felt good, and I just got in the car and my sister-in-law drove me down and it was good. I didn't think of her anymore, and I thought, Oh, no – I didn't even think of her. I said, 'That's terrible.' Yes, I felt guilty. I hadn't worried like I thought I would worry.

Out of the emotionality of the issue of separation arose a conflict that was central to Maria's concept of mothering. I categorized this as a "power conflict" when analyzing the data. Basically, it was Maria's struggle to understand the implications of power in her relationship with the baby. The practices of feeding, soothing and handling a baby must be given meaning through a discourse which conceptualizes power in some way; for Maria, this was an important issue.

Jean Baker Miller (1976) discusses two kinds of inequality. In the first kind, the overall goal is to end the relationship – that is, to end the relationship of inequality. The relationship itself is constructed in order to facilitate equality between the actors. In the second kind of inequality, the goal of the relationship is to enforce continued inequality. In Maria's account we see a struggle between the use of power to enforce inequality, and the use of power to produce equality. Maria has a clear construct about what kind of relationship she wants with her child:

You have to respect her as a person, I guess. She does have her own feelings and thoughts, and I don't want to impose myself like an authority mother. I'm starting to think of how I'm going to work out things like attitudes and stuff. I don't want to be, you know, 'I'm your mother and you do what I say and speak when you're spoken to.' I want to get her to open up and want to be, you know, a friend to her.

This overall goal produced specific behaviours toward the baby. Maria acted on the goal by assuming the locus of control of needs to be within the infant. She believed that a trusting person would emerge from an infancy in which the infant's needs were met:

> I think especially at first to have all the needs met, like now, the first period when she wants all that trust and bonding, and she'll come out of it, because she'll know that someone is there, you know, when she needs it.

How did Maria arrive at this theory? She pointed to three factors that influenced her thinking: her relationship with her parents, her early childhood education (ECE) training, and her friend Kathy.

Maria's parents brought up their children with a heavy reliance on authority. Maria was the first-born and the first to be brought up in an unfamiliar culture. Every move she made toward independence was a struggle; in her home, she was told what to do, and she had to do it. Communication, talking, openness, were not characteristics of the parent-child relationship. Maria described how she had envied other girls in school for their more open relationships with their mothers. She saw her relationship with her parents as having been organized around authority, and she did not want this to happen between herself and her daughter:

> But I was resentful that I didn't have that kind of relationship with my mother because, you know, all my friends do. Up to high school most of my friends were Portuguese and they all had the same relationship with their mother and stuff like that, right? ... but once I went to high school – I went to a Catholic school, all girls – and Portuguese was a minority there, right, so it was mostly

Canadians and they were pretty free with their parents and I thought, 'Gee, how nice,' you know. And I tried to come home and talk, but, you know, she just wouldn't come through.

Maria's ECE training helped shape her thinking about parent-child relationships:

It got really enforced with the ECE. I mean, that's what the ECE is all about, you know. Kids are people and you don't treat them just like kids.

Finally, Maria's close friend, Kathy, handled her child in a way that Maria admired. Kathy allowed for an open, respectful relationship, which gave Maria a model for her own actions; Maria, watching Kathy, was able to refine her own thinking about how to raise her child.

The development of this stance toward children was a significant change for Maria. It was an important transformation from the childhood concept of parents and children with which she was raised. We can see that she made the transformation (1) through having experienced the original concept as negative by comparison to something else, (2) by having had an emerging construct verified by an institution, and (3) by having found a personal model supportive of the transformation. The important thing we must now look at is how her concepts were continually challenged by conflict.

There were two sources of conflict; one came from within Maria, and one from people within her social network. The voice from within Maria questioned the assumption that separation was an inevitable process if needs within the relationship were being met. She sometimes wondered if she should control the separation process, or allow the baby to separate when she was ready:

I should let other people comfort her, so she'll be okay with everyone, right?

But, later,

It's good for the bonding. That she knows her mother and can relax.

Conflict from outside herself came mainly from her relatives, particularly her in-laws, who felt that she had to retain the locus of control, that she had to make the baby conform to her expectations:

My relatives say, 'Don't hold her so much; she's got to get used to it; you've got to put her down.' And people say I'm getting her so used to the lap that I won't be able to put her down – all she'll want to do is be in my arms.

Yet when I asked how she felt about this, Maria was consistent in saying she felt they were wrong, that the baby would outgrow those needs. Her practices of baby care were firmly rooted in a desire for an egalitarian relationship. We can account for the strength of her desire by looking at her first experiences as a mother.

Maria described her first few days with the baby in several ways. She experienced that period as a time of having confidence, of sensing an increased maturity, of feeling surprise and enjoyment in the relationship. My field notes from the first post-partum interview reflect my surprise at seeing a new mother who was as confident as Maria. She handled the baby with ease, and seemed to have an established relationship with the 12-day-old baby. She saw herself as having more confidence after having had the baby than she had had before:

I don't know where it came from, but ... I feel I know because I'm around her all day. I know what she's like.... I think I have all that confidence from having worked with the babies, and going through the course I have the knowledge.

I'm pleased with myself that I'm being calm and confident and I didn't think I would.

Her account shows that her confidence was built on two factors: her ability to listen and pay attention to data from daily life, and her previous knowledge and experience with babies. I would argue that the connection between Maria's development of a conceptual framework about her relationship with the baby, and her sense of confidence, is associated with her ability to use her own day-to-day reality as a basis for creating conceptions. Her conceptions are an accurate reflection of her everyday, lived experience.

Maria described feeling increasingly mature:

It's the realization that the baby is totally dependent on you.... You've got to do everything for her and that makes you feel so responsible, I guess. I guess that responsibility makes you feel mature.

I don't know, I think it's just this – that she's so dependent on you and it's such a responsibility. I don't know, she's a little human being – you have to feed her and change her and you know, do everything for her, and I guess all that responsibility just makes you feel older.

Maria described surprise. Even with her early childhood training and experience, Maria was not prepared for the reality of being the sole caretaker of a newborn:

I knew it was going to be a lot of work, but not this much and not this tiring.

I knew a newborn would be a lot of work, but I didn't imagine it to be this tiring – like I thought maybe the first week or so, I really thought a newborn would eat and sleep ... and she just doesn't.

Finally, Maria talked about the pleasure she took in her relationship with the baby. This was evident both in interview transcripts and in field notes about the interviews:

She's learned that I do come when she needs me, that she's fed when she's hungry. It's a very good feeling – the interaction, that we are communicating; we are building up a relationship.

... you know, she starts off so tiny, and you're going to watch everything, you know. You're going to watch her learn about everything, experience everything, you know. That's a great feeling, I think. It's great, you know, and the fact that she's yours. And I keep saying to Tony, I said, 'You know she was in my tummy, and I can't get over that she was inside my tummy, you know. And I remember she used to kick and everything. And now here she is, out here, you know, a little person.' You got to keep remembering that she's a little person. I think, you know, it's a little baby; you take care of it, you know. She's going to grow up into a person, you know; she's got her feelings, and she's going to have hopes and dreams and all that, right?

ISOLATION

Childbirth, physical recovery, and the development of her relationship with the baby changed Maria's personal circumstances dramatically. Accordingly, her relationship to the external world changed as well.

Maria's experience of the world in the initial post-partum phase was primarily an experience of isolation. This period, which began with a feeling of "being in the world," soon became marked by isolation and then by depression. Depression, in turn, stimulated change for Maria.

Maria's first experience of a sense of isolation was described in the first transcript, when her baby was 12 days old. She said,

> Twelve days old. I'm starting to feel so isolated – like I haven't been out in ages. I keep looking out the window – you know what it's like out there especially with the snow; I love the snow. The first snowfall has always been exciting for me and now I just watch it through the window. I don't even go into the halls to throw the garbage out because I'm usually in shorts or something. My husband's the one – he does everything.

This comment summed up Maria's relationship to the world – with a few intermissions – for the succeeding six months. She lived in a small, two-bedroom apartment; she didn't know the neighbours. Nearly all of her trips outside the house involved going to relatives' (especially Tony's parents') for Sunday visits. Isolation extended through the period of the baby's colic, when the baby was restless and frequently cried all through the day. Maria spent most of her time inside the apartment, alone with the baby.

Maria's main link to other people was the telephone. Her mother phoned her daily, as did her friend Kathy. In the early weeks, support and help were received over the phone:

> I was on the phone with my girlfriend. She was giving me a lot of moral support there, and my mom's phoning – everyone is calling to see how things were progressing....

Maria began to watch television. She felt ambivalent about watching TV, but it broke the boredom for her and provided access to a peopled world. She described dealing with the baby on a colicky day:

> I want her to sleep so I just hold her so she can get some rest, so she can sleep, so that's when I started turning TV on. I don't like sitting here feeding her watching TV. Like I like to feed her and just be with her.

Later she described using the TV to alleviate her fear of being alone at night when Tony was working late. She felt more vulnerable as a function of being solely responsible for the baby: she day-dreamed about a fire, a black-out, and so on, wondering how she would cope alone with the baby. She used TV and radio to distract her from these fears.

It is important to determine the cause of Maria's isolation. I looked at ten specific factors which contributed to producing it. One of the first factors that became obvious in the data was the role played by Tony's hours of work:

> Well, he either starts at seven or eight and he'll come home at eight if I'm lucky, you know. And what really bothers me is the days he gets off, like tomorrow, they're going to do inventory.

Tony worked all Saturdays and most Sundays. Even though Maria called him a workaholic, she felt guilty about her anger at his long hours. She knew that starting up a garage was hard work, yet after two years she saw no let-up. As well, she was annoyed when Tony elected to stay at the garage on Sundays to fix up his father's car, or complete other tasks.

Another important factor in Maria's isolation was the pressure she was under from in-laws and from Tony not to take the baby out in the cold weather. She was afraid of the repercussions if she took her out and she got sick, saying,

> I'm dying to take her outside. And, again, I'm hearing all
> these different things, like of course his side, 'Oh, don't
> take her out; she'll get cold; you'll be sorry if she gets a
> cold, bla, bla, bla.' So if I take her out and she gets a cold
> I'll never hear the end of it.

This pressure was felt at a time when Maria's confidence in
herself was waning, and it was difficult for her to deal effectively with it.

Maria didn't have a car, and that was another factor that
kept her at home. Tony would not let her drive, saying that
she was not sufficiently experienced to drive alone. He promised to let her have the car during the summer; in fact, this
never happened – he was still reluctant to give her the car.
Having no car meant that, in order to get out, Maria needed
special baby-carrying equipment. Maria had a large carriage,
but it was impossible to get it up and down three flights of
stairs, and she was afraid it would be stolen if she left it in the
ground floor stairwell. She had bought the carriage because,
before her baby's birth, she hadn't been aware that a folding
stroller is the only piece of equipment that can be used on the
bus or subway. Without a stroller, she could not use public
transportation, and, now that she realized the fact, she was
reluctant to buy a stroller because of the additional cost.

Maria was one of the first women in her social set to have a
baby, and she found that most of her friends did not understand the problems involved in leaving a baby, and the need
to get out. During our fifth interview, Maria described with
some anger a situation involving her sister-in-law and her
boyfriend, who had promised to take Maria and Tony out for
dinner if the baby turned out to be a girl. Three and a half
months after the baby's birth, Maria was ready to go out, but
she wanted to take the baby with her to the restaurant – she

thought she would sleep through the meal. But her friends and Tony insisted on bringing home take-out food, because they were afraid the baby might cry while they were out to dinner.

> We were supposed to have dinner, and we've been wait-ing so long so she could get over her crankiness so that we could go out to a restaurant, and finally we just had take-out and brought it in here.... I was dying to go to a restaurant so bad, you know. But they said, 'Oh, she might be cranky or something' – like everything for her, kind of thing. I said, 'But I want to go' but we had it at home, so I'm dying to just go to a movie or something.

She said this with anger and a sense of hurt at not having had her needs met. At a later point in the interview I asked her why she hadn't insisted on going out to dinner, and she said,

> At that dinner we should have gone out. I'm not blaming her [the baby]. I blame them for their attitudes. I did insist – I said she's asleep – of course Tony said too, she might wake up, so I said, okay, fine. It was a nice evening but I just wanted to be out of this place. Even if I could have one dinner out, one evening, I think I'd come back feel-ing a lot better.

The fact that Maria's baby was preferentially attached to her at an early age also affected her ability to take a break. By the age of six weeks, the baby had a very definite antipathy to being cared for by anyone other than Maria. She would scream if Maria left her with relatives, and Maria was reluctant to leave her, knowing no one could calm her down; further-more, relatives were reluctant to have her, because they knew she'd scream the whole time Maria was gone.

Our society has a clear bias against children in public

places. What had once been Maria's leisure activities – visiting restaurants or going to the movies – were now off limits to her because she had a baby. There are a few activities available which are specifically designed for mothers and infants, but Maria did not have much information about them, and the few programs that she did know about were difficult for her to get to without a car.

There were also physical limitations on Maria's activity. She was still feeding the baby at night, and often was up early with her. She was breastfeeding, so that her body was using large amounts of energy for lactation. She was recovering from a difficult delivery. The containment process in itself was physically exhausting. Her physical energy level simply wasn't high enough to surmount the obstacles she had to deal with in order to get out.

Finally, and overarching all the other factors which produced Maria's isolation, there was her expectation of how she was "supposed" to feel. Since she had always loved babies, her understanding had been that once her baby was born, she would love to stay home and take care of her own infant. It was difficult for her to understand why those expectations were not borne out:

> I was upset because I was feeling that way, because I had always thought I wanted to stay home, and now, I'm thinking, does this mean I don't want to stay home?

> Just the biggest surprise, that I thought I would just be home with the baby and it would be fun and, oh, I'd enjoy her. I didn't think I would have this conflict.... That was the biggest surprise and I guess that was the biggest change – just your life style. Like, you know, all of a sudden there you are at home, right, and you don't see other people as much as when you were at work day-to-day – you have contact with everybody. So you don't hear

much of the outside world, especially if I don't listen to the news.

Just naming isolation as a problem made Maria feel guilty. The fact that she found it hard to stay at home alone with the baby somehow got equated with not enjoying the baby:

It's a hard thing to deal with because automatically people assume that you don't like to be at home with your baby rather than that's it. You love the baby; you love being with the baby; but you hate the housework and being alone and all the things associated....

Thus, one of the factors that contributed to Maria's isolation was the power of the idea that mothers who love their children are not in conflict about staying home with them.

Maria's feeling of depression emerged from the experience of isolation. In her account, we see a progression of episodes of depression, starting in the third interview and culminating with a shift in the meaning of the depression for Maria. It is important to understand that Maria's depressed feelings did not subsume her whole experience; rather they marked out a trend or a path which ended in change.

During the third interview (six weeks post-partum), Maria described having had a few recent episodes of "the blues." As she explained them, her feelings had no "legitimate" causes; they were just "passing feelings." However, when I pressed for details about the most recent "blues," it turned out to have been related to a loss of confidence in herself *vis-à-vis* her in-laws. She had been feeling very good about her ability to stand up to them, to do what she felt was right, but she had been unable to do so in an incident in which she unwillingly acceded to their control. She described this incident as having triggered the blues, which made the conditions of her life appear bleak to her:

This last week it was really emotional. It was just so monotonous – the housework and stuff. And then I was upset that I was feeling that way, because I had always thought I wanted to stay home, right?

Here, part of the issue was feeling upset with herself. She wanted to be happy at home – as she had expected to be – and she was unhappy with herself that her experience somehow wasn't matching up to her expectations. However, her blue days were still unconnected to any pattern of meaning; she still perceived them as isolated incidents. She was hoping that they would somehow clear up with time.

By the fifth interview, she seemed to be at the nadir of depression. During much of this interview, Maria was crying as we talked.

I've been trying to get out – that's why I asked you how is it [outside] today. I might go out today, but I have no energy. It's always one thing or the other, but I don't know. I'm just so fed up right now.

Maria said she felt less confident than she had in the early days of motherhood. She called this "being gullible," which she defined as "... when I have my own idea and I let myself be swayed by the relatives." She said, "Now I seem to be more gullible, and they're not on me so much." Regarding her early confidence, she said "I thought I really had [changed] but I find I've gotten back to my old self again."

She was also angry with Tony, although that anger didn't come easily to her. She sounded unusually despairing when she said "I could have clobbered him." She said it almost apologetically. His long hours and his lack of involvement with the baby disturbed her and upset her on behalf of the baby. In talking about the baby making strange with people she said,

"She's the first kid – she's only got one other person [i.e., no siblings, no father – just Maria]."

It was difficult, however, for her to see these feelings as legitimate:

> I shouldn't complain that much – I have a lot of contacts. I just want a social outing. I don't want to go to the grandmothers' every Sunday.

She was angry with herself for her return to gullibility, particularly with respect to in-law pressure:

> It was just like going out – I didn't go out.

This interview was filled with pain and vulnerability for Maria. She cried continuously, saying, "I'm feeling like you've come here and I'm just wasting your time." However, potential sources of change were also evident in two of her statements. In the first, Maria responded to my question about how she felt about taking the baby out in the cold by saying,

> I would take her out, but Tony goes, 'No, it's too cold,' and everyone else. But I'm taking her out – next week, I'll bundle her up and that's that. [Said assertively.]

Here she rejected pressure to stay indoors, and decided to follow her own knowledge that babies don't get cold if they're bundled up. We can conceptualize change for Maria as coming when she can use her own data to formulate her actions. We can propose two important factors to account for this: first, the interview itself – it was clear that I was sympathetic to her need to go out. (Indeed, as she cried, I suggested that she let me stay with the baby while she went out.) As well, the art of listening is at some level an act of valuing, and, at a moment when Maria devalued her own data as a basis for action, my act of valuing her through listening sparked her ability to reassess what she knew. Secondly, Maria's situation aroused the need for change because of the degree of pain it generated, which was so great that it fueled the motivation for change.

In the second statement that reflected the beginning of change, Maria said,

> I guess I'm just finding out that I do want to be an individual again. I thought I'd be at home with her, and, fine, it would be great. But I find I do want to go out. It's a bit of a surprise.

Maria is speaking of the act of listening to herself and finding that what she hears is contrary to her expectation of what she thought she would hear.

Another change occurred as Maria reviewed her plans to take in children for babysitting in order to help out financially. Her experience of isolation, plus a new view of the reality of taking care of other people's children in her current situation, made her have doubts about her former plans. She contemplated the mechanics of taking children in:

> I want to take them [the children] out so that's the other thing. If I can leave my carriage down – you see I have the big carriage; we don't have an elevator so that's going to be a bit of a problem.... So I'll lock it up, and it's just getting the kids downstairs, and that, because I want to go out for a walk, and I don't want to be in here all day, especially once the nice weather starts. So, say if I have three kids, so there should be at least one walking, then I could put one in the snuggly and just hold one. As long as I can get downstairs then I'll just put them in the carriage and go.

But the work she had planned seemed to bring an even greater threat of isolation. Recognition of that threat eventually pushed Maria to begin thinking about going back to work in a daycare centre as an alternative.

The sixth interview took place during what was a good period for Maria. She had decided to go out to work, and that decision coincided with the arrival of a girlfriend who stayed for a month. During the girlfriend's stay, Maria went out with her (the friend had a car), shopped, and began to leave the baby on occasion:

> ... someone invited us to dinner and I thought, wow! Let's go! So my sister-in-law came and she spent the whole time – we got home at midnight and she never woke up....

This period was "good" for Maria because she was active and spending time with people. It gave her something against which to measure her life staying at home alone.

By the seventh interview Maria had begun to conceptualize herself as a mother in a new way:

> I guess that, you know, I do need contact with other people, that a baby is not enough. Like, you know, a baby is a lot and gives you a lot of meaning and stuff, but you still need your friends and the other people around you; people your own age, too. Even the part about leaving her.... I didn't think I'd need a lot of babysitting, but it's nice now when you need just to go with Tony sometimes. You need a little break.

We see this reconceptualizing of herself as a mother in her interpretation of two events. In both situations Maria saw her feelings as clearly tied to her conception of herself as a person who had needs. The first example involved Maria's depression following her friend's departure:

> It was the whole thing again ... it was after she left. I knew it was going to happen after she left. I had company and I was talking to her. And we were going out a lot and all of a sudden she left and I was by myself again and I thought, 'Oh, I had nothing to do,' and the housework was driving me nuts.

The second instance occurred when her friend Kathy took a full-time job. This meant that the support Maria had depended on from Kathy was no longer available during the day:

> My girlfriend Kathy got a job. And she was the one person who was at home and I could talk to her any time of the day. And now she's working and I have to wait till night-time to talk to her. I got really depressed about halfway through this last month. And I wanted to phone her and she wasn't there and I said, 'Oh, who am I going to call?'

In both situations, Maria related her depression to her need for people. Maria no longer called her feelings the "blues," but saw them as tied to the problem of being a person who needed people but who was alone.

As well, she began to clearly differentiate the need to be alone from the accusation that she was "not enjoying the baby." This was a major distinction for her to make, because it allowed her to experience depression without guilt.

> I know I would enjoy her. It's been great with her and that. I'm just surprised I'm getting these feelings.

Marilyn Taylor describes the process of naming the issue

without blame or shame as a crucial step in learning (Taylor, 1979). In her study, she shows that feelings of inadequacy, depression, self-doubt or anger preceded naming the issue, or moving the problem from the realm of personal inadequacy to the domain of issues to be tackled. This inside-to-outside process was beautifully described by Maria:

> That's why it takes so long, because you don't want to open up and tell people about this because you think they'll think you're a bad mother, and not enjoying your baby or whatever ... so you just sort of bottle it up and then it explodes.

With the act of naming the issue comes the beginning of finding solutions, new ways of acting. Maria did this primarily through contemplating returning to work.

> Well, first it was just financially it would bother me.... But now the financial is sort of sliding and now the social is coming out. That was coming out really strong, that was the SOCIAL thing. Not so much for the money anymore, it's just to be out for the summer, right?

Contemplating work generated its own conflict: leaving the baby for extended times. In a culture where work and home are dramatically separated, working meant leaving the baby. Maria was very much in conflict about this, because she was afraid she would lose the richness of her intimacy with the baby:

> You see I still couldn't give it up even with all this because, like you wouldn't see any of these things, you know. And you'd come home from work, and you'd have your dinner to worry about, and you'd probably feed her, give her a bath and put her to bed, you know,

and you wouldn't see all this. Yesterday, she woke up at five and she went back to sleep so I just stayed in my bed and just seeing her wake up was so funny. She took the longest time to wake up; she opened her eyes, and she'd stretch, and she'd turn around, and this went on and on. And, I thought, I wouldn't see these little things.

This issue had not been resolved when the interviews ended – six months after the baby's birth. However, at the time of a follow-up call five months later, Maria was in the process of choosing various options for returning to work, and her decision seemed imminent. She would now have to split her life between the public and the private.

We can see how the shift in meaning – from having troublesome, "meaningless" down days to naming isolation as the cause of her depression – precipitated Maria's decision to go back to work. It is tempting to see the shift as a liberating transformation; after all, it involved a woman declaring her own needs. Yet closer analysis reveals that Maria's change is in no way liberating. Her positioning in the individualistic discourse of "I have needs" ultimately constrained her in making the individualized choice of leaving her beloved baby to go to work. This will be explored at length in Part II; but it is important to acknowledge here that Maria's discovery of her needs actually *prevented* her discovery of the multiple factors which produced her isolation. And it is those factors which are key indicators of where social change must occur.

Maria had glimmers of understanding that there was something wrong with the organization of mothering. Yet for Maria to develop those glimmers into a critique of that type of organization was not possible. Three factors worked against such a transformation:

1) she had had very little time as a mother;

2) she tended to be more comfortable with self-blame than with anger; and

3) she had no network of people who might have supported the anger that is coincident with a political critique.

However, it is important to understand that such glimmers did exist, and were resources for future possibilities of making new meaning. There is, for instance, something that doesn't fit for Maria – something that chafes at her consciousness – a dysjuncture that contains great potential for change:

It's crazy – it's such an important job and there's no respect.

CHAPTER THREE

TINA

THE FIRST TAPED INTERVIEW with Tina was quite different from our informal talk before the birth of her baby. Tina was exhausted and anxious, and coped with those feelings by trying to take care of everything at once – for instance, ironing T-shirts during the interview.

For the first three months, Tina had the sleepiest baby in the study. She had to work at getting a whole feeding into her before she fell asleep. Tina also had to work at making the most of the baby's responses in order to interact with her.

There were lots of interruptions in our interviews: many things happening at once was simply part of who Tina was. There were interruptions to answer the phone, to talk to Ernie, to open the door for friends, to change locations in order to sit in the sun, or to exhort me to try the soup. While these interruptions sometimes left me wondering where my train of thought had gone, I had to be careful not to lose the real source of data by claiming the privileges of a formal interview.

I have organized Tina's account into three sections, which loosely correspond to her chronological experience. They are: 1) birth; 2) learning the baby; and 3) the construction of Superwoman.

BIRTH

I would like to begin with Tina's immediate post-partum feelings about her childbirth experience. Those feelings reveal how the birth experience changed her sense of her body as part of her self.

In the first interview I asked Tina how she felt the moment the baby was born:

> TINA Relieved, so relieved that I did it. I did it. And then when I saw her, I did it. I delivered her.... I pulled it off. I was able to; it wasn't the baby. Okay, what happened was this – the baby was beautiful; she was in a perfect position; she was right on target. The doctor didn't even have to pull.... She was born in one push, head, everything. Body, everything.
>
> AMY How does that make you feel about yourself and your body?
>
> TINA Oh, good. I feel that I'm a strong person. I have always thought ... I feel I'm very healthy. Everything operates the way it's supposed to.

Later in the interview Tina said,

> TINA This birth was somehow a good experience. It was wonderful. It was very good.
>
> AMY Could you put your finger on what was wonderful about it?
>
> TINA I found my strength. I found out how well my body worked.... I knew beyond a shadow of a doubt that I could give birth to that baby without any doctor – I'm serious. I just knew in my heart that if I had to have that baby without the doctor pulling it out that I could do it. I was strong. I felt strong.

Also in the first interview Tina said,

> What happened was, I didn't do it consciously.... I did it, I think, unconsciously. The doctor said to me 'She's perfectly positioned; she's just ready to go; your cervix is effaced; everything's clear.' What came to mind was that the baby was on a launching pad and that's exactly how she was born. She was not pulled. She was not yanked. She was on a launching pad. She came out like a rocket. It was beautiful. I really felt like I did the birth – not forceps, or the doctor pulling, or the epidural – nothing but the strength I had in my body made her come out the way she did – look at her beautiful little head – her little face was perfect.

In the second interview, Tina reflected again on the birth:

> TINA I don't know – it was such an incredible experience – I mean, I never had anything like that happen to me. To me it felt like science fiction a little but.... You know, I mean from your body comes something alive like that and that's really extraordinary even though it's very commonplace and everybody knows about it – everybody knows about women giving birth and so on. But when it happens to you then it – well when it happened to me it felt like science fiction, so out of the ordinary. This little thing here came out of my body – that to me is like science fiction, a miracle, or whatever you want to call it.
>
> AMY Has it changed your sense of your own – yourself?
> TINA Yes. It made me feel much better about myself as a woman and good about my body and so on and so forth. Now I feel like there's part two to it....
> AMY Do you have a different sense of your body as a whole?

TINA   Sure.

AMY In what way?

TINA In what way ... a good sense, a good sense – an absolutely fantastic sense of knowing that I'm very healthy. Everything is functioning. My parts are functioning the way they are supposed to be functioning and that is a lovely feeling.

In the third interview, Tina again spoke about her memories of the baby's perfect position during birth. She loved to recall these images.

In the transcripts, many references to her body relate primarily to appearance – to the attractiveness of her body and to her fears of not being slim. This was indicated in the first interview when she said,

> ... Oh – you know, I'd like to have slim hips. That's always been a dream of mine. But I'd like to firm up a bit because I've gained, but ... it'll be all right.

However, by the fifth interview, it had stopped being all right:

TINA Now it's starting to bother me. At the beginning, I was too busy to worry about – just keep my head above water and I didn't care what I looked like but now it's starting to bother me again.

AMY What bothers you?

TINA I've always had a weight problem and I've always kept it down, but I've always had this horrible fear of being fat, obsessed, you know. And now like my worst fears have been realized, I'm fat.

AMY Okay, now that your worst nightmare is here, tell me about your life in the worst nightmare.

TINA Oh dear! What do you mean, being fat?

AMY Yes. How does this nightmare play out?

TINA I can't wear anything except jogging pants.

AMY What's your worst fear?

TINA That I'll get fatter.

AMY And then what will happen?

TINA My husband is going to find me disgusting.

AMY And then what will happen?

TINA He might not – like sort of – he may be ashamed of me and sort of not take me out in public. Don't laugh, that hurts. True.

AMY Anything else?

TINA He might not find me sexually attractive and may prefer slender, younger women, who knows? Yes.

In the last interview we again see weight as a concern, in that Tina stated that she did not want to get pregnant again before losing the weight from the first pregnancy.

Okay ... my body seems to be getting back – I've got another maybe five pounds, but then ten pounds to look the way I want to look, but say five pounds will be where I was and I must exercise to get my stomach muscles tighter and so on....

How are we to understand these two conceptions of the body? One is a view of her body as strong, lovely, healthy and productive; the other is a view of her body as repulsive, ugly, and incapable of doing the work of attracting. It is clear in Tina's account that the new conception of her body which resulted from giving birth in no way changed or replaced the older conception of the body as always falling short of being good enough. During the first three months of the interviewing period, the excitement of "finding her strength," of feeling that her body had operated perfectly during childbirth, had overwhelmed previous feelings of unattractiveness. Gradually, however, the extra five pounds, the flab, the fear of losing her husband by being repulsive took over.

I think that those feelings took over because there was no framework, no structure of meaning into which her positive feelings about her body could be inserted. There are thousands of ways that conceptions of the body-as-repulsive are daily validated, reproduced, revived and remembered. Magazine ads, diet pop, tight clothes, peer pressure, husband pressure, all create a web of interpretation in which the body-as-repulsive makes good sense. There is no web of meaning which supports women's view of their bodies as healthy and beautifully functioning. Tina's positive feelings faded because they failed to make good sense in her everyday world.

The question remains, then, what happened to the feelings Tina had about her body immediately after the birth? She answered that question very clearly in our third interview:

AMY ... this is a hard question. I'm not sure how to ask – when you are feeling good and healthy about your body is that in general or do you specifically think about the birth?

TINA What you're asking is, "Is there a little compartment that I tap and I think about it and then feel good or does it generally make me feel good all the time?

AMY Yes, you know, in terms of your body?

TINA Well, no, I think that's a good point because I could certainly use it that way, couldn't I? No, I think it's something that I tap into – it's almost like a little door I open and I peek in and it makes me feel good. Yes, you know, that's it – and then I close it for the next time, but I really should let it open all the time.

AMY What would keep it shut – the door?

TINA Well, what I look like after pregnancy – like a hundred and fifty pounds.

These statements give us insight into what has happened to Tina's positive image of her body. The negative conception is dominant, structuring her practices in her everyday world; but there is a conscious recollection of the positive image that she can recover at will. That conscious, positive image finds an insufficient structure of supportive meaning in Tina's world, and this renders it too weak to allow practice to derive from it. But it continues to exist in a "box," to be opened consciously on occasion. The existence of the positive image, however encapsulated, is a resource for Tina.

It is important to understand Tina's sense of her body before childbirth; there are aspects of her history which help us trace how Tina's sense of her body after childbirth was produced. Tina described having had difficulties "being in touch" with her body previously:

> Well, I was raised in a puritan-type of set-up – parents nice Italians; you don't talk about sex, about bodies, your breasts, or anything. You just don't talk about stuff like that. And so I grew up – until I was 20-21 – and I realized that I was not really in touch with my body. I negated even that I had breasts, a vagina, you know.

Tina handled these feelings in a way that is consistent with how I experienced her throughout our interviews: she refused to acknowledge the inevitability of these feelings and set out to learn more about the problem.

> TINA ... and so I started doing it at about 25 – I just made a conscious effort.
> AMY How did you do that?
> TINA I went into psychotherapy – talked a blue streak with a wonderful, wonderful psychologist.

Tina entered psychotherapy and began to deal with the effects of the denial of the body with which she had been raised.

Of crucial importance during that time were issues concerning Tina's marriage. She had been married at the age of 20, and she described Ernie as not having been ready for marriage at that time. He began to have affairs with other women after they had been married for two years. During those early years of their marriage, Tina felt herself to be sexually unresponsive, and could not connect pleasure to her body. She began therapy at the age of 25, and, when she was 27, she left Ernie:

> So he was running around having affairs left, right and centre after about two years of marriage and at about seven years, then I left. It took a very long time because of my conditioning – you never leave your husband, a good Italian girl. So I sold the house ... we sold the house just like that. I had an apartment ... I told him I had an apartment ... come and see it – he thought I was bluffing then he realized I was serious.

Tina and Ernie remained separated for nearly two years.

> I was telling myself that I had less of a sex drive than most people, which wasn't true. I mean the whole separation was excellent – I saw other people. And, you know, I thought that I didn't need to have sex, or whatever, but, after the separation, I found out that sex was all right – I was all right – my body was all right.

After the separation, Ernie entered psychotherapy to try to understand his behaviour in the marriage.

> And he finally figured it out – it was all the conditioning, the male stuff – he's short, you know – he's not a big guy. Well, many things – anyway he got his act together quite well is what I'm trying to say – he's really very bright, and

he wanted the marriage to work. So we were talking after about a year and a half of separation.

Tina and Ernie got back together again after about two years of separation.

While direct links between Tina's biography and her experience of her body after birth can never be made, I think it is important to see that Tina refused to sustain an understanding of her body as nothing (no breasts, no vagina, no sexuality), and actively worked at "finding" her body by setting up the psychotherapy and by separating from Ernie. These efforts set the stage for Tina's discovery of her strength through birth.

Throughout the transcripts, Tina's mother appeared in ways that struck me very powerfully. I have no way of knowing if this was a function of Tina's subjective experience of her mother, or if the pattern which emerged for me was a function of my interpretive ground. I want to suggest the following interpretation about Tina's mother as tentative, in that it reflects my organization of disparate references to her, rather than Tina's stated perspective.

I have tried to understand what accounted for Tina's ability to refuse her negative body image and to actively choose to see her body in a different way. One possible explanation can be found in Tina's comments about her mother. These comments reflect a kind of good/bad split – about Tina's body as about other things – which allows for a choice because bad is always opposed by good.

Tina's mother came to Canada with Tina's father. She was at the time pregnant with her first child, and, within a few years, she had three children. Her greatest wish was to return to Italy; in Canada, she was severed from her family, the small town in which she had been raised, and her language. She returned to Italy for an extended visit, thinking perhaps to remain with her own mother; she left Canada pregnant with her fourth child, and he was born in Italy. After a while, she found that she no longer "fit" in Italy, that she was now a stranger there – a feeling which became more definite when her own mother died.

Tina's mother returned to Canada, and became pregnant with her fifth child. Soon after the baby was born, she went mad.

At that time, Tina was twelve years old. She attributed some of her negative feelings to the events of that period, during which she experienced some traumatic moments. For instance, during the time Tina's mother was psychotic, she once threw her daughter on a bed, ripped her clothes off and tried to examine her for "the sign of pregnancy":

> My mother had a nervous breakdown when I was 10 so between 10 and 15 she was really crazy, like *gone,* and what she had done was in one of her fits. Now she's fine – but in one of her fits she thought I was pregnant. I was 12 and she grabbed me, threw me on the bed and ripped my clothes off and was looking for some kind of sign on my body to show I was pregnant ... she was hysterical – that was a bad time – and, you know, she hit me and also that was part of my feeling very badly about my body. My body was dirty – she really made me feel that at that point when she did that to me – ripping off my clothes. There was nobody in the house....

Feminists have written a great deal about the problematic nature of mother-daughter relationships in patriarchy. In this data, I think we have indicators of how enmity is constructed between mothers and daughters. Given her isolation, her inability to speak English, the proscription against working outside the home, the physical toll of constant pregnancy, birth, and lactation, undoubtedly the existence of five children was both the salvation of, and a terrible oppression for, Tina's mother. This duality was inevitably played out through the body, through sexuality. The hatred of body which was engendered in conditions of oppression was passed on to Tina; it was her legacy.

But the legacy was dual; it was positive as well as negative. We find in Tina's account instances of her mother's support, which indicate the coexistence of both empowering and oppressive potential for childbearing. Tina's mother was instrumental in helping Tina to believe in the ability of her body to give birth. She told Tina not to read so much, that God had made her body so it could make babies and that she would be fine.

Her mother was also helpful in supporting Tina's ability to challenge medical authority over her body. For example, Tina felt the episiotomy performed by the doctor had been unnecessary. In discussing the episiotomy Tina said,

> TINA My mother was furious when she found out.
> AMY What did she say?
> TINA 'That's a pile of garbage.' She said, 'your body made a baby to your size – the doctor could have waited to see if your body had made a baby to your size – if the head was too big, then cut, but a 6 pound, 9 ounce baby is not an enormous baby ... you had a baby that was your size.' And I think she was right.

Images of her mother breastfeeding provided an important source of learning and support to Tina:

> ... so I remember her breastfeeding Rosa and Joe, and it was the most natural thing in the world. She wouldn't put a towel over her breast – to hide it. I remember the way she held her breast. I used to look at her breast for a long time for some reason. I don't know why – a little girl, just curious. I remember her doing this, lifting. What happened, when I breastfed her that's exactly what I did,

and the nurse went, 'Oh, that's perfect,' because the nose wasn't being blocked. I was lifting the breast so it wasn't so heavy. I didn't realize I was unblocking the nose, and lifting, so from looking when I was a child it was very easy for me and easy for the baby.

Tina's mother also encouraged her to not worry about weight loss, telling her to get stronger and to accomplish this by eating a good bowl of spaghetti every day.

The dual images of the body as dirty and as God-given were transmitted from mother to daughter. It was the positive image that Tina took to childbirth, and she used the image of a strong, healthy body, capable of birthing and feeding, to shape her experience. This was her mother's gift to her, despite the damage done during the period of insanity. And it is a gift from mother to daughter that has been systematically smashed in North America by obstetrical practice.

Tina's descriptions of the birth itself help us understand how childbirth produced her positive feelings about herself. It seems clear from the transcripts that how Tina behaved in the hospital had a great deal to do with her later sense of "I did it."

Tina was not a model patient. She was not a model patient because she constituted herself as active and self-directing during the labour and delivery. She did not play into the role of patient as ignorant, passive, and only waiting for the application of technology by experts. We see indications of Tina's ability to control decisions about her body even before she got to the hospital:

Well, you know, I'd never had a baby before so I was a little apprehensive. But I kept myself busy, had friends over, and, around 8:30 that night, I decided the contractions were 5 minutes apart, so I thought, 'Okay I'm going to go to the hospital.'

We see here that Tina assessed the stage of labour, and made a decision based on her own assessment. She didn't phone the doctor or the hospital, but retained the decision as hers.

Tina asked for information so that she could judge the progress of labour. She needed the knowledge in order to retain control of the labour:

> But I wanted to know if my cervix was dilated so I would feel more encouraged.

She was able to listen to her body and find more comfortable positions:

> I was walking the halls – I couldn't stay in bed – if I stayed in bed it felt really painful, so I was walking in and out, and I found a position, and, when the contractions came, I'd push against the bed like this and sort of walking – that seemed to ease the pain.

Nurses objected to her walking and told her to get into bed so that she could conserve her energy. What is crucial in this interaction is that Tina rejected their interpretation of her condition. She maintained her ability to "read" how she felt and to act on that reading:

> I had a great amount of energy – I knew my body knew – it was just fine. I just felt like it was a beautiful machine....

Tina was able to get angry when situations with medical personnel arose in which she felt they were wrong:

> I didn't care about any social thing – the reason I say that is because I was walking the hall – I was going into the bathroom because it was cooler. I would push against the basin because it was cool to hold on to. I remember

the nurse came in and I remember the look on her face was you better go back into your room. What are you doing here? I didn't care. I'm not hurting anybody and if people have to use the can they can use it, you know. For some reason she gave me a vibe that this is not proper; you should be in bed, you know? It was uncomfortable for her to look at someone in pain or something. It was embarrassing, that's it. I got a really strange vibe off of her – it's not kosher you know – and that infuriated me. Because I thought, when a woman's in labour, okay, it was the most natural thing in the world – if it hurts, it hurts. And I think most people, are they saints about it? I wasn't making terrible noises or anything, just that I wasn't being a routine type of person where I'd be laying in bed. Do people lay in bed? I don't know. But I imagine that's what she thought I should be doing – but I couldn't do it.

Again, at the onset of the delivery we see Tina listening to her body. She retained her sense of authority over herself and rejected medical authorities because they did not have access to the messages from her body that she did:

All of a sudden, the transition was over. I again didn't know, all I knew was that I couldn't stand up anymore – my legs would buckle under me and I needed to be down, so I lay down and I started to push by myself – I just felt like I had to go to the bathroom. Now I read in a book that that's how it feels, so when I felt like I had to go to the bathroom, well, I didn't care whether the doctor was there, the nurses were there, I didn't care who was there. At that point I had gone through so much pain that I figured, you know, this is fine; this is natural; and I'm not going to wait for someone to come and say 'Yes. You're 10 centimetres.' And, I found when I pushed, the pain stopped, and as soon as I found that out, it was terrific, and as soon as I found this out I started pushing like crazy.

It is important to note that Tina's ability to value and act on what she was feeling, her refusal to accept interpretations which didn't fit, and her subsequent rejection of medical authority, were not alterations of her usual style: they were consistent with her pre-pregnancy history. For example, Tina told me of having had an intractable infection for which rather extreme medical measures were recommended by her doctor. Tina rejected this advice and went to a herbologist, who cured the infection using herbal treatments. She entered the hospital already suspicious about medical expertise. Her suspicions coincided with a belief in her own health, and this belief grounded her conviction that her body would function smoothly in delivering her baby. This was a very different belief from that held by a "good" obstetrical patient, who, in order to interact pro forma with medical personnel, would see the body as the major obstacle to giving birth.

The reactions medical personnel had to Tina had a major impact on the birth itself: basically Tina was left alone to give birth, with only her husband in attendance. Since she had demonstrated a clear decision to manage her labour herself (refusing to lie down, or even to stay in bed) the nurses' response was simply to leave her alone with Ernie. My speculation is that medical personnel have no ways of helping that do not involve control, the application of technology, or instruction from a position of expertise; the language and skills of facilitating, listening and supporting are not included in the medical model. Consequently, when Tina displayed an unwillingness to engage in properly passive, receptive behaviour, medical personnel simply left her alone. The result was that Tina's baby was nearly born before the doctor or nurses came in:

TINA I found out later that you're not supposed to push
until the doctor tells you. Anyway, I was pushing
away, and she comes in, and she was freaking out,
and she got really excited and her reaction was ... 'Oh
my God, the baby's crowned....'

AMY Was anyone with you at that point?

TINA No – I – just Ernie – it was weird because I was
doing it by myself, which was fine.

I want to stress that being left alone with Ernie was crucial
to the outcome of the birth. The transition from labour to
delivery was the most difficult period for Tina. She was in considerable pain, and her breathing and relaxation techniques
were not helping. She was therefore most vulnerable at that
point. As soon as she started pushing, Tina found that the pain
subsided and that she was back in control. During the vulnerable point – at transition – it was Ernie who made a decision to
say no to anaesthesia. He helped her through the transition
and stalled requesting an epidural. He acted for her at a time
when she was dependent and vulnerable, exercising a choice
which he thought she would ultimately approve of.

TINA I lost my breathing; I lost my concentration; I had
never felt pain like that in my entire life, and I kept
saying to Ernie 'I want an epidural – I'm no martyr' –
and that garbage, and he was wonderful. He kept saying 'Sure, I'm going right now to get the anaesthesiolo-
gist' – he kept stalling and rubbing my back. And I
know at one point he said 'I'm going right now,' and
he left and said 'She'll be here in about 5-10 minutes.'
At which point I was going into what they call transition. I didn't know it.

AMY What did you feel then?

TINA Oh, I felt if this doesn't end soon I'm going to die. I
felt completely ... it was bad. I felt like I was at the

mercy of the pain. Actually, I had no control. At which point I didn't realize it but the transition was over.

With the end of transition, her contractions slowed, and she began to push, which made her feel better. In reflecting on the birth, Tina was grateful that Ernie "stalled" getting anaesthesia. She felt her doctor would have administered an epidural, had she been there:

AMY So you were alone, essentially, except for the last 15 minutes of the birth?

TINA Yeah, except for about 15 minutes of the birth. But it wasn't, not really alone – Ernie was wonderful, he was lovely. But, had the doctor been there, there was a strong possibility there would have been an epidural. She said to me that she is a real softy, and she's really strong. She would have just pushed Ernie aside and said 'Get out of here – you don't know what it is like to have a baby' – she's got three of her own – so she might have given me an epidural – she said it's just as well she wasn't there – so she may have given me an epidural and I'm kind of glad. I knew exactly what to do – my body knew exactly what to do because it wasn't numbed anywhere. And the baby was born so awake – she was like a little brown puppy.

We can see then that being ignored by medical personnel was significant in the production of Tina's subjective feelings of "I did it." She was helped in her most vulnerable moments by her husband, who made a decision he thought she would feel good about, based on knowing her and believing that she could make it through the difficult time.

Parenthetically, Tina's doctor's statement to the effect that "... it was just as well she wasn't there ..." gives a hint about the contradictions that exist for women doctors – that in fact she was glad not to be with her patient at the critical time so that she wasn't forced to apply help, which ultimately would not have been in the patient's best interests.

In concluding this section, I would like to discuss the issue of the political significance of the positive image which Tina keeps in her "little box." It is not an image which seemed to have a direct effect on her practice during the period of interviewing; but I believe that the image has tremendous political significance.

The sense of "I did it" – the triumph of birth that gave rise to Tina's feeling of strength – is the very feeling that obstetrical practice in patriarchy seeks to suppress. This image of strength and health stands as a direct contradiction to the image of passivity, weakness and inadequacy which our society engenders in women and crystallizes in the appropriation of birth by man-made medical practice. The fact that this contradiction exists clearly and consciously for Tina gives rise to the potential for political change.

We can see that, as Michel Foucault (1981) says, the contradiction assists

> ... in wearing away certain self-evidentnesses and commonplaces ... [so] that certain phrases can no longer be spoken so lightly, certain acts no longer, or at least no longer so unhesitatingly performed, to contribute to changing certain things in people's ways of perceiving and doing things, to participate in this difficult displacement of forms of sensibility and thresholds of tolerance. (pp. 11-12)

The process Foucault describes must happen when patriarchal meanings which describe women's bodies as weak and passive cease to be the only meanings available. When language describing women's health and strength can be heard and felt as a more accurate description of what women do in giving birth, patriarchy is weakened:

> When women no longer merely reproduce the definitions of themselves as ordained by the dominant group – as passive consumers, as subordinates required to impose order and cleanliness on chaos and dirt (Miller, 1976) – then there is nothing less than a redistribution of one form of power taking place. (Spender, 1980, p. 118)

LEARNING THE BABY

How did it happen that Tina became a "mother"? How did she become the person who was responsible for her child's emotional and physical welfare? The complexity of the task of understanding this seems formidable. The threads of the story coincide, overlap, conjoin and run parallel, seeming to defy the logical separation and ordering required to put them down in writing. It has been particularly difficult to lay out processes that, in reality, occurred over time. Clarity demands chronological order, but this order sometimes distorts the lived experience.

With this warning in mind, I will begin by showing how Tina's feeling of being responsible for her baby (a feeling acquired through the socialization processes of girls) combined with attachment, which has its foundations in pregnancy, childbirth, and breastfeeding. This combined feeling of attachment/responsibility was fully supported by the particular realities of her context, which enforced her isolation through mothering.

The knowledge that she was alone with and fully responsible for her baby helped structure the relationship between Tina and Ernie, between Ernie and the baby, and between

Tina and the baby. The result of that structuring ironically reproduced Tina as the baby's sole caretaker.

Tina described the first three days of being home with the baby as the worst. She was "... scared to death, traumatized." These feelings were most acute in the first three days and gradually tapered off into a more relaxed feeling, although this was not a smooth process. The genesis of her fear was the realization of her responsibility for the baby at a time when she didn't yet "know" the baby. It was a fear literally born from feeling completely responsible for a perfect stranger:

> TINA Trauma? A really bad shock. I don't know. When a situation shocks you.
>
> AMY How did this shock you?
>
> TINA The first few days, the day I realized the incredible responsibility – that I was responsible for this little person and I was frightened.

The feeling of responsibility co-existed with a sense of not knowing anything about the baby as a person:

> Yeah – my anxiety – anxious about not knowing whether I was feeding her enough, whether she was sleeping enough, whether she was – oh, just generally not knowing her – not knowing her. Of course, she can't tell you – I don't know her cries – I'm trying to learn her cries – she doesn't really cry. She just goes wah, wah, wah.

It was very clear from the data that the baby was Tina's responsibility. Ernie tried to reassure Tina that he, too, was responsible for the baby; the reassurance, though supportive, was unfounded. It was Tina who worried about how much milk the baby was getting, whether she was too sleepy, whether her bed was cold, and so on. I would locate the origin of this sense of responsibility for the baby in Tina's socialization as a girl in our culture. The socialization process is highly complex and beyond the scope of this book; I only want to emphasize here that Tina's feelings of responsibility for her baby began well before its conception or birth.

I would like to look at the development of Tina's attachment to the baby, which, when combined with her expectation of responsibility, formed a powerful emotional state which was activated within days of the baby's birth. I agree with Caroline Whitbeck (1984) when she argues that

> Factors other than those which are solely the product of socialization influence women and not men in their attachment to children and that these factors arise from biological differences. According to my analysis, these factors are the experiences of pregnancy, labour, childbirth, nursing and post-partum recovery. As explanatory factors, such conscious experiences contrast with a putative 'natural tendency' of women to be either nurturing or masochistic in personal relations, and with simple biological variables such as hormone levels as well as with the innate patterns of activity which are termed instincts. (p. 186)

Whitbeck rejects hormonal or instinctual explanations of maternal attachment. Instead she proposes that we consider the biological facts of birth and lactation as strong interactions which are important sites in the production of attachment. For Tina, the attachment produced by those key elements, combined with socialization processes which name her as responsible for her children, made a powerful basis for her later role as sole caretaker of the baby. In the following quotation, for example, Tina speaks of the beginning of her attachment to the baby:

TINA I think, you know, it started – the kernel of it started

– in the hospital. One night at about two o'clock in the morning, actually, when they brought her to me [for feeding], and I'll never forget it. She had been under the lights, and they had brought her to me, and they had washed her, and she was very clean I think, or just cleaned her off or whatever, wrapped her up like a little mummy. Her face was as brown as anything – she was jaundiced – so I took this little thing and said 'So, I hear you've been down South.' She looked like she'd been tanning, sunbathing. And she just looked at me, although I'm sure she couldn't see, but she gave me a look like of complete and total understanding, you know, and sort of completely zeroed in on me. I will never forget that. It was a lovely breastfeeding thing that happened that night. And it was the kernel of it. And it sort of slowly built a bit at a time. And I think at the beginning I was terrified of her, terrified completely of this little thing in bed, when she cried. And I was tired, terribly exhausted, so that the fear of taking care of her properly, and not being a good mother and bla, bla, bla and the fatigue had blocked whatever started back there in the hospital. I'm sure of that – she was three days old. Because when they put her on my tummy [after the birth] I was surprised – my reaction was just like this poor helpless thing. There was no love; I mean there was no love – she looked like a little puppy you know....

I think the feelings as a mother are so strong – the love I guess, everything that develops from that. I had no idea I was going to be like this, you know; it's so strong, the bond.

AMY Can you give me an example?

TINA No I can't. I don't think there are words to describe it, really. Just that it's an incredibly strong feeling and strong emotion. Everything rises – protection – you really want to protect her and you want to make sure she knows that you're here.

Tina was able to locate the "kernel" of her attachment to the baby in a late night breastfeeding that took place when the baby was three days old. It is important to bear in mind that breastfeeding occurs every few hours, and in the early post-partum period women breastfeed for an average of six hours per day. Mother-baby physical unity is experienced as the baby's sucking produces milk let-down reflexes, which in turn stimulates uterine contractions designed to pull the uterus back into shape. Washing and dressing a helpless infant and soothing and comforting it during distress are behaviours that favour the development of attachment.

What is crucial to understand at this point is that this attachment/responsibility emotion state is reinforced – in fact, made the only possibility – within the social context of the isolation of mothers. Tina's isolation as a mother was a critical factor in her election as the sole caretaker of her child. The first, most obvious fact was that there was no one else around to take care of the baby. Ernie returned to work; Tina was home with the baby. There was nothing and no one to distract her from the responsibility of the baby, and that responsibility remained paramount:

I have a book with me or something ... but I could watch television ... I just – during the day especially – I hate anything – crummy soaps – so boring. What do you do? But since this business with the sucking [a minor problem] and the whole thing, I haven't been able to read because I sit anxiously.

... I used to do workshops. I was doing theatre workshops, doing plays; I'd be out of the house – a course on

Shakespeare.... I would love to audit even once if I could just get someone to babysit.

But babysitting wasn't the answer. Powerful emotions, born of attachment and responsibility, made her feel too torn to leave the baby. Besides, there were complications in scheduling a baby on an unscheduled breastfeeding routine that doomed the project from the start. When I asked Tina about taking the baby with her to her course, she said that she would be sneaking into the course; by herself, that was no problem, but it was too risky to do with the baby because she would draw attention to the two of them. Here is one of the invisible lines drawn between mothers and the world: there are simply places – in fact, nearly all places – where, if you have a baby with you, you stick out like a sore thumb.

Going out with the baby was not problem-free. Tina was frightened of the responsibility of protecting the baby in what felt like a hostile world. Although she scoffed at herself for being afraid, it was clear that she perceived "out" as a place that was in some way threatening to women and small babies:

TINA: I was very nervous because I thought something was going to happen; if something happens will I be able to handle her outside?

AMY: Okay, like what is the something?

TINA: ... I have to be totally responsible for this little one and if anybody attacks her or does anything to take her away from me or something will I be able to protect her? ... a very – I think a very primitive thing, eh, when you think about it. On Bloor Street 1983, I mean who's going to attack a little baby, you know? I mean we're not in the jungle. It's not as if – really an animal thing where you're ... I think like birds protecting their little ones.... I think I felt the same way. I felt this

incredible – I feel now in retrospect a sense of responsibility coming on to me thinking I have to protect this
little one. Will I be able to do it? And instead I realized I
was terribly nervous, after going to the bathroom four
times, and then I realized she was going to die of the
heat if I didn't put my coat on.

Yet in a later statement we are reminded that indeed Bloor
Street 1983 is *not* hospitable to mothers and babies. Speaking
of feeding the baby away from home, Tina said,

I'm a good walker. I used to walk before I had the baby
... so I walk to Chinatown to see art galleries ... but then
it's always that I'm running back home to breastfeed – it's
like I've got, you know, a clock. You know, I'd love to be
able to say, okay, we're going to the museum, stroll
through the galleries leisurely and sit in the cafeteria and
have tea, you know, put her on the couch and then go
off in a little corner because the museum sets up little
couches ... but I can't feel I can do that. I'm afraid some
guy is going to come up to me and say 'Get out,' you
know, and I'd be humiliated or embarrassed, you know.

Tina tended to see fewer friends than before the baby was
born. She felt a rift between herself and her friends, because
they had not had babies and could not understand her preoccupation with, and need to talk about, her baby:

I almost feel – they don't know what I'm feeling and they
don't understand and so I wonder if this is sort of going –
like I'm experiencing something they can't experience. I
mean that's going to create kind of a rift, a small rift, not
terrible but a small rift, yes, for sure.

It – well – I have this thing about maybe boring them or

something. And, yes, I have a need to talk about it. Do
you understand?

Male friends' discomfort with breastfeeding made for difficult
social situations:

> He walked in; Amy, he did not even say hello to me. I
> was sitting there breastfeeding the little one and she
> takes an hour. I told you she was a leisurely feeder, so I'm
> not going to lock myself up into a room – forget it.... it
> makes me crazy.... so I was sitting there and I was wear-
> ing a diaper across this way, you know, just in case,
> because I mean he was coming over and he didn't even
> say hello.

I have been attempting to demonstrate the conditions of
isolation within which Tina's practices as a mother developed.
We see that her sense of responsibility for the baby, together
with her attachment to the baby, created a powerful emotional state – which existed in a social context that requires
women to be sole caretakers of their babies. A single-family
house, a husband who worked all day, cultural hostility to
women and babies, and changed relationships with friends all
conspired to produce isolation.

There is a danger here, however: the temptation to separate
Tina, as the producer and reproducer of herself as sole caretaker, from the context in which she lives, which structures
and reinforces sole caretaking. It is important to understand
that Tina's actions were formed by, and gave form to, conditions of isolation; otherwise we are in danger of accepting
individualistic ideologies, which mystify through the use of
abstractions instead of being grounded in real experience. It is
important to understand that Tina was embedded in a certain
reality: that of being the only person to care for the baby. She
was the one who got up at night; she was the one who had no

relief during the day; she was the one who was subject to the circumstances which make doing anything other than baby care impossible. Such conditions of isolation and enforced preoccupation with the baby necessarily impelled Tina to structure child-care practices in such a way as to make those conditions more tolerable. The isolation of women as mothers is a social reality that was in place before Tina became a mother; Tina's attempts to lessen the burden of that reality unwittingly and ironically reproduced it by the way they structured the relationships among Tina, Ernie and the baby.

Tina could identify the first moment of her attachment to the baby: while she was still in hospital, a late night breastfeeding had aroused her love and a deep sense of bonding. This attachment, reproduced in daily feedings every several hours, extended through the intimacies of washing, dressing, comforting, and soothing the baby, and combined with her socialized feeling of being the person responsible for the baby, meant that Tina came home from hospital having a completely different relationship to the baby than Ernie did. The already-existing intense relationship between Tina and the baby influenced the structuring of the relations between Tina and Ernie – which resulted in Tina being the baby's sole caretaker.

We see how this process operates during the second interview:

Ernie, he does this thing sort of instinctively because he's had no previous experience with children. So he will not say to pick her up might spoil her. So it's really marvelous to watch him work because she will start ... just wail or something – she'll want to be picked up or something – and he'll go and he'll pick her up and he'll put her in her own bassinet, sort of, and talk to her. Meanwhile, I will say she should be sleeping because she needs her rest so that she can rest up and then she can be awake to eat in four hours, because if she doesn't sleep enough she doesn't feed.

Here, we see Tina's enjoyment of watching Ernie "learn" the baby. He picked her up when she cried, talked to her, soothed her. But Tina interrupted and stopped Ernie's way of being with the baby, because she knew that ultimately it would be her responsibility to make sure her initially quite sleepy baby was awake enough to feed properly.

Again, we can see how the feeling of being ultimately responsible for the baby prevented Tina from allowing Ernie to develop his "style" of infant care:

> It's almost like this wonderful positive thing that happened. And I look at it and think, oh, I was very successful or whatever, and I close the door because there's all kinds of negative things that are monsters – you know, like things like am I dressing her properly, is she going to get a cold, are her routines down, is she going to be spoiled, am I going to be sorry? Ernie and I have to talk. We always have a conflict over Ernie. If you're holding her so much what am I going to do during the day-time? I have, you know – I need space. I need to have her down in the bassinet for two or three hours just so I could clear my head even if it's to do something ridiculous like dishes. I need to do that. I can't have her like this all the time. I'd go nuts. I was talking to Ernie and the discussion almost went into an argument. You know it's a hard time for the adjustment of a couple.

Tina clearly prohibited Ernie from handling the baby when he felt like it because of the fear of what the consequences might be when she was alone with the baby nine hours a day. The thought of the baby expecting to be held all day terrified Tina. The answer to the problem of being overwhelmed, then, is to teach Ernie to help her teach the baby not to need constant contact. It is important to note that in these moments Tina is the instructor, Ernie the student; that form of relationship is not conducive to shared childcare.

The data contains indications of Ernie's jealousy, particularly over the feeding situation. I have previously described nursing as one of the factors that generates mother-infant intimacy; Ernie, too, seemed to see nursing as an intimate act:

> ... because he's very interested [in babies] there's like a competition or something, I can feel it. It's like he can't – he says, 'Gee, I wish I could breastfeed.' He told me that, and I just flipped out – I said, 'What?' He said, 'Yeah – when you start going out soon we'll get some formula or something.'

Yet it is difficult for Tina to actually leave formula for the baby. It feels like leaving something bad for the baby to eat. Tina tries to express milk for her, but she is frightened to store the milk and she has a hard time expressing an adequate supply. After arduously expressing some milk to leave for a feeding, she noticed that the cream had risen to the top and threw it out fearing that it was somehow bad. This constant feeling of having to supply the best results in the following dilemma:

> I did something Saturday morning. I felt so bad after and I thought I'll never do it again. Screw the routine, screw everything – it's not worth it. She had woken up and he was playing with her Saturday morning. He brought her in here and put her on a quilt – he was playing with her; she was laughing, the whole thing. I was in the bathroom combing my hair, putting on some makeup, and I was – oh, yes, I was going to go out with a girlfriend.... The problem was, if he kept playing with her, she couldn't go to sleep and she would not wake up on time for her next

feeding, so that I could feed her then go out, because she sleeps over her feeding time when she's too tired. So I said to him, 'Put her away; you know she's got to be put asleep; you know – you've got to stop this because she's got to wake up at twelve o'clock so I can feed her. Then at one-thirty, I can be with my girlfriend because I want to go out today, period.' And he just ... took her and he put her away and I felt so badly because it was like I had cut this lovely time they had had together and she was laughing and the whole thing. Anyways, so I just felt terrible. I felt like a piece of shit.

From the third interview through the seventh, during a period in which Tina was home alone with the baby and Ernie had returned to work, we see two threads twist together: one was Tina's increasing feeling that she was parenting alone, with total responsibility for the baby; the other was Ernie's increasing insensitivity to the baby. With Tina assuming total responsibility, Ernie had no chance or obligation to "tune in" to the baby.

AMY Can other people calm her down as well as you or is that different?

TINA No, no – that is different, like I've noticed that. She has blown me away because I – she'll be with Ernie, and she'll get into some kind of ...

AMY Can I ask you a question?

TINA   Yes.

AMY Why did you lower your voice now?

TINA Oh, because I feel so badly about it. No. It's true. I feel badly – it's tearing him up.

AMY It's painful, isn't it?

TINA Yes, yes – it is because I know he felt bad about it, I think. What happens is I wasn't well – I was dizzy or something – and he was supposed to be taking care of her, and she just – she just decided she wanted to scream, right? And I thought, why on earth? And Ernie's such a joker and he loves even to joke with her you know. He'll just tease her. He'll put her on her little tummy, you know, and say, okay, and she'll say aah, aah – she doesn't like it – and he'll just leave her there and sort of laugh and then coos with her and plays with her. He says he's toughening her up. I say it's bullshit, just leave the kid – if the kid is uncomfortable, why? So anyway, I thought he was playing with her that way because she was howling, and I came in, and he just had her on his knees, and he said, 'Tina, I don't know what's wrong with her – she's just screaming.' So I just took her, and like that she shut up and she was perfectly fine – and no explanation – I could tell he felt bad.

AMY And you felt bad?

TINA I felt bad, yes.

AMY What part did you feel bad about and what does that mean?

TINA Oh, well, that first of all I have all the advantage. Like the fact I've carried the baby for nine months is the beginning and it's not fair. It's just not fair – the female gender – I've been blessed really with doing this and the male isn't. The males are not you know – I consider myself very lucky....

The gap continued to widen:

TINA I spend so much more time than he has with her, you know, because he went back to work immediately and I stayed home. But it hit me that I'm the one that puts her to bed every night – he doesn't. And the main reason is because I breastfeed her and it's like

her next feeding and she's with me and that's it, so I
might as well lay her down and so ... ultimately I'm
always the one to put her to sleep. That's quite a
responsibility, isn't it? And to make sure she's relaxed
and happy and contented and that she can fall asleep.
AMY Would it be nice if Ernie could put her to bed?
TINA You know what? He would let her cry more. He's
done it; he's done it a couple of times; and I just
haven't liked the idea of it. He's let her cry more. I
mean, she does fall asleep anyway; I'm sure the crying
doesn't do her any harm just that – there are two different personalities handling the same person.

It was excruciating for Tina to let the baby cry. Partly that
was because she was so connected to the baby's needs that
"... it just hurts me to hear her cry." Partly, as well, Tina saw
letting the baby cry as bad because she believed that "... if you
just sort of keep her more or less relaxed and happy, she'll
deal with frustrating situations hopefully in a kind of relaxed
way." In other words, Tina's practices were structured around
an image of what was good for a developing child and the
idea that she was responsible for that development. Ernie did
not feel himself ultimately responsible for the process, as Tina
did. The fact that Ernie didn't have a deep commitment to the
development process meant that Tina could not entrust her
baby to its father.

Tina began more and more to feel the burden of being a
sole caretaker:

The one thing I don't like is the total responsibility, you
know. But it does create a wonderful bond.

But we see by the fifth interview that Tina was beginning to
feel angry:

She was on the breast for three hours at a time. I was bent over with this baby here so I got angry, sort of angry – at the exhaustion. It's exhausted me and I've never been tired in my entire life and I hated being tired that way – it wasn't tired and wanting to go to sleep; it was tired of being totally drained of everything. And Ernie, I think, was sort of insensitive to what was coming down. He thought I was just being fine just because she's on my breast, and it bugged me that I had to ask him – like he didn't spontaneously say, 'Tina; give me the baby, I'll change her.' I'd say Ernie please change the baby, and he would, and that would bug me though – I hate to ask. I figure he should be sensitive enough to realize what's coming down and say 'Look I'll take the baby, you know – you've had her for three hours in a row – here, I'll change her or I'll do something with her.' He'd just sit there and enjoy – you know, watch television or do whatever he's into.

At that point, Tina's anger did not fuel struggle. The remarks quoted above were immediately followed by a discussion of what remedies could be found to combat her fatigue and allow her to be more energetic. She decided to take a yeast compound to solve the problem.

Tina felt guilty at the prospect of not being with the baby. While she called the idealization of full-time mothering a "motherhood myth," she was still under the influence of guilt:

TINA I think it's more guilt than an anxiety. I think it's part of the whole motherhood myth.
AMY Tell me.
TINA Where you know you're supposed to give completely. Somehow I think it's drilled into women, especially women of ethnic background, I think.

There are mothers who really do give themselves up completely, like my mother. She is a mother who never stopped. Now she's starting to think of herself as a person but she's fifty-nine. I think it's the whole motherhood thing that you're supposed to give yourself 100 per cent of the time.

Fitting in with the notion that mothers should give "... 100 per cent of the time" is the belief that child-care practices ultimately determine the kind of person an infant will become. If one holds those beliefs, leaving a baby becomes very difficult:

Well, if I leave she gets a little bit upset. Of course she'll stop crying, of course she'd go to sleep; of course she'll eat or do whatever she has to do, but something else will stay with her, the upset. And then it'll happen again: of course she'll go to sleep; of course she'll eat, of course. But something stays with her. It's like this person she wants to be with – and I can guarantee that she does – this person that she wants to be with is not with her, and it makes her feel that she cannot attain things that she wants, you know.

This was the emotional responsibility for the baby that Tina carried. Against that background, we can begin to understand some of the conflicts Tina experienced in her day-to-day decisions regarding baby-care practices. On the one hand, she felt compelled to be there to meet the baby's needs, to "give." On the other hand, the baby's needs presented her with the fear of being overwhelmed, of never having the time to complete her daily tasks, let alone to establish any personal space. Given this conflict, it was very difficult for her to establish a comfortable way of being with the baby. If she picked her up, she might be setting the stage for being completely overwhelmed; if she let her cry, she was being a bad mother, and would produce an insecure child. It became difficult for Tina to believe that she was ever doing the right thing:

> I put her down after a feeding and sometimes she cries and I rock the bassinet. I know I shouldn't get in the habit. When she gets a little fussy after a feed I put her down, and, if she gets fussy, she goes 'wah,' and her little eyes are open as I rock her, and so I rock her, and she sleeps. But I never pick her up. Because if I do that she'll know, and she'll get into the habit of wanting to be picked up, and maybe I won't be there. But, if she has a little gas or needs to burp, she has to go to the bathroom ... then I'll give her a bit of a snack.... I don't know if I'm doing the right thing or not.

> I can tell by her cry, you know, that she needs to be held, and, the poor little thing, I figure is something wrong with her? And I think, to hell with everything, and I pick her up so I don't know if I'm going to be sorry or not.

> She's been sleeping through but if she falls asleep at 8:00 ... then you know she's out and she sleeps till the morning and she did wake up the other night at 4:00 in the morning, but she went 'ahhh' and back to sleep so she knows I won't pick her up. Now in the daytime, however, I do pick her up. If she wakes after a ten or fifteen minute nap I do pick her up, and I try to rock her back to sleep. Well, sometimes she never goes back to sleep. That's a real problem now – her daytime naps for me have been really short.

The sense of conflict resulting from "... either she overwhelms me or I fail her ..." was impossible to resolve or ignore, and it left Tina feeling insecure about every decision.

TINA Well, I think she must need contact, obviously; she must need it and so I give it to her. I had this fear that maybe she's going to get used to wanting to sort of scream, pick her up, hold her, put her down, sleep, pick her up, hold her, you know – that whole thing. But that's why I rocked her because I want to sort of make sure that maybe at the same time she's too young to even notice it. My mother keeps on saying don't pick her up every time she screams; you're going to be sorry.

AMY What do you feel like doing?

TINA Well, I feel like picking her up, you know, but I alternate. Gee, I don't know if that's such a good thing either, because it's not sort of a consistent kind of thing, but I couldn't resist last time picking her up....

It is important to note one major way that mothering practices are shaped by sole caretaking roles: as is illustrated in Tina's data, mothers who operate as sole caretakers become obliged to teach small children not to need, because babies' needs, in sole caretaking, can come to feel overwhelming. It is very possible to imagine a scenario in which women take care of babies, and do other kinds of work as well, within a peopled setting; in that scenario, it would be possible for mothers to remain concerned about their baby's needs. Under current sole caretaking arrangements, however, mothers are forced to be preoccupied with their babies' needs, and they deal with the resulting tension by teaching the babies not to need as much: not to expect to be picked up when they cry, nor to be fed when they want sucking, nor to be rocked, soothed or comforted when they are distressed. In this way, enforced preoccupation with babies actually reduces women's ability to care for their babies.

The establishment of Tina as sole caretaker clearly affected Ernie's relationship with the baby. We have seen how his initial interest in getting to know the baby was structured by the conditions of isolation within which Tina took primary responsibility for the baby. His efforts to get to know the baby were essentially structured around relieving Tina of the full burden of child care. In this structuring process, his experience of the baby was always mediated through Tina's needs. Thus, he might take the baby for a walk so that Tina could nap, or he might play with her to tire her out so that it would be easier to put her to sleep. In this way, his direct contact with the baby was diverted. His knowledge of the baby became structured as follows:

$$\text{Tina's need for relief} = \text{Ernie and baby}$$
$$\text{rather than}$$
$$\text{Baby's need for care} = \text{Ernie and baby}$$

Ernie's feeling of responsibility became less a function of the baby needing his care than of Tina needing his help. The construction of Tina as sole caretaker was created and recreated by daily life: while it had its origin in socialization and biology, Tina's role as sole caretaker was reproduced every day in the particular forms of relationship that existed among Tina, Ernie and the baby – and those forms were themselves shaped by isolation.

THE CONSTRUCTION OF SUPERWOMAN

Eventually, Tina became Superwoman: that is, the person responsible for her baby, for going to work, for being a wife and for maintaining a social life. The need to be Superwoman was founded on Tina's role as sole caretaker of the baby. As well, though, Tina's relationship with Ernie developed in such a way that Tina increasingly had all the responsibility and Ernie was increasingly marginalized, rendered unimportant in their family ecology. From their experience, we can learn a great deal about the actual processes by which a modern nuclear family is constructed.

Tina's process of separation from the baby occurred in parallel with the processes which established and secured her position as the baby's sole caretaker. In her role as sole caretaker, she felt that the "old Tina" had disappeared. The "old Tina" was a person who was always willing to go out – to the movies, to lectures, to concerts or social happenings. The new Tina found it painful to go out, because that meant she had to leave her baby. If going out meant leaving the baby, she would opt to stay in – and, given the very real hostility of the public to babies and children, it was difficult for Tina *not* to see going out as meaning leaving the baby:

TINA As I said I haven't gotten – been able to get myself together [to go out], so, okay, Ernie says tonight you and I are going out alone. It's like I can't bring myself to leave her, it's really strange.

AMY Why is it strange?

TINA Well, because I would think that I would, you know. I have a hard time leaving her, I do.

AMY Wait, okay – you're saying – sounds like two things? You're saying you have a hard time leaving her and that there's something bad about that: weird or strange?

TINA Yes, yes. It's like that exactly. You picked up on my confusion – like why am I having a hard time leaving her? Shouldn't I? Yes, shouldn't I sort of be able to say, okay, you know, she'll be fine, and whoever takes care of her will be someone very capable and ... ?

AMY That's what you feel you should say?

TINA Yes, yes – but it's not only ever being taken care of. It's like I'll miss her, you know, and I'm saying, you know, you've got to get on with your life. This kind of

stuff but I really – I miss her. I don't know. Is it missing?
... She still needs me I think. That's it, and I need her, I
think. You know, it's still sort of being with her. The
girl downstairs is marvelous; she's terrific and the baby
just loves her and she just comes upstairs, you know,
but I can't quite enjoy myself. Still, there, that's the
thing – I can't seem to loosen up enough to enjoy
myself.

We can find in the separation dilemma a good example of
the social construction of maternal guilt. Having learned to
mother in a social context which constructs mothers as sole
caretakers, and which makes sole caretaking ideologically
"natural and normal," Tina now questioned whether her
strength of attachment to her baby was wrong. Achieving
good feelings about one's mothering is always an uphill
struggle:

Well, I have my baby and, you know, of course I care for
her and everything, and I'm taking care of her as much as
I can, but what I'm thinking – is this an overreaction or
something, am I being over-protective – am I being
overly cautious ... ?

The contradiction is that mothers, established as the only
person responsible for their baby's emotional and physical
needs, must then be happy to leave the baby to go into the
world to fulfill their other obligations (being a good and interesting person, being a social convener and so on). This produces guilt at leaving the baby, and guilt at staying with the
baby. Guilt underpins mother as Superwoman:

It's like a fear of her needing me. Now I'm assuming she
knows who I am.... She can pick up my smell or what-

ever it is, my touch, my voice that she's used to ever since conception. Like I think in the womb they must hear, and so I'm assuming that that's one thing and the other side of it is that I need to be there to fulfill that need. I need to do that.

With this reciprocity of needs established, Tina faced the issue of going back to work. Before the baby was born she had made arrangements to take maternity leave, then return to work for the last month of the school term; that would allow her to spend the summer holidays at home. Tina and Ernie counted on her salary, and, besides, Tina loved her job as a primary-school English teacher. It was difficult for Tina, while in the actual relationship with the baby, to think realistically about going back to work. She tended to dismiss the questions I asked about work, as though they just couldn't be thought about at that moment.

However, as the time approached for Tina to go back to work, her anxiety escalated. She was torn between her job and her baby:

I feel torn again. It's not a torn out of what I should do or shouldn't do. It's a torn in the guts thing. Like with the baby, a totally gut thing and, like with my job, I like it, you know, that's all. I like it."

The realities of feeding the baby were intimidating:

I don't want to stop breastfeeding and I don't want to get her onto the bottle. You know, I'm afraid I will have to – even one feeding a day. I think it's going to screw her around. She won't quite understand breast – bottle.

Finally Tina decided to leave infant cereal for the baby in case she got hungry, because the baby refused the bottle. Her child-care arrangements were settled and she was generally organized to go back to work. On the weekend before she was to return to school, she faltered:

> I almost chickened out. In fact I did chicken out. I called the superintendent on Saturday to say to him I'm not going back. And do you know what? He was away for the weekend all day Saturday, all day Sunday and if it hadn't been for him not answering that phone I wouldn't have gone.... Okay, so then I talked to my mother and my mother said 'Tina, it's going to be all right, she'll have her pablum; she'll have her milk in the morning before you go....'

And so Tina went back to work, feeling:

> The baby you're leaving ... it was so much a part of you for such a long time. It was just like ... I can't say it's like having your arm cut off because I can't talk to my arm.... There's a real deep feeling of such pain at leaving her....

The first few days back at work were very emotionally upsetting. Each morning, leaving was an agony for Tina. Upon returning in the afternoon, she felt "relief, a wonderful relief, wonderful relief" that the baby seemed happy and content despite her absence.

Doing her work was helpful for Tina:

> All right, it's helped because it has confirmed that I'm a separate entity away from the baby as well as the one who had an office who sits and plans things, that has a mind that's working on something else besides the baby, and that's what I was before I had the baby and that's how it's helped. It's just reminded me in a very, very concrete way.

Despite her relief that the baby was doing well without her, and despite her good feelings about her work, part of Tina remained in conflict. She found herself waking every four hours at night, waiting for the baby to wake and feed, even though she had been sleeping through the night for a while. Tina herself interpreted her awakening as her desire to take care of the baby at night because she was away during the day. Tina asked herself,

> I might sound crazy or something, but are we going against our nature or something by being separated from our babies? Are we going against something very, on a gut level, biological thing?

Tina's life changed in many ways after she went back to work, and those changes were part of becoming Super-woman. Her daily schedule was exhausting because she did her best to both teach and mother. Tina fed and dressed the baby in the morning, got herself ready to go and then was off to work. She taught three hundred elementary school children English every day. At lunch, the babysitter brought the baby to her. She breastfed her, changed her, played with her and then resumed teaching until 3:30, when she "... bolts out her door ..." to be at home in time for another feeding. She made supper, did routine chores and then fed the baby and put her to bed.

However, going back to work did not really make Tina feel back in the world. She was plagued with a sense of being left out. Her husband urged her to do things, to go out with him, but she was usually too tired.

> Left out. Yes. I felt so left out. He's telling me about all these friends that he met. Old old sort of college friends at Juney's – there just happened to be a bunch of them, and, you know, I just felt left out.... and yet at the same

time I don't want to go out. That's another thing.... I start to worry about myself, looking at myself, thinking why don't you want to go out? Is it safer with the kid?

It was hard for Tina to feel that she couldn't do it all. In the ideology of Superwoman, mothers can bear the intensity of children's needs, go to work, be loving wives and take part in "outside interests." This is how lives go "naturally."

Not being able to do it all counts as personal failure and provokes intense guilt. With Tina feeling constantly tired and often angry, her interest in sex declined. She felt guilty about this and worried that Ernie was contemplating an affair:

I don't know, it just bothers me and I have a feeling anyway that he's flirting or something and I told him this morning and he said no.... I know he is.... I don't know.... I don't know if he is or not.... We have not been making love because I have been extremely tired – I don't, I'm not, I don't feel like making love but I feel that we should be making love.

... and Ernie assumed that I was awake when we went to bed so he thought, 'Well, let's make love.' I thought – 'Why doesn't somebody just give me a gun, shoot me and I can forget all about it' – I mean really.

In these conditions, Tina's effort to free herself from constraints turned against her. As we saw in "Learning the Baby," Tina tended to stick to schedules so she could organize her day, and feel in control of her time. These schedules ironically ended up controlling her and reducing her ability to be in the world with the baby. Note that Tina saw this as being "lazy":

I don't want to go out because I don't – it's much easier to keep a routine with the baby; it's much easier. If I keep

on going out her sleep thing is disrupted ... her food
thing is disrupted and she's starting to become a lot more
stimulated and I find she gets distracted from sleep....
And so that's the – I guess the lazy person's way out.

Fatigue and constant demands made going out seem not
worth the effort:

> I had to go to a barbecue or something and I rush rush
> rush rush, trying to get everything ready, you know, and
> made a potato salad and so on.... Everything is done, like
> the baby is sort of more or less in gear, and the potato
> salad made and so on. I thought – what am I going to this
> thing for? I have spent so much energy getting ready that
> I don't want to go.

> Yes. It's like I need to go out, but at the same time to be
> with myself and Ernie. At the same time I need to be with
> her and to stay at home, you know.

By the seventh interview, the fatigue, the pain of separation, the feeling of being left out, the sense of being the lonely
caretaker, had all coalesced and left Tina feeling depressed
and angry. She was depressed about her loneliness and
fatigue, but she was furious with Ernie.

Tina was angry with Ernie because he was free while she
was isolated and imprisoned. He appeared as the oppressor,
she the oppressed. But it is this very construction that we need
to question and challenge, because it is a construction which
dangerously confuses freedom with being nothing. From
what, exactly, was Ernie free? He was free of attachment to the
baby. He was free of knowing his own child. He was free of
watching her growth. The major argument of this analysis is
that such freedom is a devastating form of oppression and that

it is critical to see that the construction of Superwoman is reciprocally related to the construction of Nothingman.

Let us look more closely at Ernie's freedom. He was able to follow his interests, to go out,to do what he felt like doing. In describing their child-care arrangements, Tina said,

> Oh he's – yes, he comes home and he doesn't take care of the baby. No, the babysitter is still here. He just comes in and out and makes sure, I think, I don't know, but the other day he had her. You know, it depends on his mood. If he feels like bike-riding or whatever.

Tina envied this freedom. She felt utterly tied to running home as fast as she could to feed and be with the baby. The baby needed and missed her. What Ernie's freedom meant was that the baby didn't need him.

In "Learning the Baby," we saw that Ernie never assessed the baby's needs directly. It is important to remember that his experience of the baby was always mediated through what Tina wanted him to do. He helped Tina with the baby; he rarely helped the baby. This process hindered the development of intimacy between Ernie and the baby. And, since Tina could only really be relieved of sole caretaking if another adult developed intimacy with the baby, Ernie always fell short as a helper:

> TINA You see, this is what the thing is. I said to Ernie – 'Here, take her; I have to sleep.' Christ almighty, the kid is crying and crying and crying and crying and crying and one night I was *gone* – I mean if I didn't have that few minutes – I mean on the clock five minutes – I would have fainted from exhaustion. I mean when I had my five minutes, he was in the bathroom with the door closed because he didn't want me to hear her or something, and actually the sound travels worse in a

big room, so he just put her in the bathroom. I opened the door and he was really gone. Like you know, I said 'What is it with this moron?' I got so upset....

... But I'm saying what is it with him; you know, why can't he, you know, sort this out? Well I think that was the turning point with me, and I thought, forget it – he's not handling her like, like – which is dumb, I guess. I don't know, but it was the turning point for me, and he lets her cry more than I would. Like if I'm upstairs doing something and he's got her on the couch, she's crying for a reason – pick her up – she's bored, talk to her or something – and he says, 'It's okay, Tina; don't worry about it, it's good for her.' I don't like the way he does it. So what's happened? This is the turning point. See, this is what happened that I think now I'm understanding. I need a mental break from her, but it's like, after the way I saw him handle her, and yet I know he loves her – I mean he's crazy about her – I just don't like the way he handles her.

AMY Okay, what are some other differences in the way you handle her – is it mainly that or are there other differences? Can you give me some...?

TINA Differences in the way he handles her? Is that what you're saying? He doesn't – he doesn't tune in to the baby; that's all; it's that simple to me. I just think – and it's an interesting thing, it's a thing you have to learn, a mother learns – looking out and saying okay what does she need and just tuning right in there. Ernie doesn't get upset about her crying or anything.... He won't tune into her and say, 'Well, okay, what's happening here?' – you know, check it out. It was 'Oh, just a baby crying,' you know. Well, it's not just a baby.

It is clear that not only was Ernie not needed by the baby, but

Tina in fact didn't trust him to take adequate care of her.

Being unable to "tune in" to the baby, and having Tina always intervening in response to his incompetence, Ernie was unable to understand or imagine the depth of responsibility Tina took for the baby; in other words, her work was invisible to him. When she tried to talk to him of her need not to be so burdened, of the need to share the baby, he accused her of not wanting the baby. Tina felt this comment reflected the grossest insensitivity, and interpreted it as an attempt to make her feel guilty. When Tina complained of fatigue, Ernie told her she needed to become a "doer." Clearly women's work was not "doing" because Ernie didn't do it, and therefore couldn't begin to see it.

Finally, because of Tina's anger, they fought – and began to talk. Tina pointed out Ernie's insensitivity to her role as Superwoman. He saw this, and they continued to discuss issues in their relationship. By the eighth interview, Tina felt things were much better:

> Yes. I'm fine – I don't know – I was in kind of rough shape when you saw me last. I feel much better, I think. Things are better, with Ernie taking much more of an understanding sort of status and really helping out a lot. Like it's really terrific.

> It's very good. I mean, recently he's really gotten good. He will, you know, cook for me, you know, or I will cook or no one will cook because we don't feel like it.... He started making the bed and started cleaning the toilet bowl, so it was good; and he really does take an active role with the baby, and it's tremendous....

However, the active role is as her helper. The entire eighth interview was interspersed with comments to Ernie:

Ernie; it's okay; just let her be please; she'll be all right.

Ernie, is she crying; is she crying anymore? Is she crying? No, she's sleeping? Did you go look? Did you open the door; is she okay?

Things "getting better" meant that Ernie was being a good mother's helper. In terms of the forms of behaviour that are possible in this social construction, he was limited to being a good helper – or being irresponsible. To be a good helper, he had to help with the baby and do part of the shitwork; to be irresponsible was *not* to do those things. Thus was Nothing-man constructed.

Tina's anger can only increase. Ernie cannot rescue her from being Superwoman, for that is rooted in her being the baby's sole caretaker. And how can she maintain sexual and emotional trust and intimacy with a man, who, while socially constructed to appear to have everything she does not have, is nevertheless Nothingman?

Ernie's sense of being disabled, as well, can only increase. Caught between two choices, both of which construct him as unneeded and not able, he can only continue to do nothing right or to find ways of withdrawing. He cannot rely on historical forms of authoritarian, patriarchal male roles. Being a man no longer gives him exclusive control of money, property, decisions: Tina is a breadwinner. Tina and Ernie are a democratic couple who, until now, have done things "half and half." The problem is that he has shed authoritarian practices, which historically gave meaning to fathering, and, as well, the emphasis on achieving total meaning through one's work is currently being questioned by men; yet at the same time that these two meaning structures have declined, family relations are still firmly centred on mother as sole caretaker. Hence the reciprocity of Superwoman and Nothingman. The reciprocity exists through the practices of Tina and Ernie: it is Tina who tells Ernie how to manage the baby; it is Ernie who is free to ride his bike.

The ideology of individualism is very much at work here. Liberal "humanistic" thinking has generated many categories of labels which describe people's individual characteristics, and then has held individuals to blame for those characteristics. Thus, Ernie is "insensitive" when he tells Tina to be a doer. Or Tina is "controlling" because she regulates Ernie's interaction with the baby. In generating these categories, individualism as an ideology neatly circumvents social conditions which structure the practices of being "controlling" or "insensitive." The real point of this account is to attempt to expose those conditions, so that I, Tina, Ernie and readers of the account can begin to teach ourselves how to be angry – not at each other's characteristics, but at the social conditions which produce our practices of mutual injury.

I am concerned about the distortions which my interpretations may impose on Tina's account. My concern is that, in showing how the construction of Superwoman and Nothingman has its basis in mothering, Tina's and Ernie's lives are portrayed as statically fixed in oppressive forms. The nature of my project has excluded descriptions of their overall subjective experience, which included humour, mutual caring, intimacy, respect and closeness as a function of parenting a baby. Tina was characterized by her interest in understanding her world, and in making her own meanings. They were both willing to engage in struggle, to talk, to fight. I worry that, in naming the practices which create Superwoman and Nothingman, I am "hardening" those categories in a way that replaces these real people with abstractions. I want to be especially clear, then, that some day they will probably recollect their experience of the first six months of parenting, some day, with warmth, humour and positive feelings, as well as with a sense of the life-giving nature of struggle and conflict. Superwoman and Nothingman are not descriptions of people. They are the abstractions I am using to describe a set of practices, structured by social conditions, which influence forms of social relations.

CHAPTER FOUR

NATALIE

I HAVE ORGANIZED NATALIE'S case history into sections which correspond to her experiences of birth, post-partum trauma, and achievement of equilibrium. As in the previous accounts, these experiences are presented chronologically – but in reality they overlapped or occurred concurrently to a much greater extent than can be displayed in a narrative form.

The first post-natal interview with Natalie was filled with tension and anxiety. Her usual coping mechanisms were inadequate to the task of dealing with a new baby. For Natalie, that period marked the beginning of a struggle to cope with what she experienced as trauma; I think it was because of the tension produced by this trauma that the baby remained unknown to me as a person; I knew a great deal more about the early personalities of the other two babies in the study.

BIRTH

In the first interview, I asked Natalie to describe her experience of giving birth. She said,

> NATALIE Characterize it for you? Well, it was very traumatic. It was very painful. I was totally unprepared – do you want to hear things like that?

AMY Yes. Do you feel different now after the birth?

NATALIE I'd do it again because – well maybe because the doctor said it won't be that bad next time but maybe it's a necessary evil if you want to have kids – I mean, if you have to go for the thirty-six hour package or nothing, I'd probably go for the thirty-six hour package. But there was just nothing like it. Of course, I've never really gone through pain, I mean, no car accidents or anything. Maybe other pains are more painful but I can't think of any.

AMY Any positive features or is it mostly just the pain?

NATALIE No. I can't think of anything positive about it.... No, I can't. There isn't one good thing I can say about it. Not other than this is what happens and only because I imagine things have got to get better. They certainly can't get worse.

In the second interview, she said,

NATALIE Oh, shit! Thirty-six hours of labour, are you kidding? How many different ways are there to describe it. It was terrible but something you have to go through.... If they come up with another way I'd love to try it.

AMY Looking back on it do you – just having gone through it, does it make you feel any different?

NATALIE No. Why would it? In what way?

AMY I don't know. Either that makes sense to you or it doesn't. Either better, worse.

NATALIE No. That question doesn't even make sense to me – I guess it doesn't. I can't even think of an answer.

Natalie was very clear that her feelings about her body had not changed as a function of having given birth. She put birth in the same category as car accidents – something terrible that happens, a question of bad luck. In fact, in commenting on how she would change childbirth if she could, she said,

> Well if I could change it I would obviously make it shorter, but it's not really worth thinking about it because there's nothing you can do – it's the luck of the draw.

This is a significant statement because it characterized Natalie's entire approach to birth: "There's nothing you can do." The body is something beyond control or prediction. It is controlled elsewhere, certainly not through any inner principle within oneself.

The only positive references to feelings about her body Natalie made concerned weight loss. When asked about the greatest personal changes she had experienced in the six weeks after the baby's birth, Natalie said, "Losing weight and having confidence in motherhood." It is important to note that even the positive feature of losing weight was still not presented as being under Natalie's control. She reported that she didn't really know why the weight loss had occurred – a weight loss of 38 pounds! – but made vague references to not having had time to eat, or having taken long walks with the baby. She presented the weight loss as something that had just happened to her, a piece of good luck that had left her looking good.

In parts of the transcript it became clear that Natalie experienced her body as somehow having a life of its own, whose motivations were secret, whose inner logic escaped her. This feeling pervades the following comments:

> NATALIE Certain parts of it [the body] have a certain job to do and they do it and isn't it wonderful how nature works and has a body part to do everything. That's about it. I mean, sometimes I am in awe of just everything the body can do and does do.

AMY Your body?

NATALIE The body, anybody's. Any body that has a baby. Isn't it a miracle?

The description of her body as "it" or "the body" evidenced a sense that her self was split from her body. She didn't speak of what she did, but of "... how nature [as outside her] works" – mysteriously, incomprehensibly to us, following its own course. She located giving birth as an impersonal event, without connection to her person.

How do we account for this view of the birth experience? Some insight into Natalie's relationship to her body can be developed from her remarks about her pre-pregnancy feelings about her body, and from her recollections of labour and delivery.

During the fourth post-partum interview, for example, I asked Natalie if there were any general differences in her feelings about her body before and after pregnancy. She said,

Oh, yes. I feel – well, just the fact that the weight is going off because I used to look terrific. I used to wear spike heels, skin tight blue jeans, little halter tops and when I – well one girl in the office said when I stood up every male head in the office turned around. It was very nice of her to say that. I know that I attracted attention, and I used to do everything I could to encourage that. I was a swinging single for five or six years. I was everything a swinging single was supposed to be – wearing halter dresses, going braless and swinging and dancing till three in the morning and flirting and attracting all kinds of attention and then dancing lewdly on the dance floor. So to have this three or four pounds going on every month and having to buy jeans in bigger sizes and never mind sizes, you get the pleats. I just hated myself – so now it's – the way I was physically. I mean, obviously dancing lewdly on the dance floor has got to go; a mother doesn't do this. But looking good, I mean it's so – when people look at you for five or six years because you look great and you're always getting compliments and you know that men are staring – it's hard to, it's hard not to have that anymore. I don't want to sound conceited but I had a nifty little figure back in those days and then I felt great. I've always been very – wanted to be the centre of attention. With my wedding I think it was the happiest day of my life because I was the Belle of the Ball and everybody looked at me.

For Natalie, self-esteem and confidence came through her ability to attract men. In fact, throughout eight interviews, I never heard her describe herself with more pride, more delight than she did in the above remark.

Natalie's ability to attract men was important to her because she knew that the only thing she wanted to do with her life was to be a mother, and the means to this end was to attract a man, get married, then have children. Her "nifty figure" gave her success at attracting; thus her ability to attract became a source of self-esteem.

... when I grew up I was going to be a mother and that's all. Doing this probation thing in the meantime was just putting in time. It was a job until what I wanted came about. For a while I had given up on it, figuring you're not going to meet the guy; you're not going to get married; and you're not going to have a family – that was very traumatic for me. As a matter of fact a woman at the office said 'I remember, Natalie, when a client came in with a baby, the way you handled that baby.' She said, 'I thought you were going to cry,' and I was walking around saying isn't she the most beautiful baby you've ever seen. I don't remember that incident, but it must have been about the time I was so discouraged thinking, well, you'd better re-evaluate your life because you're obviously not going to be a mother. For a while, I figured, well, then, what use is there to live for, not in a suicidal way, but so now what are you going to do with your life? – you have the next thirty-forty years ahead of you. They are going to be empty. I went through with it. I resigned myself to it and of course life went on and then I met Jim about a week after. Going through a year or so of trying to get myself adjusted to the fact that you're not going to be a mother – the depression, the discourage-ment, the tears – when I get my shit together along comes Jim.

Just as Natalie viewed childbirth as impersonal, she also saw her ability to attract men as impersonal. Her esteem for her own body depended on others, on whether or not men could be attracted by it. Even the mechanics of being attrac-tive were silenced in Natalie's account. Having a nifty figure just happened, gaining weight after marriage just happened. The work involved in being attractive is invisible – nowhere do we see an account of that work, of how one learns to apply make-up, of shopping endlessly for those little halter dresses that magically appeared on her, of the pain of spike heels. All that work is silenced through the ideology that says attraction is natural – either you've got it or you don't. Even the work of being attractive is lost to her as a resource for connecting her body to her self.

For Natalie, seeing attraction as the major function of the body affected more than just the relationship between her self and her body; it also permeated other important relationships. For example, Natalie's achievement of her life goal depended on Jim; Jim's presence depended on his decision that Natalie was attractive; so ultimately, control over Natalie's life goal rested with Jim, not with Natalie. She recognized this, saying,

It was a lousy feeling to know that what I had chosen to do with my life was something totally dependent on another person. If I wanted to be a teacher you go to school, you get education, you work hard, and you become a hell of a teacher or anything else but what I had chosen.

Natalie's "swinging singles" period began after her divorce, and ended when she met Jim. She entered her relationship with Jim vulnerable to his control and dependent on her self-less body to do its invisible work of meeting her goal of motherhood.

Issues of the body came into play in Natalie's sexual relations with her husband. Natalie was sexually unresponsive to Jim; she did not become sexually aroused, and was not interested in sex. At the time of my last – post-interview – conversation with her, she and her husband had not had sex in two years. She perceived her sexual problem as stemming from her first marriage, during which her husband had made her engage in sexual behaviour that was repugnant to her. She attempted to work out her problems with a psychiatrist, who interpreted her sexual problem as a function of her relationship with her mother. She tried to explain that it was the relationship with her ex-husband that had started the problem, but the psychiatrist ignored her perspective, so she quit therapy.

Natalie's lack of sexual response was another manifestation of the notion of a body not connected with herself – of her body as having a life of its own. Her "self" was severed from her body, and this brought guilt and a feeling of being set apart from how things "should" be. When asked what changes she would like to see in herself, Natalie said,

NATALIE I guess sexually still nothing. I'd like to work on that.

AMY You'd like that to be better?

NATALIE Yes, not because I feel unfulfilled but to make Jim happy. I'd have to say he's been a real trooper about it so I'd change that.

And

NATALIE ... well, it's okay with me. I was never that big on it anyways. I've always had problems. It's bad for Jim and I keep thinking I've got to do something about this but then I get too tired and Jim doesn't push. If Jim were more pushy about it we'd do something but if I'm tired he just lets it go too. He's so understanding and compassionate that I could walk all over the guy.

Here is a glimmer of the fear and rage of living in patriarchy, where body and self are controlled by men – but at the same time living with a husband who can be walked all over by virtue of his understanding and compassion. How can Natalie depend on a controller who can be controlled? We begin to catch glimpses of the social construction of the polarities which divide men and women.

The second aspect of a relationship based on attraction is illustrated by Natalie's attitude toward women. When one's goal is to attract men, all other women are one's competitors. Natalie said of the woman who remarked that she turned heads, "It was nice of her to say that ..." – indicating her sense of surprise at receiving a compliment from a competitor (and another woman could only be a competitor). At several points in the transcript, Natalie expressed surprise at having gotten support from women; for instance, when office colleagues gave her a shower, she was surprised, since she had felt that they "... didn't give a shit about her." Natalie did not have close women friends. She had been cut off from other women by the construction of enmity through competition. This study will not attempt to explain the origin of attraction as a primary goal for Natalie; the data available give only hints at the parts of her biography that would show us how this goal was constructed. We do not need to know how attraction came to be her focus, but must understand that it was a critical issue for her and that this focus tells us something about the construction of her subjective experience of becoming a mother. As Tillie Olsen (1965) says,

> The leaching of belief, or will, the damaging of capacity begins so early. Sparse indeed is the literature on the way of denial to small girl children of the development of their endowment as born humans; active, vigorous, bodies exercising the power to do, to make, to investigate, to invent, to conquer obstacles, to resist violations of the self: to think, to create, to choose, to attain community, confidence in self. Little has been written on the harms of instilling constant concern with appearance, the need to please, to support; the training in acceptance, deferring.... But one knows how to read for it and indelibly there is the resulting damage. (p. 46)

Natalie was admitted to the hospital before the onset of labour. She had had a migraine headache, a complaint which she had not had since before her pregnancy, and which she thought might have been caused by bodily changes signaling labour. Ordinarily, when she had a migraine, she would take strong Tylenol to "... nip it in the bud." So at 5:00 a.m., when the migraine began, she phoned her local hospital to see if she could pick up some medication there. She was told to go to the hospital where she was planning to deliver; in that hospital's emergency room she requested Tylenol for her headache, but was treated as a patient in labour:

I kept saying 'I'm here because of a headache; labour

hasn't started although it will soon, I'm sure, but that not-withstanding, give me my Tylenol so I can go home.' That's all I wanted. They had to wait for my doctor to come; they admitted me into the labour room.

The doctor came about ten or eleven and figured I was going to start dilating, I was going to start labour that day so let's keep her.

Anyway, nothing happened so they kept me there all day. I guess the pains must have started or something, I can't remember. Anyways, the doctor came back later, I think; I still hadn't done much but he wanted to keep me in overnight figuring if it didn't happen today it's going to happen tonight, so let's ship her up to the main floor and wait it out.

Natalie didn't want to stay in hospital:

Anybody that asked me how I was doing I said 'Fine. Just let me get rid of the headache. That's my top priority. If I didn't have this headache you wouldn't see me here. I'd be home.' That was my biggest complaint – give me Tylenol and let me go home so I can relax – you're all making this worse for me.

However, her wish to get Tylenol and go home was lost in a process through which Natalie and medical personnel came to an unstated agreement: Natalie would give up her auton-omy in exchange for procuring medical expertise. This "exchange" was accomplished effortlessly, without questions, without confusion to either Natalie or the medical personnel. She was an ideal patient, precisely because she had no notion that she could affect her body in any way. Her body was a phenomenon that existed outside herself; she was therefore grateful for body experts who would take charge of it for her.

During the pre-pregnancy interview Natalie had made it clear what her expectations of labour and delivery were: she didn't care about natural childbirth and had nothing special she wanted to see happen during the birth. Although she had taken childbirth preparation classes, she believed the methods of breathing and relaxation to be useless – merely a distraction to take your mind off the pain. Her idea of a good labour was a short one. The guiding assumption underlying her notion of labour and delivery was that her body would labour independent of her self; because she would have no control over it, she would need nurses and doctors to be her controllers.

Natalie's actual experience of childbirth was completely consonant with her conceptions of her body. There was an exact match between Natalie's idea of her body and medical conceptions of the role a woman's body should play in childbirth; consequently, all of her bodily experiences of childbirth were organized through the meaning of those parallel conceptions. There were no clashes, no dysjunctures, no opposing discourses, no contradictions which might have motivated change.

As Natalie described her labour, it became obvious that she lacked factual knowledge about the process. For example, when the cervical mucous plug came out, she was frightened and turned to the nurses to gain security through knowing. She said, "It made me nervous because there was just a whole lot of it. So, anyway, Jim went out to ask one of the nurses what it was, and I guess she said it was my plug...."

It is interesting to speculate about why she did not know what it was. Some well-discussed reasons clearly had at least partial effect here: for one thing, in a culture where birth happens as a private, medical event, the realities of birth are not available as general knowledge. Also, Phyllis Chesler's (1981) point about the silence among women is well taken:

Under patriarchy, pregnancy and childbirth are savage tests of your ability to survive the wilderness alone. And to keep quiet about what you've seen. Whether you're accepted back depends on your ability to learn without any confirmation that you've undergone a rite of passage.... You must keep quiet and pretend to return to life as usual. (p. 133)

The cultural silence about childbirth can partly explain Natalie's focus on attraction as the chief capacity of her body, which meshed so well with the investment by medical personnel in control through expertise. In addition, however, I question whether Natalie truly did not "know" that what she was experiencing was the loss of the plug; she had taken childbirth preparation classes where such things are taught. I believe her inability to say "This is my mucous plug" stemmed more from the lack of an image or vision, or a language, in which she could insert herself as a knower, than from the genuine lack of a fact. The plethora of books on pregnancy and delivery gives us some idea of the attempts some women make to become knowers; Natalie had not made this search. Knowledge of her body, like her sense of her body, was therefore perceived as located outside her self.

Natalie experienced a very painful labour. Medical knowledge offers one way of dealing with pain – the epidural, which anaesthetizes a woman in labour from the waist down. Methods of dealing with pain that do not rely on technology are missing from the medical apparatus, though they exist in women's traditional knowledge. Midwives, for example, commonly work to achieve comfort for women in labour by rotating a woman's position, suggesting walking, squatting, or leaning forward, applying heat and cold, massaging, and so on. Yet Natalie remained flat on her back, with an epidural held out as the only form of hope available. Of course, control of the epidural is in the hands of doctors; they finally gave

Natalie permission to have the relief she depended on, and Natalie was grateful for that:

> The doctor came in at first and checked me and said I could have an epidural at that point, just to relax.

> ... the pains were very bad, they were very sharp pains and I just wanted something for that, like once he said this is coming, you know, that's all I needed – the crutch, the hope of seeing the anaesthetist poke his little head around the door – he's the most important man in your life.

In Natalie's account, data from which to conceptualize labour are continually transformed by technology. For example, Natalie described being hooked up to a monitor and beginning to use the monitor as the source of information about what was happening in her body:

> There was a monitor there somewhere along the way because I remember watching it thinking that ... I could look at it and think that this was the crest of the pain and now it's going to go down.

Consequently, a transformation of the actual experience of labour occurred:

> ... the left side didn't take completely, so they gave me another kind; this one completely numbed me. I couldn't lift my legs; I couldn't do anything; I was just absolutely tingling and buzzing from here down to my toes. Some-body had to uncross my legs....

Natalie entered second-stage labour and was instructed to begin pushing even though, as she said, "I didn't feel like bearing down." (This was one of the few direct statements Natalie ever made to me regarding what her body actually felt like during labour.) However, for four hours she was instructed to push; finally her doctor came in and said,

> You've been a good girl, and I'm awfully proud of you, and now we're going to put an end to this.

Michelle Harrison (1982) suggests that in reality there is no second stage in labour, but only a continuous process of birthing. If the second stage of labour is indeed socially constructed, one wonders whether the dividing point (10 centimetres dilation) is merely the signal for nursing personnel to give the patient instructions to push, to summon the doctor, to wheel the patient into the labour room, to set up the stirrups, and so on.

> There were times that it helped me to push but as for this technical thing about the part of your labour where you feel the need to bear down, I don't think I felt the need to bear down. And, by the way, they had to puncture – my water didn't break on its own – that was done before the epidural to relieve pressure or something. Also a catheter, I had that. I think I had everything, you know, if I were looking at a menu, what do you want – I had all of them at least. The nurse kept saying, when you feel the contractions coming, push.

Natalie began to feel a split between herself and her pain:

> I was really working hard, but so was the pain. The pain was working harder than I was but it was neck and neck all the way. I don't know who won.

She became disconnected and was unable to concentrate:

... they kept telling me to keep pushing, keep pushing, keep pushing. I was getting closer and I did keep pushing but I eventually became too disconnected to even – I didn't even know what a contraction was anymore. When they said to wait till the next contraction, I couldn't even remember what it was I was waiting for, so I was pushing at the wrong times, and, because I hadn't gotten in front of a contraction to push, it was painful as hell to miss it, but I didn't even know what I was there for anymore.

When her doctor ordered more epidural medication, she felt,

Relief in sight – get me that anaesthetist – and not only was he going to get me the anaesthetist, he was going to give me the second drug, the one that made me numb and tingly all over.

At the point of delivery we again see the transformation of the experience through technology. Natalie was re-anaesthetized; she said,

The pain had stopped, and I was feeling fine. I was in a good mood. The baby was coming. We're all here – my favourite doctor, my husband was here, my parents were waiting outside. Everything was great – no pain. I kept saying, like get this show on the road. Come on I'm ready. I don't want to play labour anymore. Let's play having the baby. So he turned it around [with forceps]. I could feel a vacuum – he was pulling. I guess that's the closest I ever felt to bearing down, and that's not even bearing down, that's just a little something. I was curious, I couldn't see anything – there was no mirror. I just saw a little bit. The baby was born, 7 pounds, 1 ounce. I didn't see her for a long time.

She was with a nurse being cleaned up and weighed. Jim could see her but I really couldn't.

I tried to find out how Natalie had actually felt about the birth:

AMY How did you feel when she was born?
NATALIE I don't know – I can't come up with a memorable moment.

Then I tried to sort out the sequence of events following the delivery of the baby, but much detail was simply lost for Natalie in a fog of disorientation:

NATALIE Oh, because I – a lot of it I don't remember.

No, no, I don't know when I nursed her.

I was wheeled out and she was with me. I don't know.

Well she was up on the ninth floor with me when we went up there, but I don't know when she left.

I don't know. No, I don't. I can't remember. I don't know what happened. I don't know when I slept; I don't know when I fed her.
AMY How were you feeling when you got up there?
NATALIE Obviously stoned.
AMY Anything you remember?
NATALIE Blank.
AMY Okay, let it go.
NATALIE Yes, isn't it amazing? I never even thought of it. I'll have to check that with Jim. Where was I Wednesday night?

Regarding seeing the baby for the first time, Natalie said,

They gave her to me all wrapped up and I'm trying to look, peek over all this stuff and see. I'm surprised I wasn't more overwhelmed by the whole thing. It was just on to the next step, now this is done so let's go on.

It is clear that the events of labour and delivery as Natalie experienced them could not become data capable of altering Natalie's pre-pregnancy sense of her body. In fact, it is striking to see how Natalie and the medical system were able to collaborate, with great skill, to produce an experience of childbirth that would reproduce Natalie's sense of her body as out of her control and needing the take-over of technology. Natalie's experience of childbirth was managed so as to meet the needs of the medical system for control, and at the same time to verify Natalie's culturally-based notions of passivity and powerlessness. In other words, a perfect birth.

We are left with the question of how Natalie herself mediated the hospital experience. At several different times in the interviews I asked Natalie how she would have liked to change her labour and delivery if she could. She was able to point to only one thing: she had laboured in a room with a woman who had just had a Caesarean section, and she had felt unable to make noise for fear of disturbing her roommate. She also commented that the nurses hadn't supervised her adequately.

Natalie made a few vaguely negative references to the doctors and nurses, but any expression of dissatisfaction about them was inchoate, unpatterned, and immediately discounted by being appended to a rationale showing that the staff was good rather than bad. There was simply no pattern, no image, no language available to Natalie which could make sense of her nebulous feeling of disturbance. In the absence of such language, a "discourse of excuses" had a clear field:

Well, I can't – well there's a couple of nurses I'm not

crazy about – on the other hand, I didn't really push anything. One of them was busy, said she was busy, and she was.

When asked what she would have changed about labour and delivery if she could have, she said,

Well, off the top of my head I would change the labour and then have another doctor or something but another doctor couldn't make it easier, and it might've meant a C-section and I wouldn't want that.

I really enjoyed my hospital stay. I found it more like a hotel than being in the hospital, and, if it wasn't for the pain of having a baby, I could look forward to going back for my next, my next delivery.

The discourse centring on women's control over their own bodies was totally lacking in Natalie's language. Instead, she spoke a language that maintained her as passive, alienated from her body – one in which her body's actions didn't depend on her or belong to her, but were dedicated to the service of those who had power over her.

How are we to understand Natalie's total lack of woman-centred language at a time when such a language is being heard by more and more women? My speculation is that this lack can partly be attributed to Natalie's isolation from other women, partly explained by the jobs Natalie and her husband had chosen, and partly understood through Natalie's biography. I do not claim that these three sources provide a complete explanation, but only that they offer the most pertinent information that appears in the data.

Natalie did not have close women friends. For her, women had been cast as competitors: people who aspired toward the same goal of being chosen. Since Natalie's life goal had been getting a husband so she could have children, competitors in the race toward that goal were understood as mortal threats.

Isolation was reinforced by Natalie's job. She was a probation officer: she supervised from an adversarial position; she sought evidence of disallowed behaviour; she gave advice to people who most often didn't want to hear it. The job was one in which she exercised social control, predominantly over women; Natalie came to see her clients as *needing* control. For example, she was hostile to teenage mothers who ran out of money for formula or disposable diapers, feeling that they hadn't "tried." "Trying" meant breastfeeding and washing diapers. Hence, Natalie defined these women as "users" who depleted her. After spending the day "shooting the breeze" with those people, when she went home from work, she wanted nothing more to do with people. She described this job-related irritation with people as a significant reason for the fact that she and Jim had few friends.

Jim's job, too, was one of exercising social control: he was an R.C.M.P. officer. Both Natalie and Jim had jobs that located them as protectors of the dominant social order. To "hear" oppositional discourses, therefore, would have meant dealing with contradictions to the discourses which they themselves formed and by which they were formed every day at work – a very difficult balancing act.

Finally, we know from Natalie's biography that her mother's life was one of tremendous hardships; only her struggles and resolute actions allowed the family to survive, and eventually to prosper. Natalie showed a similar quality of persistence – I think as a result of family experiences – saying over and over in the interviews, "You do it because you have to." This attitude had helped her overcome some very difficult obstacles; however, it also kept her in situations in which gritting her teeth and "... going through it because she had to" were her only available choices. With something less of a commitment to persistence, she might have found that she didn't "have to," and she might therefore have begun to question her basic framework. All Natalie's considerable energy was spent "doing it"; if she had had a little less strength, she might have discovered the advantages of stepping outside the frame, simply because she could not have gone on "doing it."

TRAUMA

Natalie endured a period of shock or trauma following the birth of her baby. This trauma began in hospital, seemed to be most intense during the first and second months of the baby's life, and then gradually tapered off into a state of relative equilibrium through the fourth, fifth and sixth months.

At the first post-partum interview, held ten days after the birth of her baby, Natalie greeted me as she opened the door by saying with real resentment as well as some humour, "Why didn't you tell me it was like this?" She was pale, exhausted, and filled with a kind of nervous energy that made it difficult for her to rest.

NATALIE I didn't know it was going to be like this. Oh, God.
AMY Like how?
NATALIE Totally not prepared for – nothing at all. I don't know what the hell I'm doing.

My field notes from the first post-partum interview describe Natalie as totally overwhelmed by what was happening to her. When I was sorting out the interview data, I found that the major categories of the first two interviews were "Shock," "Being unprepared," "Panic," "Anxiety," "Not knowing" and "Feeling out of control."

Much of Natalie's anxiety centred around the feeding situation. Natalie came home from hospital without any confidence in her ability to feed her baby. She panicked at each feeding. I saw an instance of this when, during the first interview, the baby whimpered; Natalie's whole body stiffened and her face contorted with anxiety. I asked her if there was any way I could help her feed the baby, and she said no, she would wait until she absolutely had to feed her, because she couldn't face feeding her until she had to.

The situation was so tense that at the end of the interview I felt that I couldn't leave without making some effort to support her, so I asked her if it would be helpful to her to see the milk which she was sure wasn't there. She said she thought it would, so I helped her express some milk; she looked at it and explained it as "fluid." She was simply unable to believe in her capacity to nourish.

When I asked her to describe her feelings of panic around feeding, she said,

> NATALIE It's this feeling of 'Oh, my God, what now?' So I feed her and if I do is it going to work or is it going to be one of those bad feedings and it's not just – if it doesn't work now – if it doesn't work now then it's going to affect her tonight, it's going to affect her indefinitely so it seems as if each step is all important. You can't isolate each individual feeding, each change, it's all part of the whole picture....
>
> AMY What makes you panic?
>
> NATALIE My baby, everything about her. The – like she's – whenever I hear her whimper it means I've got to do something and will I guess right? Will I do it right? You know when you've just fed her and she's crying and you figure, well it's got to be a wet diaper and you're just hoping when you poke in there it's going to be soaked or something, which reminds me she hasn't had a bowel movement that I know of for at least two or three days.

Natalie had firmly believed that "... there are only three

things that can go wrong with a baby: she's wet, she's hungry, or she's thirsty. Now if you've got those three covered then she's happy." The reality – that babies' needs can't be neatly packaged – made Natalie feel totally out of control.

Yes, but there's – nothing falls into place. You've got to make your own place and just because you've made your own place it doesn't mean it's the right one. Anyways you might just have to leave that place and try another one, and that can go on indefinitely.

When the baby was hungry at an unexpected time, Natalie felt,

Then things can be out of control for the next day before you get done – this morning I thought it's going to be a good day and maybe tonight I'll get her back on schedule. When I woke up at night and found she'd been sleeping for those hours, I thought great, now we can start all over again. Clean slate – back on some kind of tentative schedule and already she's off her schedule.

The work of trial and error with new babies was something that Natalie found difficult to tolerate. The idea of a need for any change appalled her.

My mother kept saying, 'Come on, sit up in a rocking chair and you'll like it,' and I kept saying, 'No, no, no, I just barely got her nursing laying down. I'm not going to try anything new at this point.' It's, well, like as insecure as I was, as soon as I had anything that was the least bit close to making her happy, I'd stay with it, so she was taking to nursing lying down. Lying down was shitty, but at least she was nursing, so I wasn't going to try sitting up.

170

You know, there's something about night-time. You don't take chances at night, but during the day – when the sun comes up then that's better. And again my mother would be saying, 'Try feeding her sitting up,' and I'd say, 'Tomorrow, maybe in the daytime but not now.' Insecurity about the dark.

At that stage, almost all Natalie's statements about her relationship with the baby involved feeling sorry for her. There were no statements of enjoyment or closeness – I think because the experience of caring for the baby required that all of Natalie's resources be directed at sheer emotional survival. The closest she came to describing good moments with the baby was the following remark:

She – I was thinking that another low is when she looks so cute because she looks up with those big eyes and I have to look after you, you poor little thing; you don't realize I don't know what the hell I'm doing. I feel so sorry for the poor little thing because she's got – she's got to count on me and as I said earlier I don't know what the hell I'm doing.

How was such a traumatic experience of early motherhood produced? Given the restrictions of the dominant language of individualism, it is difficult to produce an explanation which avoids presenting psychological and contextual factors as independent of each other. Natalie's case history, however, provides some spaces in which to make the attempt. Such an attempt must ignore the boundary-posts of language and thought which are used to demarcate "inside" and "outside," and begin to describe the inside and outside as co-constituted.

The first indication I had of Natalie's trauma came from my phone call to Natalie in the hospital, which had been made to set up the first post-natal appointment. She told me that things were going "lousy" – the nursing wasn't going well. According to Natalie, she herself had felt things were going well, but the nurses had decided that the baby wasn't latching on to the nipple properly; they had taken the baby off the breast and were feeding her glucose and water. Natalie was convinced that she had no milk, although she described her breasts as engorged; she was unable to hear my suggestion that the engorgement was due to milk filling the breast. My notes of the phone call read: "Natalie had no sense of herself here – she was just relying on reactions from nurses. I mentioned that if the baby was a lazy sucker that sugar water in a bottle might not be the best approach and she said, 'Well I thought so too, but that's what they do here.' Her own centre, sense of autonomy, was obliterated."

Once again we see the perfect fit between Natalie and medical personnel. Natalie in effect believed that there was no way she could affect what was happening or control the situation. She handed her autonomy over to the nurses, as people she believed – or had to believe – could control the breastfeeding process. The nurses took control, which of course precluded the possibility of Natalie's taking charge of feeding her baby. It was a nurse who informed Natalie that the baby was sucking "improperly" – as if there were one model of sucking that all babies had to follow. Until she received this information, Natalie had felt that things were fine; she was shattered by the nurse's statement. She no longer had any basis for believing in her own sense of how things were, and no longer had a sense of being adequate to feed her baby – a feeling which was manifested in her inability to believe that she could produce milk. Nurses fed the baby bottled sugar-water; the bottle, carefully rationalized as medically necessary, was a means of assuming control through technology, and also a statement about Natalie's inability to feed her baby. Natalie heard the message as confirmation of the fears and doubts she had brought to the feeding situation. In fact, Natalie became instantly dependent on, and grateful to, the nurse (E) who had informed her that the baby wasn't sucking well. It was E who would help her; E on whom she relied; and Natalie was in a state of panic when E went off duty.

NATALIE When the good nurse, the one who was looking after me, went off shift, [she] said she would leave notes with this other nurse. Well, when I went to this other nurse to say E told you about me, that I'm going to need help nursing, she said: 'Yes – sit over there and I'll keep an eye on you.' Well, I've never nursed her sitting up; it had always been lying down, let alone in this nursery, this – you know, where everything was bright and I was exposed – I can't nurse in public. I feel bad nursing at home because my father doesn't leave the room, but there's no other way.... So in this nursery with all these bright lights, even if nobody passed by, just the bright lights. It was just obvious that she wasn't going to do anything for me but I couldn't really blame her with all these other kids – babies to look after – I opted for going to the pump [electric breastpump] myself because I was afraid if I didn't I would undo what E had taught the baby, so it was just as well I guess. It was awfully discouraging though. I was sitting by this breastpump and nary a drop. I think about, I'd say not even a quarter of an ounce, an eighth of an ounce came out after 15 minutes of pumping.

AMY And what were you feeling at that point?

NATALIE Totally discouraged, abandoned, not a mother. If I was any kind of mother I would be able; I would be able to fill the bottle up right away. Just, not even to have to be in that room in the first place. You know, what kind of mother are you anyway. Doing that was better than undoing what E – I had so much faith in E that I wasn't about to do anything that was going to change what she'd been doing.

Even now as I write, after having seen this quote countless times, I am unable to read it without feeling anguish. I feel this anguish because the incident is somehow a "perfect" moment, which allows us to see the kind of relationships which structure the reproduction of oppression.

Natalie came to breastfeeding believing that good mothers breastfeed:

> If you are a good mother you nurse your baby. If you're a good mother you don't use Pampers.... It goes back to my job. Working for the probation department, so many girls when they phone and say they don't have money, they say right away I don't have Pampers for my baby. I think deep down inside it made me kind of think that they are kind of lazy.

Matched with Natalie's belief that good mothers breastfeed was her lack of confidence that she herself could produce milk, that she would be able to breastfeed. Historically, she had experienced her breasts as the paraphernalia of sexual attraction, rather than as potential sources of nourishment.

The nurses who took care of Natalie were inculcated with the belief that they were in control, that they held the knowledge, the expertise necessary to make women into adequate mothers. But breastfeeding is a process which can be facilitated but not controlled. As well, nurses' knowledge of breastfeeding – apart from any personal experience – is limited to medical knowledge, which has always ignored the only reliable source of breastfeeding information: women's experience. Attempts to impose control are made in the form of statements about improper sucking, by introducing bottle feeding, by suggesting breastpumping. The assumption of control by nurses helped to obliterate whatever potential there had been for Natalie's belief in her ability to breastfeed, and she was left incapacitated by what she perceived as nothing less than her failure as a mother.

We can clearly see the double bind which applies to mothers: mothers are invisible and inexpert; but, though they are powerless, they are at the same time responsible for all failures. In Natalie, for example, we see someone who was unable to speak for herself, to name her reality, to feel centred – yet who at the same time held herself responsible for a breastfeeding difficulty which probably didn't even exist.

This was Natalie's experience in hospital. The stage was set. She and her baby went home.

After my talk with Natalie when she was still in hospital, I was very surprised, at the first interview, to find that she had persevered in breastfeeding. I had fully expected to see her bottle-feeding. In fact, despite the hospital problems, she had no intention of bottle-feeding. Her perseverance came from an ultimate sense of "having to": when the chips were down, you just "did it." When I asked Natalie about the decision to stick to breastfeeding, she said,

> Probably because I would've had to. That's all there is to it. You do things because you have to. I used to say to lots of girls, you're going to make it because you have to and that's life – so I would continue breastfeeding because it's easier than formula, it's better for the baby and you find a way.

All through the eight months that Natalie breastfed her baby, nursing was fraught with difficulties. She never fully believed in her capacity to make enough milk, but took satisfaction from the fact that, on unsupplemented breastfeeding, her baby had doubled her birthweight at three months. Probably as a function of engorged breasts (a condition that often occurs because of infrequent feedings structured in hospital), Natalie developed a cracked nipple, which caused bleeding and excruciating pain all through the months that she breastfed.

Why did this difficulty never get resolved? There were two co-constituting factors: one was Natalie's ignorance of her own physical functioning; the other was that, ironically, she was cut off from adequate sources of breastfeeding support precisely because of her belief in expertise.

Natalie quite openly attributed her difficulties to her own ignorance. As she had not placed herself in the "underground" women's network of information, however, she had to rely on "official" channels for learning about how her body functioned – that is, on school, family, popular and formal medicine, and so on. Clearly, neither school nor popular nor formal medicine disseminates breastfeeding knowledge, while Natalie's mother was of the generation – an entire generation! – that was labelled as "not having any milk." Thus, Natalie ended up saying,

> NATALIE I think it's just – a lot of it's just – I don't know enough about my body or the body in general.
> AMY Could you tell me more?
> NATALIE Well, not even knowing exactly how it worked that the milk came out. Just things that people learn when you learn about – I think I told you I needed a class that would be from the very beginning to the very end.

When problems occurred, she turned to the expert for help: to her doctor. However, the very specific breastfeeding advice she needed wasn't available through socially appointed experts. It is usually available only in a network of women who have breastfed and who have organized around their interest in breastfeeding. Natalie was not part of such a network; her relations with other women had always been limited to a competition around the ability to attract men. As well, in her fear of being judged and found wanting as a mother, she isolated herself from other women.

So Natalie placed her faith in her doctor's advice. He dispensed a prescription, she used it – and neither of them questioned the lack of positive results. Neither of them raised into consciousness the possibility that he didn't know how to help her. Natalie simply got used to – was no longer panicked by – the feeding difficulties which in the first month of her baby's life had provoked such high levels of anxiety.

Another factor that contributed to the trauma of Natalie's early experience of motherhood was her pre-childbirth image of what the work of mothering entailed. For example, in the first interview with Natalie – before her baby was born – I asked her what she felt would be the worst thing about having a new baby. She replied that missing the office Christmas party was the worst thing she could think of. When I pushed her on this point, she said that there were three things that could make a baby cry: it was either hungry, thirsty, or wet. There was very little material regarding any other expectations of mothering.

Phyllis Chesler (1981) and other feminist writers have spoken about the lack of real, detailed descriptions of the work of motherhood; what *is* talked about is in fact produced from the double bind of "everything and nothing." In the discourse of psychology, which filters down through popular versions in the media, we hear of mothers as everything: criminality, neuroses, psychoses, anxiety, sexual difficulties, and identity problems are modern plagues that are all laid at the door of one's early interaction with Mom. At the same time, the real work and the mothering person are invisible, are nothing. Women's magazines rarely reproduce the reality of mothering, because to describe the reality of mothering would necessitate describing women's knowledge. Validating that knowledge by allowing it language would grant women power through the relationship that exists between knowledge and power. Granting such overt power to women obviously contradicts the meanings ascribed to "women"; suppressing such a contradiction, therefore, through suppressing a language which describes the work of mothering, is essential. It is important to bear this in mind in learning about Natalie's expectations, because her myths are cultural myths. The crisis which resulted for Natalie from the discrepancy between reality and myth gives us some insight into how the fluidity between inside/outside acts to construct experience.

> I figured that motherhood was natural, and, you know, it all falls into place. You know, either she's wet or she's hungry or she's thirsty, or, you know, you look after things there, and you're just fine – but it's not that way – they are just moody. Like we were thinking yesterday one of the reasons she wasn't sleeping is that it's a whole new environment. Like she's used to the thickness of the mattress at the hospital, the smell of the air in the hospital. Everything is a change and maybe that's why she's upset. There are just so many things that it could be, and I always had it narrowed down to three. I always pictured I was going to be the most natural mother in the world. I pictured that so perfectly that I convinced everybody that Im just cut out to be a mother. I'm so goddamn maternal, you know, mother nature. No.

The essence of Natalie's expectations was that all things connected to motherhood were natural, so she would naturally know what to do. And, because the process of breastfeeding was natural, it was naturally beautiful:

> Well, the way it is in the book it almost seems as if it's something only the Virgin Mother and Jesus could have

gone through. There's an aura surrounding any nursing mother that it is the most wonderful feeling in the world, and it's not. The baby is hungry and you've chosen to breastfeed, so you feed her; that's it, and, if it goes well, great, if it doesn't, shit.

I think the important part is to let people know it's not natural. I was really surprised to hear that. I just – I just thought everything was going to fall into place so when it didn't, and I didn't know it's not supposed to yet, that's when I felt inadequate. It works for everyone else; what's wrong with me? When I found out that 90 per cent of women don't take to it naturally then, oh, well, that explains it right away – this wave of relief that everything's okay. I'm not the one – the one out of a million who isn't doing it right.

When asked how she had thought things would be, Natalie said,

This was just a scene – I kept picturing myself sitting at the pool weighing about 115 in a black bathing suit with a little baby [in a] chair beside me who'd be perfect and we'd be catching some rays and I've got a long tall one and everything is wonderful.

Everyone says there are only three things that could be wrong with her – well there's a fourth, and the fourth is I don't know, and that's the one she is going through most of the time. What's wrong with her? I don't know.

Let us look now at the reality of Natalie's everyday life, and at how her expectations differed from that reality.

AMY You were going out every night?

NATALIE Yes. We were taking her places because the car ride would calm her down.

AMY So you just, you'd go to the mall, right?

NATALIE Yes, every night.

It is interesting to contrast Natalie's image of "... sitting by a pool ... because it all comes naturally ..." with the following statements about the reality:

It was pretty painful [expressing breast milk]. It didn't kill me but it was the first time I'd ever done it. I had two bruises on my breasts for three days running because I'd been squeezing in the same place; it was the only place that had any effect.

It's all so encompassing time-wise. I guess that's what gets me down. When you're a mother or a parent all the time you can't put it down. I guess that's it – that bugs me. It's so overwhelming.

When it's been a long day, and I wish I could have a nap, but even when I'm napping my mind's not on – I can't completely nap because I'm always waiting for that little cry....

Well there's always folding diapers, or just taking her out for a carriage ride requires so many things; there's a snowsuit to put away and there's a fur piece that goes in her carriage and the carriage has to come apart in pieces because it's also the thing she sleeps in. I spend ten minutes just putting everything away that's involved in taking her for a walk. As it is now, quite often, by the time she comes up the steps from the walk or from the stroller ride, she's already awake and reaching to eat. So all I can do is walk in the house, take my boots off, take off my T-shirt, and everything else because my nipples feel cold – I guess as do everybody's. So I'm bundled up, and it takes me two full minutes to undress and this is just throwing things all over the place, not having to worry where things land, and feeding her, and then I have all these things to pick up and put away again.

Natalie's life goal had always been to have children. She believed she would find this natural, would not need to learn anything about mothering, and would easily and instinctively adjust to having a baby. When this turned out not to be the case, the immediate post-partum period was experienced as a crisis.

As part of the account of Natalie's experience of trauma, we need to look at how Natalie herself mediated this period of "shock." She framed her difficulties mainly in terms of her own inadequacy. Usually, she saw this inadequacy as a kind of global lack of preparation; but nowhere were there questions about *why* she was unprepared, about *why* she felt so inadequate. She felt that the inadequacy *was* her, and she did not move in the direction of understanding how her inadequacy was produced.

The idea of "ideological spirals" seems appropriate as a description of how Natalie's sense of inadequacy was produced and reproduced. I would like to try to describe how this ideological spiral operates. I start with the assumption that Natalie experienced herself – not at a conscious level – as very vulnerable, very fragile. Authority figured very heavily in her biography, and that may have contributed to Natalie's core sense of vulnerability. It is difficult to supply data to substantiate this assumption, as it is based on intuition and my feelings when I was with her: I usually felt that I needed to be very gentle with her. As well, small things – such as her difficulty naming her attachment to her baby, although she obviously adored her – gave me the feeling that acknowledging attachment triggered her vulnerability.

In any event, it is clear that the use of control and certainty was characteristic of Natalie's way of being, and I think this stemmed from her inner sense of fragility. We have numerous examples of how important control was to Natalie:

Well, with her it's such an unknown factor. You never, you can't count on her sleeping; you can't count on her being hungry at any particular time; so I'm totally out of control, and I'm not good when I'm out of control. As long as I'm on top of it, great, and when I'm not I know it.

I'm in control again, and I'd always been in control, and that was what threw me the worst was that everything was out of my hands, but now it's back in my hands again – that's fine.

Up till now the only time I was happy with her was when she was asleep or I was nursing her because I knew exactly what was going on at the time....

Clearly, for Natalie, having her baby created a situation that made her feel out of control – a very dangerous feeling for her. Her response was to give herself over to experts, to authorities. She left herself entirely, and searched among experts for answers and solutions to this new situation:

NATALIE I really don't listen to myself. I don't have anything to contribute here. All I can do is pass on information that my doctor gave to me. My mother will say something or she'll start doing something and I'll say well, the doctor said or the nurse said.... That's all that

is there – there's nothing I can – that I feel I can con-
tribute to this.
AMY Because?
NATALIE Inexperience.

It was clear that she felt it was all right for me to come to
interview her chiefly because she could ask my advice. When
I asked her if there was anything important she'd like to talk
about, she said,

> No. The only things I save for you are advice questions.
> It's nothing about how I feel inside because I figure what
> I'm going through is what everybody goes through so it's
> no big deal and what do you expect? It's just advice
> which I turn to you for.

People who were not experts were simply nuisances to
Natalie. They had no value to her if they couldn't tell her what
to do.

AMY Who would you tend to see during the day?
NATALIE Nobody.
AMY How do you feel about that?
NATALIE Great! Right now they'd put me out. Having to
worry about what she's like. I mean it might be nice to
have some conversation at this point. I've got four
people on hold who want to come over; but I've had
to say not right now and I'm glad I can say not right
now because I don't want to see them anyways. I
don't know. There is her fussiness and not knowing
what to expect from her....

And so, the people who were important to her were authorities – primarily her doctor, and sometimes people she read
(e.g., Burton White). Thus what she "knew" from experts had

an ideological character. She was dependent on dominant sources of knowledge, and those sources are part of a super-structure which organizes knowledge in the interests of maintaining relations of domination.

The ideological spiral was made reflexive by virtue of the fact that Natalie could never assume a sense of her own expertise. Her dependency was permanently maintained, because expert advice never speaks directly to local, specific, concrete situations, and hence can never be fully adequate. However, Natalie explained the failure of such expert advice as a product of her own poor mothering. For example, in dealing with the baby's difficulty sleeping in the evening, Natalie saw the baby as "testing" her and let her "cry it out" for two nights. I asked her how she felt about letting the baby cry and she said,

> I figured I had to do it. The second night again, I had to do it so it wasn't bad. Then reading the book from La Leche League it says they are insecure at this time. Well the La Leche League book says, NO NO NO – they need security so this is why they are crying that way. That made me feel guilty having made her cry for an hour.

The gap between what she actually did and what she was "supposed" to do she interpreted as her failure. This interpretation, in turn, substantiated her core feeling of vulnerability, and the circle repeated itself.

The important focus, for Natalie, was her own failure. She could not interpret expertise as inadequate; given that she felt she had no answers herself, to do that would have been too frightening. To interpret the gap between her own actions and what one "should" do as anything other than a proof of her own failure would have been the location of a "revolutionary moment" for Natalie. She was not able to make such an interpretation.

CIRCLE OF VULNERABILITY

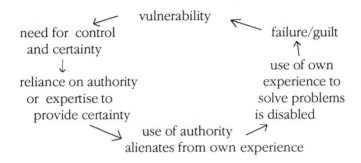

AN EQUILIBRIUM OF CONFLICT

As the period of shock and trauma receded, Natalie was left feeling more in control and more confident. However, her equilibrium was characterized by the concurrent presence of constant conflict.

In general, conflict did not appear to lead to resolution and change; rather, it became part of the ideological spiral in which Natalie's own names for her reality were repeatedly silenced. The task of this section, then, will be to describe the conflict in Natalie's equilibrium and to show how the conflict was both embedded in and sustained by a process of silence.

The period of trauma began to wane when the baby was about three weeks old, and gradually an equilibrium was reached at about the third month. It was experienced by Natalie as a diminished feeling of panic and an increased sense of confidence. I asked her to tell me how her growing confidence had come about. She said,

NATALIE Practice makes perfect, I think that's all it was.
AMY How do you know you have more confidence?

185

NATALIE Well, I still get – like when she would start whimpering I could actually feel my heart going into my throat. Now, it's – I'll get this feeling, quick feeling in the pit of my stomach, and then realize you don't need it. It's just there out of habit, but by the time I finally feel it I've also realized there's no need.

In the fourth interview, Natalie said,

Being with her, you know, looking forward to the day and not – and then getting into a panic about things that are going to happen, and a routine is getting set up. I'm in control. I've lost 38 pounds.

Probably one of the major reasons for the lessening of the crisis had to do with the baby becoming a "good" feeder. Natalie recognized this:

So anyways she knows how to feed now so it's easier on her side and so consequently easier on mine.

Although Natalie still had pain while breastfeeding, and doubts about having sufficient milk, she saw the baby gaining expertise in the feeding situation and was reassured.

Another important factor in the move toward equilibrium was Natalie's perception of the baby as human, as a person. This was important to her, and really marked the beginning of attachment, for Natalie. Until she perceived the baby as a human person, Natalie felt like a "faithful butler" – almost like someone who was doing a job because it was a job, rather than someone whose actions were motivated by attachment.

Well, I feel she is a daughter now. For so long she was a little – little more than a slug. Even now, I mean sometimes she seems like such an insect the way she slithers around and can't move, and her movement so far is so primitive it's almost insulting or disgusting to look at. It is and that's lousy but she's just so basic, you know, grovelling and all that kind of stuff you know.

She was – I guess she became more of a person all of a sudden. She was just pleasant to be with. She was responding. I think she's going to be affectionate. Some kids like to hug and be hugged and others don't. I think she's going to be fine.

She's becoming more than a slug. She's becoming people and that's interesting and when things go wrong with her I have a handful of things I can try now. And, just knowing that if one doesn't work there's still two or three or four things I can go through, that makes me feel better. As I say, hope is eternal.

We can see here a glimmer of a process that seemed to go hand in hand with Natalie's perception of the baby as a person: the replacement of Natalie's belief that there were only three things that could be wrong with a baby with a more realistic understanding that her baby had many needs, some of which were difficult to interpret or control. Once she understood this, Natalie developed a repertoire of responses to the baby's needs, which allowed her to feel that she knew what she was doing.

The following quotations show Natalie learning the work of responding to the baby; they also show the connection between her growing sense of relationship with the baby and her ability to "know" the baby and respond to her in a variety of ways:

She doesn't cry to be changed but I'll change her. She likes to take a tour; she likes to walk. I don't even have to jiggle her or really do anything – just kind of walk, you know, like this is the plant, here's the buffet, and you walk around the whole house and she keeps looking.

Now she's holding her head up when she sleeps on her stomach. I can't put her to sleep on her stomach because she spends the whole time holding her head up and she won't lay it down again.

She likes to sit and she doesn't like to be held upright against you. She likes to have a little seat of her own right here so it's like she's a tourist, you know, and this is the tour, and this the great spot.

Yes. She just walks around and looks at everything.... She likes looking up there at the drapes, and I thought it was the ruffles....

Knowing how to respond to the baby gave Natalie some sense of control:

She's ticklish right around here, right around her mouth and a big sort of smile so that's a good feeling knowing that you've got some control over her mood.

I can put her in her swing and know that she'll fall asleep, if she's in a lousy mood I can coax her into a smile. She responds to play she didn't used to, understandably. You can just kind of do things with her now that you couldn't before because she's becoming more human, not much but, I think, knowing it's starting and this opens a whole new world.

Natalie's growing confidence and ability to cope with the baby not only made daily life better, but also provided relief that she had been able to achieve her life-goal of becoming a mother. The easing of trauma brought relief from the fear that perhaps she wouldn't be able to handle motherhood:

> You've got a job to do, and you do it.... I think it makes me feel good too because this is what I waited for all my life – always wanting to be a mother. So I guess from the beginning, when things weren't going great.... You want something for so long and you finally – I guess it's like working toward a certain promotion or a certain position in a company – you finally get it, and you find out you're not suited for it. Or you go to university to study social work, and you find out you can't stand it. Anyways, I waited all this time and ... it would have been lousy if I found I couldn't and had to go back to work and have a nanny or something. I think I would have been totally devastated. And what else do you live for after that?

So equilibrium derived from a sense of having control, of knowing how to respond to the baby. This in turn facilitated feelings of attachment to the baby and brought relief that she was, after all, capable of realizing her life goal.

Yet despite the lessening of trauma, the equilibrium period was filled with conflict. When Natalie had overcome the crisis phase by learning how to meet her baby's needs, she entered a new phase in which the issue of needs was at the heart of ongoing conflicts. We see this in two general areas: her conflict about meeting her husband's needs, and her conflict about meeting her baby's needs.

When the baby was five months old, I asked Natalie if she could identify what her needs had been since the baby was born. She said,

> Oh, yes. I may have told you that this came up. Jim and I were talking about her and Jim said, 'When are you

going to have....' He said, 'everything is the baby, when are you going to have time for me?' And I said I don't even have time for me – after time for me you're next and you'll know.

This seemed to be a clear statement about whose needs were to be met, and when. But at several points Natalie contradicted herself and gave evidence of the presence of conflicting discourses; for example, during the interview I attempted to reflect back my understanding of what she had said:

> AMY There are, you know sort of three sets of needs and the first need if I heard you correctly was the baby's, then yours, then Jim's.
> NATALIE Yes. That's the way it is. That's not the way it should be.
> AMY How should it be?
> NATALIE It should be me first, I think.

This statement about her needs coming first may perhaps be a part of the popular injunction to take responsibility for one's own needs – to be a person, to look after oneself – as a basis for feelings of self-worth. Yet this discourse does not provide the logic for Natalie's actions, since the proposition to look after oneself is felt by Natalie as something she *should* do (but doesn't), a way she *should* be (but isn't). It is empty rhetoric. In the following quotation we see no evidence of her putting herself first, but only guilt about not having enough to give:

> NATALIE Oh, again a bit of guilt, and, you know, poor Jim, he's not getting what he needs and me not knowing why – blaming it on being tired and it's not really tired – I guess it's like there's only so much affection

that can go around, and your tap runs out. So Jim will just have to get me earlier. Whoever gets me first gets it all.

AMY Does that make you feel stretched?

NATALIE No, because Jim does without. If there were only ten allotments of TLC to give out and she got all ten, it's not as if I would search within myself and pull out half a dozen more – I would just stop at ten. With Jim it's so easy just to say no I can't or this or that and he doesn't bother me. Yes. He lets it go.

AMY Is that good or bad?

NATALIE Well, it's both. I take advantage of it. As I say maybe I should search within myself and produce six more units of TLC so I can give him some but, because of the way it is, I don't.

It is interesting to note that at no point in Natalie's commentary do we hear any sense of expectation that Jim should meet her needs. There is not even a sense of what her needs are, except to be free of the guilt of not giving enough. Basically, her lack of expectations around her own needs, and her guilt about never giving enough, were rationalized through her understanding of work roles. In the final analysis, Natalie believed it was her job to look after the baby, and it was her job to protect her husband so he could do his job:

NATALIE Well, as in being tired and I should take a nap, I should hand her over to Jim and say, here, get out of here; take her, and I'll lay down for an hour. But I won't. I'll just keep persevering and figure, well, at nine o'clock she'll be asleep.

AMY Why do you do that?

NATALIE I don't know. Maybe I figure, oh, it's not so bad. I don't know. Sometimes it's not worth it. Jim's great when she wants to play, but, when Jim's had enough, he's had enough. And, then it's me, and it's not worth me saying to Jim, take her, and Jim saying I've just had her – saying 'You want me to go for a walk; is that it?' something like that, just that tone.

AMY So it becomes an argument with Jim?

NATALIE No, no. It won't be an argument because he'll go. It's just, I don't know, maybe I think it's my job to have to do all that and Jim works and he should be able to relax at home; not always, and he's got obligations with her too, but I guess I feel that because he's out working he should have as much relaxation time – and it's my job to be with her, to handle her.

Later, she said,

Jim was sleeping and even though I was sick I couldn't wake him up. I felt I had to handle it, so I'll take her out. So I guess the bottom line is the pressure to take her out and not to leave her so that he can sleep. It's this damn job, and always having to be on your toes because anytime you're going to have to pull a gun or something.

There are times that he's slept downstairs just so he doesn't have to hear her crying – sometimes it gets on his nerves; sometimes it's just that he doesn't have time for it because he's got to go to work and he's got to get his sleep and that's all there is to it. Being in the R.C.M.P., you know that at any given time you might have to pull out a gun or your life is on the line. It's not like usual work where you just get to shoot the breeze all day. His life is on the line so he's got to get his sleep.

It's interesting to note that there are two categories of meeting Jim's needs: the first is "silence," a form of meeting his needs that is defined as her job – that is, caretaking activities;

the second is being an intimate companion – going to shows, holding hands, offering TLC. Natalie saw the first category as a matter of "doing her job" – not as giving; it was only the second category that she saw as "meeting his needs," and about which she felt guilty when she failed him. Since the work involved in basic caretaking of Jim was not defined as "meeting his needs," but as only "doing her job," when she couldn't produce enough affection she felt that she was giving Jim nothing. Thus Natalie didn't perceive the fatigue of being the constant caretaker as the reason she couldn't produce those extra units of TLC – and she was left seeing herself as a person without much to give.

Natalie experienced conflict, not only around the question of meeting Jim's needs, but also in dealing with the baby's needs. She was constantly in conflict about the issue of spoiling the baby. She was caught between two discourses: in one, the idea is that meeting babies' needs will spoil them and since all people are out to obtain power anyway, a spoiled child will become a tyrant; in the other, it is assumed that a baby's needs should be met, because doing so will create a secure individual who will not need to exercise excessive power and control over others.

These two discourses are traced historically by Anthony Synnott in an article appropriately entitled "Little Angels, Little Devils: A Sociology of Children" (Synnott, 1983). Synnott cites a 1580 essay by Montaigne as a foreshadower of the permissive discourse which provides meaning for Natalie's practice of demand feeding. He also describes Calvinist and Puritan expositions of the idea that the parents' duty is to crush the natural evil to be found in children, a discourse which supports Natalie's decision to let the baby cry because she is being "manipulative."

This contradiction is imbued with the anxiety that has been generated by the age of the child-rearing "expert." As Synnott says, "… the threat of irreparable damage to the child due to 'bad handling' is absolutely clear" (p. 88). This threat produced tremendous anxiety for Natalie. She was caught between two discourses about what was best for children, all the while understanding that if she made the "wrong" choice, the terrible damage that followed would be her fault. Given her particular difficulties in naming her own reality, we can readily understand how intractable the conflict was for her.

Natalie bounced back and forth between these discourses, presented to her through what she read, by her doctor, by her pre-natal instructor, and by me. She could never feel that what she was doing was right: if she met the baby's needs, she worried about spoiling her, and, if she left her to cry, she felt guilty about creating insecurities. This conflict was expressed in the following remarks:

NATALIE My gut feeling is to pick her up, but then, based on having read that it's okay to, even if it's, you know, way down deep inside, subconsciously.

AMY Is it really? Is your feeling about picking her up based on what you've read, really?

NATALIE Yes. I think so – not all of it, but it's there. When she was fussy for those ten days when she was about a month old, after I realized she didn't have gas the third night – the first two nights she had gas and was sick – and, when I realized the third night, I picked her up anyways and cuddled her and held her because she was just crying and wouldn't.... The fourth night I thought, oh no. She's not sick any more, and now she's gotten into the habit. At a month old I thought she already had me pegged so I didn't pick her up, and she cried for forty-five minutes....

AMY How do you look back on that now?

NATALIE Oh, I feel so lousy.

AMY Why?

NATALIE Because I don't – I may have read this but they

don't – that's too young for them to be able to manipulate you. They don't know enough to cry and relate it back to you. They want to be picked up at that age, whereas – well I feel so bad now – like I blamed her for it and I.... Can you imagine? The poor little thing like that, and all she wants is.... She's not secure yet about her own environment so she's crying because she doesn't feel safe and secure and I made her cry for forty-five minutes.

AMY And what would you, inside you, without anybody else around, say, do?

NATALIE I would have picked her up.... BUT, I was afraid I'd get her into this thing with being picked up all the time. She went through a three-month growth spurt. Shortly after she did, all of a sudden I was being awakened at one in the morning again and she used to sleep from about ten to about seven or eight.... Well I talked to Joy and she said, 'It sounds like a three-month growth spurt, so just go with it; don't worry about it.' So I would get up and feed her. Now that went on for ten days. Then I phoned Joy and said, how long does this go on? And she said actually only a few nights.... I said it's been ten, and she said don't worry about it; it will work itself out. Well then I had an appointment for her shot with Dr. C., and I said, I'm not going to worry about it, and he said, 'Well just don't get into the habit of getting her or feeding her at one o'clock in the morning or else she's going to keep getting up,' so right away I was in a panic again. Joy had made me feel that it would pass, and it's okay, and go with it. And here I pictured myself for the next six months getting up at one in the morning just because Joy had said that. What does he know?

I read somewhere that they are finding that a lot of

criminals are – well, they've related the way they are now to the way they were raised as kids. And they didn't get enough attention and actually took it right down to ... whether they were picked up or not right away when they cried....

Natalie had read in Burton White's book that "... you can't spoil a child under seven months." This brought her some relief, but also terrorized her about what would happen at the seven-month mark:

> NATALIE Well, now the professionals say you can't spoil, and now I do anything I want, and it's okay. But as soon as I hit seven months I might be doing something that's going to negatively affect her future.
>
> AMY And what would that something be?
>
> NATALIE By picking her up too often and spoiling her so she won't grow up to be well-adjusted, mature – handle the responsibility you're supposed to. Did I tell you that I still send a Christmas card to our lawyer because one of my kids might be a juvenile delinquent and need legal services?

Those comments give us an idea of the horrifically debilitating effect that floundering between discourses had on Natalie: she was so convinced that she would harm her child that she kept in contact with a lawyer so there would be yet another expert available to help when the ruination she had perpetrated became manifested in her child's adolescence!

And so we see that the equilibrium established after the period of trauma was one filled with conflicts – but conflicts which never led to resolution or revision. Two statements show us the fatigue and tension that such endless, inconclusive conflict caused in Natalie's daily life:

NATALIE Did you see *All That Jazz?* Well, where he started every day with putting Visine in his eyes and popping some speed pills and saying, 'It's show time!' and that was another day – so that's what I feel with her.

AMY Well, what do you do to get your own needs met?

NATALIE I drink. Well, it started as being my reward – the day is over; she's asleep; the day is over.

During the crisis period, Natalie's sense of vulnerability in new circumstances led to a need for control, and she looked to outside expertise in her search for that control. This ideologically based "help" was never useful in creating change, and its failures were accepted by Natalie as further proof of her guilt and inadequacy – leading to a still greater sense of vulnerability.

This ideological spiral appeared in a different form once the crisis had passed: Natalie was still vulnerable, not because she needed control per se, but because she needed a rationale, a logic, with which to frame her practices of childrearing. For that rationale, she once again looked outside herself and turned to experts – and, once again, the inevitable difficulties that arose in applying dominant ideological solutions were seen by her as indications of her own inadequacy.

In organizing the data on Natalie, I marked one category of her statements "No centre," because they seemed to indicate an absence of any sense of a core self. I do not have sufficient biographical data to understand the etiology of this state of affairs, but have selected data which indicate the nature of her vulnerability. For example, I asked Natalie to describe herself at her best as a mother. She said,

Best at – I guess when there's something wrong with her and she's crying and I can soothe her without nursing because nursing is such a catch-all that it's too easy – it's a cop-out, yes. I mean, I know that it solves everything, and that's not fair because men can't, so to resort to that just because she recognizes it's me and it makes her comfortable and she's relaxing [isn't fair].

This is a statement that can be interpreted in many ways, but I tend to see it as Natalie putting herself in a no-win situation. If she can't comfort the baby, she is a failure; if she can, then it doesn't count because it must be too easy if she has been able to do it. Her inability to acknowledge that she has done something right indicates her fragility and vulnerability:

I'm still not sure how long I'm supposed to wrap her up because she swings her hands and that wakes her up but she likes it and in the morning she – she'll be there for about an hour....

Here, Natalie described her experience of the baby – what she did, how she liked her hands free, and so on. Yet Natalie didn't feel that the decision about whether or not to wrap the baby should come from her own observations: she looked for the decision externally, from what she was "supposed" to do. Her experiential data were not enough.

I had difficulty assessing the relationship between Natalie and her baby. When she spoke of her feelings toward the baby, Natalie was unable to talk about loving her; the closest she could come to it was to say she was "nuts about her." Yet in practice Natalie was clearly very attached to the baby and – particularly later in the interview series – seemed to adore her. Yet at the same time, she seemed frightened of acknowledging attachment to her baby, as if such powerful emotions might leave her feeling out of control, endangered through being attached.

Her sense of her own vulnerability led to a belief in expertise outside herself. Her decisions would be made by search-

ing out authorities who "knew better"; this search was beautifully co-constituted by the existence of numerous authorities
who also believed that they knew better than she did what she
should do. They were part of the ideological structures which
shaped and defined the scope of responses that constituted
Natalie's mothering:

> It's like – it reminds me of all these books I've read that
> say you can't spoil – Dr. White especially – you can't
> spoil a child before seven months. After that maybe, but
> not up to seven months so I can see Jim and myself cross-
> ing off the days to seven months and then at seven
> months....

Reassurance came not from her assessment of the baby's
health but from "real" authority. I asked Natalie in the seventh
interview about her increased confidence:

> I guess doctor's appointments: he said everything was
> fine. Kid is doing great.

But confidence, of course, can never really come from the
process of being told what to do:

> I don't know. I'm not there yet. It's hard to say because
> right now I am affected by what I read. I know I am. You
> see that's why I get the books because I don't feel
> confident and I'll check what somebody else who knows
> better has to say about it.

Problems, everyday decisions, begin to feel like a merry-go-
round of events requiring expertise:

> When I woke up in the morning and found she had a
> rash, my whole day was ruined. It would be on my mind

all day how to get rid of it. And what am I going to do? Call the pediatrician. Call Dr. C. again. When things are great I'm great, but they're never great – as soon as something goes away something else comes up.

Natalie experienced intense and pervasive guilt in relation to the baby:

NATALIE Oh, I could feel guilty about anything. There's just too much I could say about it.
AMY What are the sources of guilt?
NATALIE The baby. The major reason is the baby. I can feel guilty about anything. If anything is wrong it's my fault because I could have done something. She was lousy – if I hadn't wanted to go to Florida she wouldn't be in that situation. If I hadn't wanted to go to the drive-in this wouldn't have happened.... If it hadn't been for me she wouldn't be in this position, the poor little thing.

This guilt seems tied to the discourse of Mother-as-Everything. For post-Freudian mothers, every pain, all suffering is injurious, and a mother's responsibility is to prevent pain – thereby preventing risk to a child's psyche, which is fully formed by the age of five. Natalie's practice is well-shaped by this discourse:

NATALIE I'm looking forward to her being able to roll over so she can decide what position she wants all by herself. I guess all these things I feel guilt over are things that I know she will eventually assume responsibility for herself. I just wish she'd hurry up, hurry up and get it because I can't stand all this guilt.

... I don't like her to have to go through any discomfort

200

because at this point I think any discomfort that she feels is our fault. If she's not comfortable it's because we've put her in the position, or if she's got gas it's because of something I ate, or if she can't sleep maybe it's because we're putting her down too soon. If she's got really tired, we're reading her signals wrong, trying to conform her to what we want, and it's not fair. You wouldn't believe the guilt I could impose on myself if I really wanted to.

AMY About what?

NATALIE Anything.

AMY About her being happy?

NATALIE Yes – it's all my fault in the long run.

This Mother-as-Everything discourse was underlined by the fact that, realistically, Natalie was the only person in the world who felt responsible for the baby. Her life had been spent waiting to achieve motherhood. The baby was her job:

NATALIE If I put her down for a nap at the wrong time so she screams and yells – Jim has no patience with her. I just can't believe it. He's great with her as long as she wants somebody to play with. As soon as she starts crying he just – he just goes crazy and I'm left.

AMY What does he do?

NATALIE He starts pacing and stands like this, and he'll clench his fists and say, 'Baby, what's wrong with you?' He just can't take it, and I've got to tell him to get the hell out or something, and I'll take her because I have to.

AMY You have to? Why?

NATALIE Well, there's nobody left. I'll do what I have to do.

And, in the fifth interview,

AMY What's the difference do you think, or do you – is there a difference between the way Jim relates to her and you relate to her?

NATALIE Well obviously because I see her and he doesn't.

AMY What's the difference, though?

NATALIE She needs me; she doesn't need him. I think that's – off the top of my head – that's all I can think of because I really pushed her on him a lot.

AMY Why did you do that?

NATALIE So that she would be just as comfortable with me and with him.

Although Natalie had said that she and her husband believed the baby was her job, and that she saw and cared for the baby more than he did, she explained the difference between mother and father in terms of the currently popular hormonal explanations of why women mother:

AMY How do you account for the differences between the way you and Jim see her?

NATALIE I see her more; I have more patience; and, you know, I'm the one who has an ulcer. I think that basically – there's got to be something about I'm a mother.

AMY How?

NATALIE I don't know. It's as if it has something to do with having carried them and – well, Jim read somewhere where there are hormone changes that a mother goes through....

Operating from intense guilt, Natalie projected her self-criticism onto others, giving experts and authorities the capacity and the power to criticize her. The only way for her to feel comfortable was to please those who had the power to judge her – by taking their advice, learning the discourses, adopting the practices, all of which were ultimately ideological. To modify those practices with her own experience would be to displease, and the guilt would then be overwhelming. In the following quotation, Natalie described taking the baby to the drive-in, which she felt guilty about doing:

> We had the worst time getting her to sleep. I may have to talk to somebody about this. Anyways ... I took her into the washroom twice and walked her up and down, you know, in this colic position, rocking her, and she fell asleep – it always does put her to sleep. But I felt guilty thinking if anybody walks in they're going to say, poor little baby – mother dragging her to the drive-in. So one girl did walk in, and I had to say – I had to substantiate why I was there. She didn't say anything.

The explanation for why she was there had to be one that proved Natalie was a good mother – one which placed her solidly in acceptable discourses of good mothering practices. Thus, the guilt-projection process ensured Natalie's regulation through ideology:

> You know, I feel so bad when she's crying because people are thinking what a lousy mother.

So in order to feel like a good mother in other people's eyes, Natalie had to produce acceptable mothering behaviour:

> Well, in my own way I'm okay that way. I worry what other people think though. Like with that diaper rash – if other people saw this then I figure they would think I'm not a good mother.

Isolation abetted the guilt-production process: in the early period of having the baby at home, Natalie couldn't tolerate having visitors or going out to see people. She explained this by saying that she was worried that the baby might cry, or that she might have to feed her. She was also concerned about her appearance: she needed a "perm"; she needed a haircut; she needed new clothes. However, as the crisis abated, Natalie didn't become more social. She didn't seem to crave social contact and, in fact, stuck quite closely to seeing people who would give her advice – her doctor, or me. Natalie did not identify being alone with being isolated:

> I don't think I ever felt isolated because I knew there was lots of places I could go. It's just that I wished I didn't have to use those resources, that things would be comfortable enough at home that I didn't have to spend half an hour getting ready to take her someplace else to be amused.

Natalie's main outings were to the local shopping plaza, where she would browse, looking mostly at clothing, and then go home. Natalie tended to use the TV as a marker to give shape to her day:

> Well I saw the whole day ahead of me. Every time the clock came to the hour again it was like one down, five to go, and then another one down and four to go, and I watched two soaps in the afternoon. I think they are important to me because it means the day is half over, but I don't necessarily look at them that way anymore – the last week or so. But up 'til then it was like 'I made it,' and on to the next half of the day. This was when Jim was on afternoons and I had her all alone. Jim would sleep 'til eleven, so I had her all morning. Then Jim would take maybe a couple of hours and he's off to work and I'm all by myself again.

Although Natalie did not feel isolated, the lack of sociality cut down on her opportunities to talk about what was happening in her life. If learning is a social event, then the climate of isolation with which Natalie surrounded herself wasn't conducive to validating her own experience or exploring new ideas and new approaches to mothering. Her isolation ensured that her exposure to oppositional discourses that might better explain her lived reality would be minimal. Instead, she was positioned to receive only medical opinion and media representations of mothering. Both have traditionally been powerful regulatory discourses of mothering.

PART
II

INTRODUCTION

In the first part of this book, I have tried to demonstrate how the experience of mothering is socially constructed and that mothering practices in our culture are not "natural and normal," but are socially organized through the needs of capitalist patriarchy. Understanding that, we can now see how those mothering arrangements produce "Woman," the category on which the oppression of women is built.

In this second section, using the experiences of Maria, Tina, and Natalie, I will show how the body of Woman is produced through the experience of birth and how the caretaking function of Woman is produced through sole responsibility for children. It is important to bear in mind that women become Woman in many different ways; I do not want to pinpoint birth or sole caretaking as the only sources of Womaning; rather, these sites must be recognized as two of the many and diverse routes to becoming Woman.

To understand the production of Woman through mothering, we have to take a critical approach to the data. This means that we have to disconnect cultural images of women from the "natural and normal" in order to see how such images produce Woman. As we have seen throughout the three accounts, ideologies of individualism and biologism provide ways of making meanings, which permit us to overlook the fact of the social production of mothering.

To be able to work outside individualism toward the goal of understanding mothering, as it both organizes and is organized by women's actual experience, demanded a new theoretical framework capable of answering questions about how we come to be well-intentioned people who, nonetheless, within our everyday lives produce relations of domination between men and women. As well, if we dismiss individualism and biologism as ideologies which obscure our vision of the social organization of mothering, then we need an alternate perspective which can offer a political agenda for liberating mothering from its implication in the production of patriarchy.

A major stumbling block, for me, in trying to develop such a perspective was that I had been trained in the language of the individual. This meant that my early attempts to articulate the problem of the co-production of mothering always ended up cast in language which made a conceptual distinction between the individual and the social. There was the fact of individual mothers "in" a social context, but there was no theoretical position that could adequately deal with the concept of "in." I spoke and heard academic language which sprang from the traditional social sciences; it is a language of the individual. All questions somehow came to roost within a person/feeling state: behaviour and attitudes were all the property of the individual. Thus, anything I could say about learning was attributed to the individual person – yet this was exactly my criticism of traditional research on women. I tried to counteract this individualization (which always required a victim) by introducing the notion of the effect of social context on the individual, expressed as "How the social context impinges on the experience of learning." This approach perpetuated a distinction between the individual and the social, and left me working with the notion of a social context as some kind of intentioned force that acts on individuals. The concept of "acting on" fell apart under analysis.

For me, neither psychology nor theories of ideology contained a real possibility of dealing with the complex experience of the organization of mothering in patriarchy. Psychological explanations inevitably not only left out historical and material experiences of the individual, but could not explain how psychological processes in mothering conveniently met the needs of capitalist patriarchy. Nor could psychology begin to deal with the issue of conflict between the needs of women and children, on the one hand, and the requirements of the reproduction of patriarchy, on the other. Theories of ideology seemed always to stop short of the crucial issue of identity, and therefore failed to explain how real people – thinking, feeling, sensing people – came to do mothering "normally": the way it should be done, the expected way, the taken-for-granted way of raising children.

I turned to what is called post-structuralist theory to find a theoretical framework capable of dealing with these problems. When I use the phrase "I turned to," my language obscures a very rocky process and makes the act seem an insouciant gesture of the well-informed. It is important for me to document the problems of using such theory before I describe its contributions; I do so because I do not want to be positioned by readers of this book as "knowing post-structuralism," but rather as a collaborator in the search for theories which will best serve our mutual, most urgent goals.

When I read post-structuralist books, I am usually afraid of the writer, because I am so easily persuaded by the text that he knows and I don't. I stop being a knower and, instead, use my energy to receive more and more knowledge. I become frantic in the search for what can explain me best. In this way I reproduce Woman.

This is the danger of post-structuralism – or any other powerful new theory of understanding – which must always be kept in mind along with the enormous value of such a theory in helping to explain the construction of patriarchy. The danger lurks in the kinds of questions which tend to falsely dichotomize the issue: Do I not understand this because I am stupid? Do I not understand this because it is written to signal membership in a particular male club called "The Post-Structuralists"?

I think that the answer to the problem does not lie in our stupidity or their male chauvinism, but in the reality that such theory is a new paradigm, a break with our pasts and, therefore, is not yet fully accessible to our language and consciousness. As such, it is not fully accessible to either the reader *or* the writer; but it is a knowledge which is in process of becoming better articulated, and, thus, better subject to critical analysis. At the same time, I am becoming more experienced in the language, and better able to make connections between my reality and the theory. My ability to be critical grows.

I think that in any exploration of new territory, a woman must try to keep a balance between *suspending* previous "frames," in order to admit new learning, and *maintaining* a stance as knower, in order to retain the locus of control within herself. This is a very difficult tightrope to walk, especially when women have for so long been constructed as Other. It is a tension I am very aware of as I describe how post-structuralism contributed to my analysis of the construction of Woman through mothering.

There are two words which I use frequently and with very particular meanings in Part II: "subjectivity" and "discourse." By defining these words, I hope to show why they are important to discovering the construction of Woman through mothering.

"Subjectivity" refers to the conscious and unconscious, emotional and cognitive ways one makes sense of oneself and the world. At first glance, the broad scope of that definition may seem to render the term rather useless. However, the value of the word "subjectivity" is the signal it gives to the reader that we are talking about something that is *produced*, not given.

Historically, social and psychological theories of the individual have maintained that there is a core self within individuals on which the social context acts. In other words, there is an inborn individualism within each person. Post-structuralism challenges that notion, saying that there is no fixed or essential nature within people, but that people are constantly in the process of being formed and of producing forms themselves.

Right away, we can see one advantage of post-structuralism

to this project: it eliminates the individual/social distinction –
a distinction we have criticized as embedded in the individualism and biologism which support ideologies important to
the regulation of women as mothers. In using the word "subjectivity," we are stating that the individual *is* social and the
social *is* individual. This statement is very close to the feminist
tenet that "The personal is political." We can begin to see why
feminists have embraced post-structuralist analysis.

Crucial to the issue of subjectivity is how it is formed: if we
can understand its formation, we have access to an understanding of change. It has been commonly thought that
people make up language to express thoughts and ideas;
post-structuralism turns this notion around, claiming that language structures people's thoughts and ideas (subjectivity).
We are formed by the possibilities that are available to us in
language: we are unable to think about what isn't in language.
There is nothing of which we are conscious that is not in language. Therefore, our subjectivities are produced in language.

Language makes up *discursive fields*: areas of thought or
ideas bounded by language. Within these discursive fields are
discourses: things that can be said – or not said – about a certain thing. Secretly, when I think of a discourse, I think of a
cookie cutter, whose shape determines what dough will fall
inside the form, and what will fall outside the form. The discursive field is like all possible shapes – Christmas shapes,
heart shapes, or plain round ones, including those that
haven't yet been invented – and subjectivity is, of course, our
cookie dough. Our dough does not begin with a "natural"
desire for a particular shape; shape is given by the cookie
cutter (the discourse.) All discourses exist as part of history,
and they are visible through *discursive practices*: our actions,
when we understand all action to be organized through language.

When we understand that subjectivity is our way of making
sense in the world, and that discourses are the available

opportunities in language for making sense, we can begin to understand how crucial these two concepts are for analyzing the operation of power. Who makes the cookie cutters? Why do they make them in those particular shapes? Why do we use particular ones to shape our experience? How do the cookie cutters come to cast some of us in shapes that are seen as subordinate to others? How do we come to *like* the shapes that ultimately form our subordination? How are new cookie cutters made?

It is important to understand that, although every cookie cutter has potential power, any given one may or may not be impressed on the "dough" of our subjectivity. That is the message of optimism from post-structuralism: *change is possible because discourses are multiple* and, indeed, frequently in conflict or contradiction among themselves. Many cookie cutters compete for the same patch of dough.

That remark brings me to the limits of the usefulness of the cookie-cutter analogy, because we cannot envision dough having any effect on which cutter stamps it. But people are not passive lumps of dough merely waiting to be stamped by whatever cookie cutter happens by.

Post-structuralism calls the idea that people are entirely created through discourses "discourse determinism." While the notion is still a subject of debate among post-structuralists, I believe that people are not determined by discourses just because the discourses are there; people have ways of *investing* in discourses – in weak ways or strong ways, in conflicting or wholly committed ways.

My concern, then, is to try to understand why a person's subjectivity takes one shape rather than another. I have tried to account for it in three ways: by looking at the histories of each of the women I interviewed; by understanding the effect of the practical, real, current world in which each person was embedded; and by locating the discourses which were available to each of the women. (I take it as given that the discourses available to all of us have particular histories in capitalist patriarchy, and that exploring these is a study beyond the scope of my book.)

For example, if I walk into my kitchen to find yet another mess of peanut butter and honey, there are many discourses in which I might invest to form my response to the situation. Which one I choose will depend on my history as a person and on the real, particular world around me. If I had been held back from independence as a child and now resented it, I might enjoy the results of my child's attempt at independence. If I had been held back from independence as a child but had never recognized that fact, I might tell the child to let me make the sandwich next time; however, if a cleaning lady was just about to walk in the door, I might not care about the mess. Furthermore, if I had been doing something important to me while the mess was being made, and the child had made the mess as part of an attempt not to interrupt me, I might praise her.

When discourses conflict with or contradict each other, they create the possibility of change. If I use both the discourse of "mess" and the discourse of "independence" at the same time in responding to the situation in my kitchen, putting the undesirable "mess" beside the desirable "independence" may sponsor change in me; I may reject the notion that "Mess is always my responsibility."

Working with the concepts of discourse and subjectivity has allowed me to put to use my conviction that the power to construct us as Woman works through ordinary, everyday life. As well, it is not a power that can coerce, but a power that works by producing within us the desires that shape us as Woman. Power is operating when I choose to avoid the hassle of getting a babysitter by not going to a meeting on how to get grants. That power can be seen in the production of *my* choices – everyday choices which ultimately define me as Woman. Thus, my purpose in using words which I know are possibly alienating, such as subjectivity and discourse, is to allow both me and you, the reader of this book, to get closer to our own experience, to get closer to where the power to define us as Woman operates, rather than farther away into abstractions which make us feel like Other.

A note of caution at this point: it is sometimes difficult to use an analysis of discourse in a way that also displays people's capacity for change and growth. Discourse is a way of freezing a moment in order to analyze power; but it does not imply that the *person* is frozen in the moment. The choice of moments is mine, and my intention in choosing the moments is not to represent a person, but to understand that person's relation to power at a particular moment in time.

CHAPTER FIVE

BIRTH

HISTORICALLY, DISCOURSES ABOUT women's bodies organize meanings in terms of disgust and revulsion. Practices of the body, when organized through such discourses, have been practices of restrictions and regulations. Adrienne Rich (1976) speaks of these discourses as follows:

> It is these grown-up male children who have told us and each other: in Mesopotamia that we were 'a pitfall, a hole, a ditch' (a grave?); under Hindu law, that we were by nature seductive, impure and required to live under male control, whatever our caste; in the Christian Era, that we were the head of sin, a weapon of the devil, expulsion from paradise, mother of guilt; that as Eternal Women, we wore the word 'mystery' inscribed on our brows and that self-sacrifice was our privilege; that our wombs were unbridled breeding-places of 'brackish, nitrous voracious humours'; by the Victorian medical experts, both that we had no sensuality and that 'voluptuous spasm' would make us barren, also that 'the real woman regards all men ... as a sort of stepson towards whom her heart goes out in motherly tenderness'; in the aftermath of the Bolshevik Revolution, that we were the victim of our own 'biological tragedy' which no legal or

social changes could undo; by the neo-Freudians, that 'the syndrome of decay, the evil tendency in man is basically rooted in the mother-child relationship'; in the People's Republic of China that the love of women for women is a bourgeois aberration, a function of capitalism. (p. 189)

Such discourses give meaning to women's bodies, and we come to understand those meanings through restriction of women's bodily potential. Practices of restriction of that potential become practices through which we organize our experience of our bodies in the world. Such experiences in turn extend beyond the body and permeate our entire subjective experience of being in the world.

Current medical practice of obstetrics incorporates such a restriction of bodily potential. Medical discourses hold a woman's body to be a passive, alienated object which is the site of the male organized, technologically accomplished removal of babies. Such practices command women's dependency, and reinforce the subjective experience of helplessness – all in the guise of "helping." Rich (1976) says,

No more devastating an image could be invented for the bondage of woman: sheeted, supine, drugged, her wrists strapped down and her legs in stirrups, at the very moment when she is bringing new life into the world. This 'freedom from pain,' like 'sexual liberation,' places a woman physically at men's disposal, though still estranged from the potentialities of her own body. While in no way altering her subjection, it can be advertised as a progressive development. (p. 166)

The medical organization of birth stands as a set of instructions for the regulation of the female body – instructions which tell us about who we are as Woman. I asked Maria,

Tina, and Natalie to tell me about their experience of child-birth in order to find out how they mediated this set of instructions. I wanted to find out how their own histories, their aspirations, their ways of making meaning, their current life situations interacted with the discursive practices which organize birth in our society. In studying this interaction, I hoped to understand something about how the body of Woman is produced, so that we can open up that process to change.

NATALIE

For Natalie, giving birth – as a new experience – caused no contradictions or conflicts; consequently, the act of giving birth offered no starting point for change or revision. Her first experience of giving birth seemed to offer her no new information, with the exception of the degree of pain she experienced. When I asked her if the birth made her feel different in any way, she said, "No. Why would it? In what way?" She couldn't imagine what I was getting at. How can Natalie's experience of birth be understood so as to explain her puzzlement?

R. D. Laing (1960) describes the "disembodied self" as resulting when an individual is in a position where he / she "... experiences his self as being more or less divorced or detached from his body. The body is felt more as one object among other objects in the world than as a core of the individual's own being" (p. 69). Natalie's account shows that her identity is marked by such a sense of disembodiment. Laing describes the fear of engulfment as one of several primary insecurities which tend to produce the sense of disembodiment. In engulfment:

> ... the individual dreads relatedness as such, with anyone or anything, or indeed, even with himself, because his uncertainty about the stability of his autonomy lays him

open to the dread lest in any relationship he will lose his autonomy and identity. (p. 44)

In Natalie's biography we have only hints at the construction of the strong fear of engulfment which is responsible for her disembodiment. We can see her fear of engulfment operating through her need to be isolated, her fear of being out of control, her difficulty with intimacy. Although my sketchy knowledge of her biography is not intended to serve as an account of that fear of engulfment, there are features of her history that give us possible explanations of the strength of her investment in disembodied positions.

The constant theme of Natalie's childhood was authority. Hardships and deprivation marked her early childhood, and obedience was the means used to cope with them:

> I would let her know that I was hungry and my mother said, 'All I had to say to you was wait. Johnny gets fed first.' And she said, 'You would be down on the couch. You'd kick around with your little feet up in the air, and you'd be laughing and smiling, and you'd wait until your brother was fed. And then it was your turn.' She said the whole time she was raising us it was perfect.

We see here the conflation of "being perfect" and "doing what you're told." Poverty and isolation could only be withstood by making "perfect" children: children who obeyed, who didn't argue, fight back, or contradict.

Indeed, it seemed as though Natalie's history showed itself to me in the present when I watched her feed solid food to her baby. She fed her baby the way her mother had fed *her* children when they were infants: she lay the baby on her back on the floor, pinned her arms down across her stomach and shovelled food into her mouth. This was the way to do it with no mess or fuss. I couldn't help wondering whether this method of feeding was one of the many experiential bases for Natalie's fear of engulfment and, consequently, for feelings of disembodiment.

Natalie's description of life in a two-parent family was heavy with the idea of authority. Her father had been the master of the house, the enforcer of discipline, someone to be feared, a man who was emotionally remote. He used the belt as actual and threatened punishment for wrongdoers. Natalie describes not only her parents keeping the children in line, but the entire close-knit Lithuanian community in which they lived taking part in enforcing traditions of obedience. Both the community and the family held up the need to respect state authority in the form of police, law, schools, etc.

My speculation is that a bright little girl, required to be perfect in order for her mother to survive, with a highly authoritarian father, and living in a community which required obedience from its children and which valued "legitimate" authority, could logically be expected to have difficulties with autonomy. Lacking a developed sense of autonomy, as an adult woman Natalie feared engulfment and experienced disembodiment. I am not trying to locate the production of Natalie's adult experiences in her childhood; rather, I am trying to show that certain aspects of her childhood influenced her investment in the discourses which structure her adult practices.

Disembodiment informs every one of Natalie's descriptions of bodily experience. The birth of her child happens outside her, through the intervention of medical authorities. The weight loss she experienced after the birth of her baby "just happened," as did the gain of two pounds per month she experienced after she married. That she used to have a "nifty little figure" was luck. We can see how disembodiment, as part of Natalie's identity, was produced, and how it, in turn, produced her further investment in dominant discourses of women's bodies.

Themes of the body, such as birth, sex, and femininity, need to be understood in terms of their connections to each other; consequently, an understanding of how Natalie's sexuality was produced discursively and historically can shed light on her experience of childbirth.

Natalie's life-goal was to become a mother. This was her *raison d'être,* and all other activities she saw as a means of filling in time before she became a mother. She couldn't wait to quit her job as a probation officer, and in fact it almost seemed as though, for her, the job symbolized not being able to get what she wanted. We have no evidence of her having any particular fondness for children; indeed, her greatest fear about being a mother was that she might discipline too harshly. As well, she had had very little contact with children prior to her own child's birth, as evidenced by her unrealistic understanding of baby-care. Although mothering was the only activity which she felt could legitimize her life, in our interviews, whenever Natalie talked about the real lives of children, it was apparent that she feared them – because, as externalized parts of herself, they could be seen and therefore judged.

We cannot know the meaning the goal of motherhood had for Natalie. One could speculate that it is connected to security, position, or achievement of femininity. I would intuitively agree with this, but cannot substantiate it through the data. I think it is safe to assume, however, that the meaning of motherhood, for Natalie, extended beyond the question of a love of children.

If Natalie's life-goal was motherhood, the way to that goal was marriage. She married, but the first marriage was unsuccessful: her husband gambled and drank. After agonizing over the decision and being hospitalized for a "nervous breakdown," Natalie left the marriage. She entered what she calls her "swinging singles period." This consisted of what seemed to be concerted efforts to attract a man through dancing and drinking at downtown singles bars. It was a period of her life that was punctuated by moments of despair at the distance between her existing reality and her goal of becoming a mother.

Natalie was firmly invested in the need to "get a man." Wendy Hollway (1984) describes this as the have / hold discourse, in which men are the objects of women's need to get and keep their man. In this discourse, sexuality is the means to accomplishing that goal.

To be locked into the discursive practices of the have/hold discourse means disembodiment for women. Natalie's mind and body were split; her mind was made up of a male gaze which was constantly checking her female body for sexual perfection. Too fat? Too hairy? Too smelly? Her body was produced, as always, for men's sexual gratification. There was no space for her own pleasure, or her own sense of how her body should function. Her body had become the regulated body of Woman – the servant of the critical male gaze.

Just as Natalie was trying to come to grips with not having a man and with the fact that she was getting older, she met Jim. As a gentle, compassionate, unassertive R.C.M.P. officer, he probably presented no threat to her inner fears of engulfment. (In fact, she described him as someone she could walk all over.)

Natalie and Jim married. Over time, their relationship stopped being founded on the socially valued discourses of femininity and masculinity:

> The available assumptions about men are that they are, for example, powerful, rational, autonomous, in control and self-confident. Those features are positively valued in sexist discourses. The effect is to foreground men's qualities and conceal their weaknesses and to do the opposite for women." (Hollway, 1984, p. 253)

Jim was dependent, Natalie seemed stronger. In reality, Natalie's seeming strength was a rigidity born from fear of engulfment, but the form the relationship took was a polarization between weak and strong. In this dynamic, Natalie could not remain positioned in the have / hold discourse, because Jim was holding on to *her* through his dependency. Since Natalie's sexuality was defined by the have / hold discourse, when she lost her position in that discourse she lost her sexuality. She had never had a sexuality *for herself* – only a sexuality that had the function of attracting men. She stopped engaging in sexual activity – and saw that as indicative of her own inadequacy: there had to be something wrong with her. Disembodiment had been produced through her social relations.

We can now begin to see how the birth of Natalie's baby was orchestrated in such a way as to leave Natalie unable to imagine how childbirth could in any way affect one's sense of body. Medical discourses position medical personnel as the subjects of the discourse and patients as its objects. For example, "The doctor does the delivery" (on the patient). This positioning is extremely powerful: doctors and nurses are the experts of the technology that has come to be seen as necessary to giving birth. That technology enforces passivity in patients: the numbing of women from the waist down, the application of forceps, the use of equipment that enforces supine positions during labour, episiotomies, and the constant threat of Caesarean sections. The power of the subject (medical personnel) over the object (the labouring woman) is firmly cemented by the woman's overarching desire to have a healthy baby. Intimidation and guilt provide the strength of women's investment in medical discourses of childbirth.

Such an object position tends to produce disembodiment: a split between self and body. It requires that women give to medical personnel control over, and knowledge of, their bodies. Natalie, for example, read a monitor to see how the contractions "felt." Natalie's self is thus seen to have observed her (separate) body. She laughed and joked as her baby was being born; anaesthesia separated her from the work that was being done by her body, detaching her from the fact that *she* was giving birth. Such detachment leaves space open for medical personnel to administer the birth.

Natalie took up her position as object in the medical discourse with no sense of discontinuity or contradiction between her experience of childbirth and her previous experiences of the body. She came to the medical discourse having previously been located in other discourses which required the same splitting of body and self. Disembodiment is her historical experience; it is "normal and natural." Positions as objects and positions which produce disembodiment define Woman.

How do we explain this in light of Natalie's attendance at childbirth education classes which stressed natural childbirth? Natalie went to her classes faithfully, but it is clear that in no way did she take up a position in natural childbirth discourse. The childbirth teachings did not even produce contradictions for her, because she had no position in the discourse. My sense of this is that her historical identity of disembodiment, and her location in legitimized authority, made a take-up of such a position impossible. Basically, she found ways of discounting natural childbirth teachings regarding control of the body. Learning to breathe, she felt, was useless because she believed at best it was "... just a distraction, something else to do." She just hoped her labour would be quick and painless. In fact, she hoped she would be "lucky," as no efforts she could make would alter the course of the birth.

We can see that even a fairly intensive exposure to a different discourse regarding women's bodies did not influence Natalie's use of that discourse. It is Natalie's personal history, her social location, and her location in dominant discourses of women's bodies that influenced her positioning.

Historically, Natalie had always been located in discourses which legitimated dominant authority. Her parents had taught her right from wrong and she would do that with her children, too. Her children would be severely punished if they ever called the police "pigs." She was a probation officer, and Jim was a member of the R.C.M.P., a profession she totally respected. Located as she was in these discourses, for her to challenge medical authority was literally beyond imagination. And so she handed her body over to the doctors and nurses so that they could "deliver her," and made jokes while they were at work.

Natalie's difficulty in imagining how childbirth might produce change in her sense of her body brings us to an interesting conclusion: if we were to permit ourselves to slip into the individualistic mode of diagnosis, Natalie might be labelled as having schizoid tendencies – at least as defined through Laing's discussion of disembodied people. But trying to view her account as socially produced forces me to confront the fact that dominant discourses of women's bodies themselves produce "schizoid tendencies" through the necessity of disembodiment in the assimilation of positions in those dominant discourses. Here we see a massive contradiction displayed: women who, without conflict or contradiction, take up positions in the "normal and natural" discourses of women's bodies are in fact "abnormal." It is clear that taking up the struggle to combat or to contradict these "normal" discourses is an essential step toward health for women.

TINA

In contrast to Natalie's experience of childbirth, Tina's experience of giving birth provides an important contradiction to dominant discourses of women's bodies. Tina describes the experience of childbirth by saying: "I did it"; "I found my strength." How does it happen that Natalie is unable to understand how she might be altered by the experience of child-birth, while Tina expresses pure joy at having found her strength through it? To answer this question we must turn to the differences in the ways Natalie and Tina mediated their experiences.

Well before the birth of her child, Tina was positioned in complex, multiple discourses about women – while Natalie knew only a limited position within dominant discourses. Positions within multiple discourses generate opportunities for contradictions and conflicts. Contradictions and conflicts shaped both Tina's experience of childbirth and her subsequent mediation of it. When Tina says "I did it," and "I found my strength," how are we to understand her feelings? I am first tempted to think about her words as expressing a healing of the self / body split that is demanded by discourses of women's bodies – but it is not. References to the birth are interspersed with metaphors which allude to the mechanical functioning of the body: "My parts are functioning the way they are supposed to"; "My body was like a beautiful machine." There is still the sense of a split between self and body, with the self watching the body operate well. Phrases such as "I was strong," and "I felt strong," give us glimpses at a sense of embodiment, at an undichotomized body and self; yet immediately these statements become part of the body-as-beautiful-machine discourse, thus reproducing the dichotomy. I wonder if the embodied statements, such as "I was strong," give us clues about the potential of birth to unite self and body. That potential remains unrealized, though, because there is no discourse which gives meaning to a united body and self. Tina's expressions of joy are fleeting moments of interruption in the constancy of the self / body dichotomy.

The major contradiction that surfaced during the interview period was the contradiction between the I-found-my-strength discourse of birth and the body-as-object position of dominant sexual discourses. When Tina first came home from the hospital, feelings of pride in her body and of accomplishment were prevalent. I think it was possible for her to feel pride because it could be attached to a self-conception of "a person recovering from birth" or "a new mother just home from hospital." But gradually, as things "got back to normal," those conceptions had to change. She recovered from the birth, and the excitement of the new baby faded as she became used to it. Discourses which support the idea of "I found my strength" ceased to exist as time went on. At the same time, "getting back to normal" means getting back into the world where dominant discourses define women's bodies as objects designed to get and hold a man. During the interview period Tina gradually re-entered those discourses.

It is important to account for Tina's resumption of positions in those discourses. That shift was strongly influenced by her relationship with her husband. After the birth of her child, Tina was tired, and saw herself as not being a particularly stimulating partner, socially or sexually. She felt socially left out, but was too tired to put herself into social life. She began to fear that Ernie was flirting, was finding other women more attractive. Tina dealt with that anxiety by holding her body accountable: it was not doing its job because she was too fat. Once again, she split into a "self" – as a male gaze – observing an inadequate female "body." The body in which she had "found her strength" was now her enemy.

As well, to re-enter the world after the withdrawal necessitated by birth and recovery means to re-enter the dominant discourses of women's bodies. To go out in the street, to look at store windows, to read newspapers or magazines, or visit with friends is to be re-positioned in a web of interpretation which attempts to standardize unique bodies. That web of interpretation tells Tina that she is not being good enough. Such an outcome is no different from the past; the difference she feels comes from her despair at being so far from the

unattainable goal, and the increased fear (of loss of love) that
provides the investment in the discourse.

Tina is positioned in contradictory discourses of the body.
On the one hand, she retains an image of her body as instrumental in her discovery of her own strength while giving
birth. On the other hand, her body is seen by her "self" (her
male evaluator) as a passive object, never adequate. It is to the
mental organization of this contradiction that Tina refers
when she speaks of keeping the birth image in a little box: a
box that she opens occasionally in order to recapture the joy
of a strong creative body, then closes again in order to exist in
dominant discourses of the body as weak and unattractive.

A review of Tina's biography can help to explain how it
happens that Tina takes up positions in contradictory
discourses. In fact, such a review immediately makes it clear
that Tina comes to the experience of childbirth with a history
of multiple positions. During the years of her mother's illness,
she was simultaneously a mother and a daughter to her
mother. She was a mother and a sister to her baby brother. She
was her older brother's sister and protégé. She was a Canadian
girl at school and an Italian girl at home.

But the crucial point is that, within these multiple and contradictory positions, she was forced to learn the lesson of
refusal: that one has to refuse one identity in order to take on
another; one has to refuse one experience in order to under-
take a new one. The most obvious example comes from her
refusal of her father's authority.

Tina's location in Canadian culture caused her to see possibilities for a different way of being – a differentness she valued
for herself. To be different involved struggling with – refusing
– the image of "nice Italian girls," which was part of her identity. Tina's ability to refuse that identity was energized by her
equation of her father's definition of life with death. Accepting
her father's image of life – frustration, bitterness and distrust –

was simply more frightening to Tina than refusing it. As well, the silent support of her mother and the active support of her brother enabled Tina to refuse without risking abandonment – a major difference between her situation and Natalie's.

Let us look at specific instances of refusal in Tina's history. Tina's descriptions of interactions with her mother give a historic dimension to the development of a contradictory image of the body. Once, for example, in a fit of psychotic fear and rage, Tina's mother ripped off her daughter's clothes to search her body for marks or signs of pregnancy. Tina identified this episode as having given her a sense of hatred and fear of her "dirty" body – a girl's body, where vagina and breasts were condemned, made bad through silence about them. On the other hand, her mother was a deeply religious woman who also saw aspects of the body, particularly in childbearing, to be God-given, something to be respected.

The early years of Tina's marriage saw her caught in the interplay of dominant discourses. In order to hold on to Ernie, her male gaze always had to stand guard over her body's sexual attractiveness – creating a disembodied state in itself. At the same time, sexual attractiveness was a quality condemned by her mother's fear of the body. That conflict precluded Tina's being comfortable with her sexuality, and she was made to feel guilty for her inadequacy by the "experts," who claimed that normal women are all sexual – in ways that meet men's needs. Tina's response to the double crisis of her lack of sexual response and her husband's affair was to both refuse and invest. She recognized her depression as something she had to refuse; she took it seriously at the point when she found she could no longer connect to nature – to weather, temperature, scenery – and she entered psychotherapy. At the same time she started to study yoga. Her object was to recover her negated body. Again, we see her mother's support: the evening that Tina separated from Ernie, two years after beginning her exploration of issues of her body, she sat at her mother's table, depressed and unsure about her decision. Her mother was heartbroken about the separation, but supported her decision.

Given Tina's history of refusal – of belief that something better is possible – and of support for that refusal, the construction of Tina's experience of giving birth becomes understandable. She was imbued with the knowledge that rejection of authority is the alternative to spiritual death. With practiced ease she rejected the interpretations of her body by nurses, and insisted on responding to her body in her own way. She had spent a great deal of effort investing herself in discourses which emphasized the activity of the body. She believed in the possibility of something better than that which was offered by authority. This made her a "difficult" patient, and medical authorities essentially left her alone. The space was therefore opened up in which Tina could give birth without intervention.

We can now understand Tina's joy in her experience of childbirth. It was derived from two experiences: one was taking a position of independence from authority. Statements such as "I did it," "I just knew I could do it without any doctors," "It was only the strength of my body that made her come out like that," ring with the joy of autonomy. For Tina, this kind of independence feels like the choice of life over death. The second experience was the validation and legitimation that the birth provided for the positive discourses of the body with which she had already been involved. The yoga, and the psychotherapy, as discourses which spoke of her body as productive, healthy, and part of her self, were discourses that in fact helped her produce an independent birth.

Of course, Tina had no physical problems which might have required medical intervention, so that it was possible for her to be left alone with her husband to have the baby. Had this not been the case, medical intervention would have brought the full weight of medical discourses to bear on Tina's experience. In that case, it would have been very difficult for her to have refused an object position in the discourse. In the interests of avoiding "discourse determinism," it is important to acknowledge the tenuous hold we have over the nature of our experience. For Tina, slightly more pain, a little longer labour, might well have altered the experience of childbirth as a validation of positive body discourses.

MARIA

Where Natalie recalled giving birth as an experience of giving her body over to experts to deliver it, and Tina recalled childbirth as a joyful discovery of her bodily potential, Maria remembered her experience of childbirth with a sense of disappointment. Her disappointment helps us to understand the construction of the subjectivity of Woman through the body.

More than either Natalie or Tina, Maria had had definite expectations of what she wanted to happen during childbirth. When those expectations were systematically disappointed, Maria understood that disappointment in the context of her body as an obstacle: that "it" – her body – hadn't performed the way she wanted it to; that it was "too bad" she had to have all those things done to her. But, in some way, this disappointment is framed within the "natural and normal." Bodies are unpredictable; these things just happen. How, then, does the desire to stretch one's bodily potential, when shattered by medical violence, come to be felt as disappointment?

Maria had clear expectations of what she wanted during the birth. She wanted to feel the delivery; she wanted the baby placed on her stomach after birth; and she wanted the doctor to wait for the cord to cease pulsating before cutting it. Maria, like Natalie, had been to childbirth classes where "natural" childbirth methods were valued – but, unlike Natalie, she was open to the discourse of natural childbirth. Although she didn't position herself in the discourse, claiming she was no "nature freak," she saw aspects of the natural childbirth discourse as providing "Canadian" space for her.

Maria's biography shows that she had experienced many different discourses as having common positions toward which she would like to move. She gravitated toward those positions, feeling that they offered her a better life. At the same time, a multiplicity of practices compelled her to retain her Portuguese identity. Within her day-to-day life, not only did she have no support for "Canadian" positions, there was active opposition to her tendency to move in those directions. This is why the issue of "gullibility" loomed large in our early interviews. Being gullible, for Maria, meant acting as the relatives wanted her to: doing things their way, the Portuguese way. Maria experienced giving in to those pressures as "gullibility." If she were gullible, she would not be able to move toward positions she felt were better for her.

In effect, Maria had positioned herself as Portuguese, but always with the sense that what was outside Portuguese space – i.e., inside Canadian space – was better. Her expectations of childbirth were unsupported by her family, and unsupported by her husband, who was designated as her "supportive person" at the birth. Her expectations were also given absolutely no weight by medical personnel.

The pivot on which Maria's experience of childbirth turned was the fact that she had a prolonged labour. Unlike Tina, who was able for the most part to deliver herself, Maria needed help, and that help could only be offered by medical personnel – in the form of violence. Medical techniques of childbirth have been developed on the principle that they must control women's disgusting, impure, unreliable, dirty bodies. Not surprisingly, such techniques reflect the violence of that principle. There was no other form of help available to Maria: violent control of birthing bodies *is* the only in-hospital practice. Without a contradictory discourse, there was no possibility of conflict. To the extent that Maria could not position herself in natural childbirth discourse, she could not really experience conflict. Given an absence of conflict, how else could she conceptualize her delivery but through vague, shadowy, elusive feelings of disappointment?

The central problem here is that the discourse of natural childbirth pertains only to births which do not require intervention and help. When a woman needs help in the form of technology, the discourse falls apart and dissolves into that of medical control through violence. One is not given a choice between violent control and facilitative help: the need for technical help automatically shifts the birth onto the terrain of control ultimately based on men's fear of women's bodies.

Maria never described her delivery as violent – as I do – and I am curious about that. In accounting for this difference, we again head toward questions of women's sense of identity.

Because Maria does not have a discourse with which to contradict that of violent medical control, she is virtually forced to remain in the discourse of the body as obstacle – as bad. She cannot say, "I am angry at these doctors and nurses who robbed me of an understanding of my bodily potential," because there is no model through which she could envision them offering her something different: no model of facilitative technology exists. The natural childbirth discourse locks itself into the avoidance of technology. Since Maria herself had decided she needed the technology, the only way she could understand her subsequent childbirth was through the conception that her body wasn't good enough.

The conjoining of medical discourse, which positions her as a diseased object, and individualism, which holds her to blame for her "bad" body, produces shame. Primitive, inner, continuously produced and reproduced shame structures women's participation in the various removals which constitute femininity: hair, smells, organs, babies, voices, spaces. Maria's account shows us just one of the infinite number of ways by which women's concrete experience of her body is made to produce Woman. Shame, as a layer of identity, is what compels her to define the experiences which produce Woman as "natural and normal."

We also find, in Maria's account, glimpses of what I think of as feelings of pre-anger. These appear in the form of questions, little doubts (such as wondering about having her placenta pulled out) – pieces of thoughts that are difficult to anchor to the conception of disappointment. If Maria had been able to find a conception that would allow these bits to make sense, she would have found an opening for the full expression of anger. In patriarchy, such anger is prohibited through a multitude of practices, since it threatens women's pervasive identity of shame, thus threatening patriarchy itself.

Naomi Scheman (1980) gives us three reasons why women have difficulty discovering anger, and these are germane to an understanding of Maria's experience:

> One is the myth about the emotions, women's emotions in particular that tells us they are irrational or non-rational storms. They sweep over us and are wholly personal quite possibly hormonal! ... A second feature of our lives that keeps us from putting the pieces together is our own insecurity. The central cases of anger are judgmental, a way of feeling that someone (or some group) has acted badly. In order to be straight forwardly angry one standardly has to trust one's own reactions and be in a position to judge. That can be very hard to do from a position of dependency, where one's welfare and happiness depend on pleasing others ... A third thing keeping us from seeing ourselves as angry is the picture we are likely to have of what the good life for a woman consists in. Anger is 'object hungry': if there is no one and nothing to be angry at it will be harder to see oneself as really angry. If the life one has is just what one has expected

would be most satisfying and fulfilling, and if one's sacrifices are seen merely as the transcending of childish dreams, then it will be hard to find anyone or anything to be properly angry at. (p. 177)

If Maria had been able to think that her disappointment in the management of the birth of her child was caused by medical practices, she would have had to become angry. She would necessarily have had to think that someone had acted badly toward her, and this would have created anger. Contrariwise, restriction of anger also restricts the concept which gives the anger meaning (i.e., that someone acted badly to her). Anger and meaning co-produce each other. To restrict one is to restrict the other.

I would like to look at the ways in which, during the birth of Maria's child, Maria's anger was restricted – with the consequence that no meaning other than shame, no meaning which depends on anger, could come into being.

Being ashamed requires that one adopt the position of one who is judged. This position precludes the possibility of being the judge – the position required in order to be angry. The very practices which produce shame (being judged) also prevent the production of anger (being the judge).

The "object-hungry" character of anger made anger unavailable to Maria. The hospital personnel did her delivery; they produced her healthy baby. To be angry with them would make Maria seem like a carping ingrate – to be angry would make her feel even more ashamed. The political distinction between "giving birth" and "being delivered" pales in the relief of having a healthy baby. Matters of personhood seem silly and inconsequential next to the reality of the baby. After all, Maria got what she wanted.

Maria was also blocked from discovering her anger because her pain made her vulnerable. Pain meant that she needed help – and that help came in the form of doctors and nurses whose practices were produced through dominant discourses of women's bodies. In a condition of vulnerability it became difficult to distinguish help from control. Indeed, help and control came to mean the same thing, so that Maria couldn't get angry at the control because she needed the help.

But, once out of the hospital, no longer vulnerable, shouldn't Maria have been expected to discover anger as she thought about the pieces that were hard to attach to the idea of shame? Logically, perhaps; but, realistically, that would have been most unlikely for a woman who lived in a social network that did not recognize the personal as political. There was no one to support the emerging glimmers of feelings which she described as a "little bit of resentment" or a "little anger." Thus, as Scheman (1980, p. 178) says, "What is primarily keeping us as women from acknowledging our anger is an inability to interpret our feelings and behaviour in the proper political perspective." We see that the difficulty of gaining a political perspective in a social environment which doesn't support political redefinition is one of the elements that prevents Maria's production of anger.

For Maria the only possible mediation of her experience of giving birth is disappointment. Her subsequent way of dealing with that disappointment is to act in what common sense tells us is a "healthy" way: she tries to forget about it, to get over it, to hope for a better delivery the next time. In short, she tries to return to normal.

And "normal" has already been established for her. Normal is to get her flat stomach back, to start looking good, to lose that extra weight. Normal is to look like she did before pregnancy. So Maria turns her energies to getting back to normal: exercising, trying not to eat too much, looking for new clothes.

Again, as with Natalie, we see the full force of insanity in these "normal" discourses. We see that "getting back to normal" rests on bodily shame and excludes the possibility of transformation by *not* getting back to normal. "Not getting back to normal" would allow one to glimpse the organization of systematic practices which produce bodily shame as part of feminine identity, and thus would allow one to feel rage at such practices.

It is difficult to resist the urge to end this chapter by providing a global statement neatly packaging three such different experiences of childbirth as those of Natalie, Tina, and Maria. But I believe that the very differences which are evident in the construction and mediation of their experiences of birth argue powerfully for working with diversity rather than falsely subsuming difference into a general abstraction.

The accounts of childbirth presented by Maria, Tina, and Natalie, notwithstanding their commonalities – first births, in the same city, in the same hospital – speak to different realms of feminist theory and action.

Maria's account brings to the foreground the question of strategies for confronting institutions, and shows why developing such strategies is critical: the violence done to her during childbirth she turns back on herself in the form of rage-crippling shame. The ascendancy of patriarchy depends on such shame.

Tina's biography, on the other hand, illustrates how her learned ability to tolerate contradictions gives her the possibility of refusal. Tina's practices are structured by investment in conflicting discourses; the resulting contradictions allow her to refuse medical practices of birth and instead exercise her right to bodily potential. This experience of the body doesn't alter her identity, because she is constituted in dominant discourses of the body as well. However, the act of experiencing bodily potential gives her a strong contradiction to such discourses, once again providing the potential for refusal.

Natalie, invested in dominant discourses of women's bodies, shows us how practices which are structured within those discourses necessarily produce disembodiment, which, in turn, as part of her identity, continues to inform her investment in those discourses. This process maintains her in spirals of shame and dependence, creating the natural and normal identity of woman in patriarchy.

There are implications for feminist action in the women's stories. Tina's story makes it clear that feminism must maintain and strengthen its attack on the discourses of femininity, so that people like Tina can have social support for keeping her contradictions alive as sources of refusal. Natalie's lack of a sense of personal power makes it clear that, for feminists, locating the construction of Woman, and acknowledging that it exists only as a social fabrication, is crucial if we are going to take on the project of producing individuals who value contradiction as containing the possibility of freedom.

CHAPTER SIX

ISOLATION

TO BE PRODUCED AS A WOMAN in capitalist patriarchy is to be circumscribed by a particular function: taking care of others. The major element of caretaking assigned to women is the primary responsibility for child care. This sole-caretaking function justifies women's location in the private sphere – in nuclear families and away from and outside the making of culture. Women's sole responsibility for child care does not just affect women who mother; it provides a reference for discourses which affect all women. Thus, women without children are either selfish or not quite whole. It is difficult to overstate the degree to which women's sole responsibility for children grounds discourses which regulate the concept Woman.

And isolation is the factor through which women's practice of mothering is organized – and that organization grounds sole caretaking. In all three of the accounts that make up Part I, we have seen that isolation had specific effects in structuring sole caretaking – which, in turn, produces Woman.

MARIA

Maria did not question that the gender division of labour in child care was "natural and normal." Two factors are important in explaining Maria's conception of her responsibility as a mother: first, her occupation as a child-care worker gave her skills and experience which provided her with a sense of expertise with her baby; second, she clearly had a project in relation to her baby – she wanted to raise her baby differently from the way she had been raised. This involved "treating the baby as a person," which meant rejecting the authoritarian methods used by her own parents.

Neither of these factors held true for her husband. Tony had no expertise with babies; he couldn't even change a diaper. As well, he was not involved in a direct project with the baby; rather, his project was clearly to make a success of his service station. He loved his work and spent over twelve hours a day at the garage. Labour was thus sharply divided: Maria mothered; Tony "worked." It came as a surprise to Maria when this arrangement didn't meet her needs.

For Maria, early motherhood was an overwhelming experience of isolation. Maria's mothering as sole caretaker was a direct outcome of that isolation. In Maria's account, I located ten factors which were responsible for her isolation:

- Tony worked from 12 to 14 hours a day;
- Maria didn't know her neighbours in the apartment building;
- the family pressured her not to take the baby out in cold weather;
- she had no car;
- she had no suitable baby-carrier for travel on public transit;
- her peers didn't want to go out with the baby, but pressured her to socialize at home;
- adult recreation and leisure activities do not welcome babies;
- her baby was very attached to her;
- she was tired from getting only interrupted sleep;
- she felt guilty about feeling isolated.

Interestingly, when we look at this list, it adds up to what is "natural and normal" about mothering. Each item is just part of "the way things are" – not practices that add up to the isolation of women in the private sphere as part of the organization of capitalist patriarchy. And yet it is precisely these elements that, together, make the family a central site in the everyday practice of capitalist patriarchy.

Much has been written in the literature about the isolation of women as mothers (see for example Dorothy Hobson, 1978); yet little of that work has actually focused on isolation as a constitutive feature of mothering itself. Most analyses have simply described isolation as boring, oppressive and undermining to solidarity among women. Maria's account is important because it allows us to see isolation as *in itself* a condition which is implicated in the construction of Woman in the practice of mothering.

Tony works away from the home nearly all his waking hours. He has next to nothing to do with his child, and cannot perform the practical tasks around which relationships with babies are built. Maria doesn't know the neighbours, because families are the locus of privacy and intimacy at the end of the workday; in Maria's building, the long narrow corridor lined with shut doors tells us about that privacy. Maria doesn't have a car – Tony keeps meaning to leave her one, but he doesn't trust her to drive. He is afraid she will smash up his car, and cars are his work, his pride, connected to his masculinity. Maria's friends would hate the embarrassment of going to a restaurant with her and the baby and having the baby cry. They and the relatives, who use the excuse of fear of cold weather, actively pressure Maria to stay in the private sphere, at home. Maria's baby prefers her; after all, no one else knows the baby. Since Freud and object-relations theorists have told us about the exquisite fragility of babies' psyches, it would be impossible for Maria to leave her baby with someone who might not take quite as good care of her as Maria herself does.

Finally, to stay home and look after an infant is the fulfillment of womanhood, which should enable "adequate women" to overcome even the worst social context.

Mothering involves listening, trial and error learning, changing one's rhythm, working simultaneously at different levels, uncertainty, and physical exhaustion. Such work requires a tremendous fluidity of identity: suspending one's own identity to momentarily "be" the baby in order to understand her needs, dissolving one's boundaries to admit a different rhythm, thinking with a constant sub-thought of "baby" – all this means that mothering involves rather extraordinary transformations in identity. I think what new mothers tend to call "shock" is the fluidity of identity that a newborn requires in its caretaker.

In conditions of isolation this fluidity is experienced as a loss of self – not because babies are so voracious, but because the social situations in which one's identity is normally continuously re-constituted simply disappear. Mothers are left without the social interactions which construct and produce identity; at the same time, they are expected to perform work which demands a kind of diffusion of identity. In a very real sense, mothers feel they have "lost" their selves. They have lost the world in which selves are co-constituted with and by other people. Instead, their identities are defined every day in relation to absolutely dependent infants.

In this situation, the baby's needs become *the* figure against an unpeopled ground – there simply aren't any other figures on which to focus. In isolation, the work of listening to a baby is made more stressful because the baby is the only thing we can hear. In isolation, altering our own rhythm means becoming absorbed by the baby's rhythm. In isolation, to be uncertain about the baby means feeling *generally* uncertain, because there are available so few social situations in which we can feel certain.

The baby comes to be experienced as insatiable. Here is the

pain that Maria feels as she pleads with me to understand that it is not the baby that drives her back to work, but the impossible situation of being always alone with her. We must acknowledge the consequences of isolation in the creation of relationships between mothers and children. Such isolation structures the contradiction, "I lose myself with you / yet you are everything to me."

Nancy Chodorow (1978) labels this contradiction "overinvestment":

A mother's sense of continuity with her infant may shade into too much connection and not enough separateness. Empathy and primary identification, enabling anticipation of an infant's or child's needs, may become unconscious labelling of what her child ought to need, or what she thinks it needs. The development of a sense of autonomous self becomes difficult for children and leads to a mother's loss of sense of self as well. (p. 212)

Maria's account shows that the contradiction, "I lose myself with you / yet you are everything to me" – what Chodorow terms "overinvestment" – is created and maintained in conditions of isolation. I think it is important to locate the dis-ease in the social arrangements of mothering. The danger of individualism is that it can lead us to search for individual perfection, for the eradication of our flaws, without understanding that the social situation produces the interactions that damage us. I would like here to repeat Maria's account of a normal day, which previously appeared in Chapter Two, in order to show how her isolation grounds overinvestment:

5:30 a.m. She woke up. I changed her and fed her.
6:30. She falls back to sleep and so do I.
8:00. She wakes up. I change her and play with her a little. She is happy and smiling.

8:20. I feed her.

9:00-9:30. She sits in her chair, on the kitchen table. She is 'gumming' some toys while I have breakfast and tidy up.

10:00-10:30. She starts fussing. I change her and try to rock her to sleep, but it doesn't work. She is searching for the breast, so I give her some (just one side).

11:00. She is crying. I try to rock her to sleep, but again rocking alone doesn't work, so I feed her the other side.

11:30. She is asleep again. I write this and begin rinsing another load of diapers.

11:40-12:10. She is awake again and I attempt to put her back to sleep – but she refuses and is wide awake. I notice that she is wet right through so I go change her and give up fighting her to sleep.

12:10-1:00. She sits in her chair in the bathroom as I rinse out her diapers. She is very quiet because she is so sleepy, so I don't even talk to her and she listens to the sound of running water. Then I notice she has poohed right through, so I change her again.

1:00-2:00. I carry her with me in her chair as I go up and down three times to the laundry [three floors down]. Her chair sits on top of the dryer and she falls asleep from noise and vibrations. So I carry her upstairs gently leaving two loads of laundry in the dryer and one load in the washer.

2:00. I let her sleep right in the chair, and I come to lie down on the couch. I'm quite tired from all the stair climbing. I get one short phone call from Tony, and I'm thinking about what to have for lunch when I hear her cry!

2:10. I take her out of the chair and begin to rock her – but she is searching, so I come back out to the couch, and I feed her. I myself am falling asleep while nursing

her so for the second side I transfer to the bed and
nurse her lying down.

2:45. She is finished eating and asleep, so I just leave her
on my bed and close my eyes. I would love to take a
little nap, but I know my clothes should be ready now
and my stomach is growling.

3:10. I get up and go get the clothes downstairs, leaving
her asleep. Then I make and eat lunch. I'm starving
and also exhausted. I come and lay on the couch and
write this. Believe it or not I hear her crying.

4:00. She is up and takes a temper fit on me. She doesn't
... [Maria doesn't finish – the baby is too demanding
and she is too tired].

The diary tells us that Maria is the baby's whole world. We
see that Maria is alone with the work of mothering. The diary
gives us clear examples of that work. From 10:00 to 10:30 we
see the work of trial and error, which is accomplished through
constant listening to the baby's needs. At 11:30 we see her
adjusting her work rhythm to match the baby's sleep pattern
and stopping her work when the baby wakes. At 12:10, when
she takes the baby into the bathroom to keep her amused
while rinsing diapers, we see her working at different levels.
Throughout, we see the physical forgoing of self which ends
in exhaustion.

In conditions of isolation, this work makes the baby seem
devouring. A simple need for the baby to go to sleep becomes
an exercise in "fighting her to sleep." This is a function of isolation, in which the fussy stretch of time between the moment
when the baby begins to get tired and the moment when she
actually falls asleep becomes unbearable. When that period of
time is the primary focus, the fussing, the rocking, the nursing
become intolerable because there is no distraction from it.
Maria's identity becomes sucked into the baby's fussiness,
with no other source of affirmation of boundary, with no way

of *not* focusing on getting the baby to sleep. These terrible periods of time structure the "message" to the baby, "You must sleep so I can survive." When the baby sleeps Maria can have her self back for an all-too-short period of time.

One of the problems for isolated mothers is that these moments lead to the feeling of "I need help." The minute that need is felt, it is immediately contradicted by the certainty that only the mother can nurse, that the baby wants to be only with the mother when fussy. Being helped is felt as the solution, but this is immediately rejected as impossible.

What we must come to understand is that the entire character of the work changes in a peopled landscape. When the challenge to identity that is manifested through the work of mothering is tempered by forms of social interaction which reaffirm identity, one does not experience the sense of loss of self from motherwork. It becomes possible not to attend to those fussy stretches, because there are other loci of interest which prevent the total absorption of the mother into her baby's discomfort. With other people around, one does not have to worry about whether the baby would feel abandoned if one were to leave the room to rinse a diaper. Even if all the tasks of motherwork remained the same, doing them in a peopled setting would mean that the work need not be experienced as a decimation of the self.

For Maria, it is clear that there was only one escape route from isolation, and that was through returning to work. It was the only alternative which her relatives would accept, since making money was a way of helping Tony out, of getting ahead in Canada. And so Maria returned to work as a daycare worker in an infant room. She took her own infant to Tony's grandmother to be cared for while she herself took care of other working mothers' babies. The condition of isolation in fact structured Maria's need to leave her baby. It is a terrible irony that Maria could enjoy her work as an infant care-giver because it was structured as public – there were other people present, who gave her a sense of accomplishment and validation, who provided cooperation – while the isolation inherent in being at home with her own baby, and her consequent sense of dissolution of self, made staying at home an impossibility.

Maria's return to work in no way affected her identity as sole caretaker: going to work was something she did *in addition to* carrying out her primary responsibility for the baby. It was Maria who made child-care arrangements with the grandmother, picked up and dropped off the baby, kept track of naps, food, and clothing. The baby's time with the grandmother was interpreted as "doing without mother," or "waiting for mother to come back," rather than as actually being with the grandmother.

Maria's return to work raises an important question: how did Maria understand her need to go back to work in a way that defended her against seeing the organization of mothering as oppressive? Maria's experience of early motherhood was one of constant isolation. As the weeks went by, Maria began to feel more and more depressed. She explained the depression as "down days" or the "blues" – in other words causeless, random feelings. The factors that caused her isolation she perceived as random also – nothing that would suggest a patterned arrangement. Eventually, she had to deal with her depression – the feelings were too pervasive and occurred too frequently. However, the relationship between the specific factors which isolated her and her depression was severed, because those factors were perceived as random. If her isolation – and its consequence, depression – was causeless, how could she oppose it? To see the specific as random prohibits the formulation of a sense of pattern, an explanation which could transform a neutral relationship to anger at the oppression of women through mothering.

The abstraction Maria used to conceptualize her depression was the discourse of individualism. She observed that she was a person who had "needs"; she could not continue to operate in isolation because she needed to be with other people. The contradiction between her expectation that she would be a happy contented mother at home with her baby and the reality of her isolation was resolved when she positioned herself in a discourse which was developed in early popular feminist writings – probably the best example of which would be Betty Friedan's *The Feminine Mystique* (1963). Friedan acknowledged that depression was produced by women's isolation in the home, and let women know that it was okay for them to have needs to be with people – and, in fact, that women must get out and join in public life. Friedan said, however, that it was the responsibility of individual women to seek solutions to a condition of isolation imposed by the social construction of mothering. In such an ideology of individualism, ultimate responsibility always lies with the individual.

In view of this, we need to look at what the statement "I have needs" means to Maria. To discover that she has needs really means that she is able to define herself as normal rather than abnormal: abnormal people are depressed, normal people have needs. Thus, the effect of the discourse "women have needs" is to normalize negative feelings. Everything becomes fine once it is normalized – the only thing left to do is to take responsibility for one's needs. And the condition of enforced isolation of women in the private sphere is left untouched, undiscovered. Thus what is presented as a liberatory discovery of the "needs of women" in fact works to focus attention on the individual rather than on the actual conditions which produce the problem.

Once positioned in this discourse, Maria had to "choose" an individual solution. For Maria, the "choice" between leaving her baby – who needed her and whom she needed – and being grossly depressed through isolation was, in reality, no choice at all. The only other option which might have relieved her isolation was a mother-baby "class" or activity – in which the public / social is made private in order to accommodate women's needs, in a way that does not threaten the "real" work of the world. However, this option was not open to Maria, since her relatives would have been shocked at such a frivolous use of time and money. Women have to pay for activities in a private public space, and Tony would have disapproved of that. Also, I think Maria herself probably felt too shy and too culturally estranged from such activities to seek them out; they felt too Canadian. So the only solution for her was to go to work.

One might have predicted that Maria would experience a great deal of guilt at going back to work; after all, she was leaving what she saw as her primary responsibility. However, this did not happen because of the influence of her ethnic background. Maria was raised within a value structure that held "getting ahead in Canada" to be a major priority. Her relatives, and Tony as well, approved of her work because it helped her family unit economically. Thus, through work, Maria could meet her needs while still doing the socially approved thing.

To me, this represented an interesting moment in the process of change. The oppression of isolation created by staying at home was so great that Maria, supported by ethnic values, went back to work. As a working mother, different possibilities arose for her. On the one hand, she faced the Superwoman position, as sole caretaker of her baby and full-time worker. On the other hand, working put her in a position of lessened financial dependence and brought a status which allowed her to feel justified in asking Tony for help. We cannot predict how all this will act to produce change: Maria may move toward a new kind of oppression; her relationship with Tony may move toward equality; or, in fact, both things may happen.

TINA

Tina's account gives us insight into how the fact of isolation underlies the relationship between Tina and Ernie. Despite their conscious intentions, their relationship produced Tina as primary caretaker.

In Chapter Three, I described the beginnings of Tina's feelings of responsibility for and attachment to her baby as having occurred during her hospitalization. Once home, she had an entirely different relationship to the baby than Ernie did: she had already taken up the role of primary caretaker. We can see the day-to-day practices that maintained her in that role in the structuring of relationships as Tina and Ernie began parenting.

Tina's transformation from being a person who was constantly out in the world, at galleries, concerts, or lectures, to someone who stayed at home almost all the time was an abrupt one. The fact of having a baby quickly placed her in the private sphere, and, after that, each venture into the public realm felt like a transgression. For example, Tina could no longer drop into courses because to sneak in alone would be "okay," but to transgress from the private to the public with the baby would not. The image of such transgression is well cemented in women's consciousness: public is equated with important, private with unimportant. Tina interpreted her sense of transgression as a fear of being attacked in public with the baby: an interpretation which meant that she could dismiss the issue as a function of her own craziness. However, to contaminate the "important" public world with the "unimportant" needs of mothers and children is to make a political statement which, in fact, does leave one open to attack.

Tina's friends dropped away. Most of them were childless single people who had access to the public realm. Tina no longer did, and this meant that whatever their previous common interests, she and her friends now had different, incompatible projects. When Tina talked about mothering to her friends she felt trivial; when her friends talked about their lives in the public world, she felt excluded and marginalized. The gap between Tina and her friends was filled with tension, and she ceased to have much contact with them.

Cut off from friends and outside activities, Tina stayed alone at home with the baby. She was engaged in the same work that Maria's account details: Tina changed her rhythm, listened, engaged in continual trial and error learning, experienced the baby's needs as her own, worked simultaneously on different levels. The boundaries of her identity changed to incorporate the baby, and those boundaries remained fluid because of the work of baby-care. Because this work was done in isolation, Tina too, like Maria, experienced a loss of sense of self: there were no people around who could help her reconstitute her boundaries in the shape of her recognizable self. Consequently, we see Tina set up patterns of defense which helped her to cope with this decimation of the self – particularly evident in her attempts to create schedules or routines for the baby. The routines were a way of mentally organizing activity in order to have a sense of control, a sense of being proactive, in a world which daily threatens the self. Tina needed to protect time for herself; to know that the baby would be asleep at a certain point held out the promise of time in which she could be herself. For Tina – as for Maria – loss of self didn't happen because of the voracious needs of her baby, but because the baby's needs were experienced in the absence of the self-constituting effect of other people.

But, paradoxically, the need to establish routines and schedules reduced Tina's freedom to be with other people. It is difficult to organize "going out" if one must first make sure an infant is fed and asleep. Nevertheless, Tina feared breaking routines because doing so felt like opening the door to personal chaos.

How did Ernie fit into the picture of Tina's sole caretaking? He helped her by caring for the baby when she went out or when she needed a rest. In doing so, he became Tina's helper. Since she was the primary caretaker, she was obliged to tell him what the routines were, how to do baby-care – essentially how to be like herself. He could not be different from her, because to be different would have meant establishing different routines, different rhythms, different patterns and logics with the baby. This was intolerable to Tina for two reasons: first, differentness would have made her feel overwhelmed and out of control. Isolation had deprived her of her sense of self; if routines could be held constant, then perhaps the spaces for the self, felt ambivalently as "being without the baby," could be made predictable or reliable. Second, in the division of labour, Tina had always been the primary caretaker. Such a division of labour meant that Ernie was not fundamentally responsible for the baby; it was Tina who did what Ruddick (1984) calls the "maternal thinking," Tina who knew the baby's routines and had control of them. As a function of having left maternal thinking to Tina, Ernie became less sensitive to the baby. He played roughly with her, left her to cry, didn't "tune in." This is the beginning, I think, of what Dorothy Dinnerstein (1976) describes as the root of patriarchy:

It is obvious we all have character traits which make us less than perfectly parental. What is not faced head-on is the fact that under present conditions, woman does not share man's right to have such traits without loss of human stature, and man does not share woman's obligation to work at mastering them, at shielding them from their consequences. Women will never have this right, nor men this obligation until male imperfection begins to impinge on all of us when we are tiny and helpless, so that it becomes as culpable as female imperfection, as close to the original centre of human grief. Only then will the harm women do be recognized as the familiar harm we all do ourselves, not strange harm inflicted by some outside agent. Only then will men really start to take seriously the problem of curbing, taming their own destructiveness. But this can happen only when the early core of human rage can no longer vent itself on the mystical figure of the early mother, when we all take on ourselves the blame for the damage we do each other and the responsibility for stopping it. (pp. 237-38)

In the division of labour between Tina and Ernie, only Tina, not Ernie, is responsible for the baby's development. This creates a problem of trust for Tina. Since she believes in the caretaker's impact on a baby's development, and since she is responsible for maternal thinking, how can she tolerate Ernie's unmaternal caretaking? She does not trust Ernie to care for the baby, and this causes her to continuously instruct him, a form of relationship which is inherently unequal.

Over time, therefore, Tina became established as the more gratifying parent. The baby stopped crying when Tina picked her up; she cried when Tina left. Tina knew what pleased her, and it was Tina with whom the baby experienced the pain of separation. Throughout the six-month interview period, Tina, Ernie, and the baby all agreed that the mother was sole caretaker in that family.

This form of relationship, structured through isolation and rooted in maternal primary caretaking, fuels Tina's anger at Ernie. He can never truly relieve her of the burden of being Everything: he can only help, and the help which he offers must always fall short of taking responsibility. Assuming responsibility is precluded because Tony's behaviour toward the baby has always been mediated through Tina's need for help, rather than deriving from a sense of his unique relationship to his child.

With a tremendous sense of ambivalence, Tina returned to work. Tina's project had always been to find more in life than her mother and father had been able to acknowledge. In light of that project, we can understand how being confined in isolation was impossible for Tina. Still, her definition of mothering focused on primary caretaking; the thought of leaving her baby was a nightmare for her, particularly since the timing of the separation was determined by the school's schedule, without reference to what the baby needed.

After returning to work, Tina became responsible for both her job as teacher and her job as primary caretaker. She was chronically exhausted, and torn between the demands of the job and the demands of the baby. In that state she watched Ernie, who had time and energy, going out, seeing friends and maintaining a public life. His freedom both angered and depressed her – reactions which are inevitable in mothers isolated in the private sphere. That anger, however, while painful and divisive, can also fuel a struggle for greater equality in the parenting roles.

Even while she sought greater equality as a parent, Tina continued to explain her mothering through biologistic references to instincts and hormones. She did this through a process of "double consciousness." By double consciousness, I mean situations in which one explains an event through an ideological abstraction, despite the existence of a contradiction between the abstraction and the real event. This produces "double consciousness," because there is a lack of "fit" between what we know has actually happened and the interpretation we attach to the experience. Double consciousness is an important resource for learning about how we are produced as Woman, because oppression happens to us in the real event, but the discourses available to describe that event interpret it as "natural and normal." If we are to resist definition as Woman, we must analyze the production of oppression through discourses which are able to name – i.e., correctly interpret – oppressive events.

Biologistic explanations of women's mothering figured heavily in the meaning Tina made of her activities. She described many barriers to going out: she was afraid of being thrown out of a public place if she breastfed; she was afraid of being attacked and then being unable to defend her baby; she was afraid of not having any place in public where she could adequately care for her baby. When I asked her to explain her fears she attributed it to her hormones: she likened herself to a mother bird protecting her young – there was some "natural force" in her that produced fear.

My contention here is that the hormonal explanation is ideological: that is, it is an explanation of reality that serves to regulate women in order to support their continued oppression. We can see that the hormonal explanation acts in a way that justifies the limitation of women to the home – to the private and invisible. Tina didn't understand her fear as a response to the real examples of cultural hostility to women and babies that she has experienced; she interpreted it as caused by a little spurt of hormones – the very hormones that made her the only person equipped to take care of children in the home. To use the hormonal explanation is to relegate one's body to a particular space, to assign it a particular function – and such a space and function help to constitute capitalist patriarchy.

How was a double consciousness put in place? For Tina, it began with her knowledge of actual events: she knew women had been humiliated for publicly feeding their babies. She knew there were few places where she could change her baby. She understood the difficulty of taking a baby on public transportation. Yet she interpreted all of these obstacles to a public life through discourses which gave them a random character, so that they became things that just happened, without intention or underlying organization. Experiences of a public domain hostile to women with babies were explained through reference to "... an insensitive person," or the "fact" that "... babies are difficult to travel with." These experiences were described as specific and singular occurrences; one might say that Tina's experiences took on meaning through discourses which ascribed random individuality to events. As random events, they did not warrant inclusion into a conceptual pattern. Thus her fear had to be explained through some concept other than her own experience: in this case, the ideological hormonal explanation. This was the moment of regulation, in which her personal experience was lost to her as a basis for understanding her fear.

Double consciousness links power and subjectivity. It helps explain how we participate in our own oppression. Foucault (1982) explains this kind of power as the power of the state to simultaneously individualize and totalize. Tina sees her body as individual and unique. This is paradoxical, in that the body is the site that culture acts on to produce Woman – as we saw in the preceding chapter – yet it is simultaneously individualized so that the concept Woman is obscured.

Let us look at another example from Tina's account. Much of the early interview data was an account of how Tina learned to mother. She learned how the baby liked to nurse. She learned to bath, soothe, and comfort her baby through trial and error learning. Yet she explained her knowledge of mothering as a function of her instincts and hormones. Again, the double consciousness: at the level of the actual event, Tina told me about her everyday learning to be a mother – about the mistakes, the unknowns, the desire to find the right way. At an abstract level, however, she described her ability to mother as due to instincts. Her explanation of reality did not refer to the real experiences of her daily life, but was named through an ideological construct. Again, Tina interpreted the details of learning as individually random. These details, therefore, did not have to be given any meaning, and, consequently, Tina failed to connect the process of "learning to mother" with the outcome of "knowing how to mother." Instead, she attributed her knowledge of mothering to instinct.

NATALIE

Natalie's experience provides a very different perspective from those offered by the accounts of Tina and Maria. For Tina and Maria, isolation was a threat: for Maria, it meant pressure to exist within Portuguese culture, which she experienced as restriction; for Tina, isolation meant she could no longer engage in her constant search for "life," which for her meant enjoying struggle, conflict, and contradiction. Ultimately, isolation fueled both women's return to work.

Natalie, on the other hand, actively collaborated in her own isolation. She did not want people to visit her. She shunned casual contact with other mothers. She went to shopping malls nearly every day, as a way of getting out of the house while still avoiding social contact. An active desire for isolation structured her practice as a mother.

Natalie acted from feelings of extreme fragility and vulnerability in the world. My speculation is that this vulnerability probably derived from early family relationships, in which Natalie was the object of different modes of authority within a context of parental poverty and isolation. Natalie emerged from her childhood as a person who operates without a sense of self-determination, without a conviction of her own authority. She has great difficulty naming her own reality. To name one's reality is to experience oneself, if only for a fleeting moment, as legitimate. This experience is missing from Natalie's life, and that lack is directly implicated in Natalie's desire for isolation.

Natalie looks outside herself for the meaning of her experience. She does not use her own location, her own senses, to make meaning. She does not experience herself as a knower; she ignores her own perceptions as she scans authority for the meaning of her reality. Thus, the potential for empowerment that exists in the experience of mothering is lost to her. She uses abstractions that are derived from the dominant ideologies of mothering to structure her experiences. She concentrates on surviving within discourses which themselves create a problem of survival. As long as she has no power of naming, Natalie's practice of motherhood can never challenge ideology.

Given this background, we can begin to understand the trauma a new baby represented for Natalie. She faced a massive contradiction between prescribed meaning and her experience of reality. Her ideological framework for mothering was that mothering is natural, instinctive, and unproblematic. However, the actual practice of mothering posed a contradiction to the ideology. Natalie didn't know what to do for her baby. She didn't know how to breastfeed – which, according to her discourse, all good mothers know. This reality could not be obscured, denied, repressed or forgotten, because it existed in her forced relation with the baby as a separate but totally dependent person.

This was traumatic because without the power to name, Natalie had no way of handling contradiction. The contradiction between "mothering is natural" and a complex, real baby was the basis for Natalie's feeling of being totally out of control. A dramatic change would have been required, however, for Natalie to perceive – name – the contradiction, and such a change was not possible for Natalie. Instead, she interpreted the contradiction as evidence of her inadequacy. She felt bitter.

During this period of early motherhood, almost the only people with whom she had contact (excluding her family) were people Natalie invested with authority: her doctor, pop psychologist Burton White, her pre-natal instructor and me. The problem for her was that these "experts" were located in conflicting discourses, so that she could never settle in with a particular set of instructions. And as the power to name rested always outside herself, she herself could never invest strongly in a position. As we saw in the account, for Natalie, equilibrium never came from a sense of comfort with any expert's advice; rather it came from the gradual regularization of the baby's life, particularly with respect to sleeping and feeding.

Natalie's desire for isolation was tied to her intolerable level of self-criticism and self-loathing. She dealt with the pain of these feelings by splitting her contempt off from herself and projecting it onto other people. In this way, she constantly felt criticism and judgement to be coming from other people, from outside her. She feared other people, who might criticize the baby's diaper rash, just as she feared comment from the woman in the drive-in washroom who might criticize her for taking a baby to the drive-in. Isolating herself from people reduced the possibility of feeling criticized or judged by others. She felt safe at home because there was nobody there on whom she could project her condemnation of herself.

How then did isolation structure her practice as a mother? I have argued previously that mothering in our society is organized to meet the needs of capitalist patriarchy, rather than the needs of women's reality. To mother at this time, in this culture, requires constant negotiation of the contradictions between one's immediate reality and the dominant ideologies of family organization. This negotiation was problematic for Natalie. Lacking the ability to handle those contradictions, her practice as a mother consisted of searching for the "loudest" ideology, the most accepted way of doing things, the most legitimate course of action. What she "heard" was necessarily the dominant way of organizing child-rearing. Her practice was always structured by dominant discourses, at the expense of her own sense of reality. She abandoned her own opinion that her baby was feeding well when the nurse informed her that the baby was sucking improperly. She could act on her desire to pick up her crying baby only after reading Burton White's dictum that a baby can't be spoiled before the age of seven months. She reproduced dominant forms of organization which do not acknowledge women's needs and interests.

Learning is a social process. Dialogue is necessary in order to deal with the conflicts and contradictions from which change derives. When Natalie isolated herself through fear of condemnation, she precluded the development of conditions favourable for learning. She was left to interact with ideological forms which only served to validate her sense of inadequacy. She could never rest easy at having done something right, because a louder, contradictory ideological voice might come along at any moment. In short, out of a feeling of disempowerment, she cut off interaction which might have led to support or validation. Instead, she listened to the experts, a process which reproduced her disempowerment.

Well, one might ask, so what? How do the problems of an insecure woman affect us, we who are better equipped to handle conflict? Why can't we dismiss her as a casualty of upbringing? The reason we must allow ourselves to be taught by Natalie's experience is that it is important to understand the contradiction lodged there.

The isolation of women in the home is "normal and natural." To be at home bringing up the kids is what women are supposed to do. The mythical normal woman is happy, contented and fulfilled at home. To be a perfect ideological mother, one must tolerate isolation. Natalie teaches us that tolerating isolation is rooted and maintained in the disempowerment of women. Only through crippling our most basic sense of authority can we be the kind of mother required by capitalist patriarchal organization. To be produced as Woman is to be crippled. This has a familiar ring to it: it is the same contradiction that we found in discourses of the body.

When I first attempted to look at the question of how sole caretaking came to be produced in Natalie's subjectivity, I felt stuck. When I studied her account, I saw Natalie operating as the perfect subject for regulation through dominant cultural definitions of mothering. She had no capacity to resist ideology, and was therefore inseparable from it. For Natalie, the boundaries between self and other didn't seem to exist, as they did for Tina and Maria, and this is what made analysis of her subjectivity hard: in Natalie's case, it was difficult to distinguish subject from non-subject.

The complex contradiction that occurs is that, in being the most perfectly suited candidate for regulation, Natalie turns out to have the least well-regulated subjectivity. Since her capacity to name her own reality was minimal, one would have expected that the cultural definitions which regulate women as sole caretakers of children would be the only meanings used to construct her reality.

Yet, contact with Natalie two years after the birth of her baby showed a very different picture. The baby was then living with her grandmother outside Toronto, and had been for over three months while Natalie and Jim were renovating their house; it was not clear when she would come home. Natalie told me that the eighteen months following the interview period had been filled with anxiety and tension for the couple. Marital difficulties had emerged, coped with chiefly by the use of tranquilizers and alcohol. In other words, much of Natalie's behaviour contradicted the dominant ideologies which organize motherhood.

In Natalie's account we do not see double consciousness, as we do with Tina or Maria. Instead, Natalie had two different ways of making meaning. When an external source contradicted what Natalie believed was true, Natalie was "shattered." Shattered, for her, meant that the full extent of her vulnerability was exposed: contradictory external opinion meant to her that she never even knew what she was doing. For instance, in the hospital, Natalie at first had felt her baby was feeding with no problems. Then a nurse informed her that the baby was sucking improperly. Immediately, all legitimacy was wiped out of Natalie's experience. She abandoned her own experience to take up the nurse's opinion; she had lost control, and the only way to get it back was through following the advice of experts. The discourse that organized her baby's feedings as "going well" immediately changed to a discourse which positioned her as having been fooled, been wrong, been inadequate. In taking up the nurse's position that the baby was sucking improperly, Natalie turned herself against her own experience – which made her feel she had been a fool. Only in being positioned with the experts could she hope to control the fool and become less vulnerable.

In this dynamic, double consciousness is precluded. Double consciousness requires that a subject be able to attach legitimacy to the experiences of the body. It requires being able to rely on or validate one's bodily experience as the origin of investment in discourse.

Natalie did not trust her body sufficiently to believe in or legitimize such sensations. This was the ultimate source of her vulnerability: she was alienated from her bodily experiences, so she was at the mercy of external definitions of those experiences. Dominant discourses of women's bodies produces alienation, and such alienation, in turn, prevents women from using their bodies as a resource for creating meaning. Without this resource, there is no experience which motivates us to go past ideology, to search for patterns which could make our experiences coherent.

A profound alienation from her own experience can also be seen in what constituted conflict for Natalie: she experienced conflict when two external sources didn't agree. Conflict was then experienced as panic caused by the need to choose which external source to follow. She could not make such a choice; on what basis would she do so, when she felt her own perceptions were not trustworthy? Thus we see Natalie leaping desperately from position to position among conflicting discourses, her subjectivity in chaos.

An example of this can be seen in the difficulty she faced about letting the baby cry. Natalie had decided to let the baby cry at night so that she would learn to sleep through the night.

To pick her up, she felt, was to spoil her. Then Natalie read Burton White, who provided the information that babies couldn't be spoiled before the age of seven months. She immediately dropped the "spoiling" discourse, and positioned herself with Burton White. She then castigated herself for having let the "poor thing" cry. Again, she had been a fool, inadequate.

This way of handling conflict tells us about the fate of contradiction for Natalie. Since her bodily perceptions could not be trusted, establishing a sense of control in her life depended on suppressing those perceptions. She relied on experts to provide her with the knowledge that could not be gained through her own perceptions. In the face of conflict, she immediately bypassed her own body and depended on external knowledge. Where conflict or contradiction always signals being out of control, being endangered, the possibility of occupying multiple subject positions is precluded. Change or growth is limited. The chaos is handled through tranquilizers and alcohol.

What we are talking about here is the lack of capacity for resistance, since resistance requires some degree of trust of one's bodily senses. It depends on giving some validation to what is felt, heard, touched, or seen.

I want to return to the irony of Natalie's experience. At first sight, Natalie appears to be the perfect subject for regulation and control: she can speak only with an ideological voice. Yet regulation fails with her: she is *in chaos.* She is too frightened, too vulnerable, too concerned with maintaining control to maintain her position as sole caretaker.

I think this irony contains an important lesson. We can begin to see ideology and the control which is manifested through ideology, not as an independent force, but as inseparable from consciousness and inseparable from resistance. Without resistance from Natalie, the work of ideology fails. Regulation cannot be sustained. Cultural meaning in which ideology is inscribed depends on resistance for the possibility of meaning; without resistance there can be no real acceptance of meaning. I am unable to move this idea further within the limits of this book; to go further would require data that illuminate the failure of power in organizing subjectivity. However, I am struck by the importance of the experience of resistance as key to individuals' capacity to take on meaning.

This seems very clear in Natalie's account. Her inchoate distrust of her bodily perceptions prevents her from having a base from which to differentiate one discourse from another. She has no basis for positioning herself within a particular set of meanings. Not being able to resist meaning, she also loses the capacity to accept meaning. The discourses she takes up, since she cannot charge them with acceptance or resistance, lose their meaning and become absurd. Absurdity stands outside regulation. Her baby could equally well be with its grandmother or with Natalie; either choice is absurd because neither relates to any real sense of meaning in her consciousness. Alcohol and tranquilizers make just as good sense as any other means of coping.

If we were to describe the major differences between Natalie, Tina, and Maria, we would have to locate those differences in the varying degrees of legitimacy each participant gives to her bodily experience of coherence or dysjuncture. We can see that for Tina and Maria, the acceptance of bodily experience permits a strong investment in ideology – but also the basis for resisting ideology, should one's perception of the randomness of experience be transformed. For Natalie, however, alienation from the body robs her of the feeling of coherence or non-coherence, and thus ensures a weak investment in ideology – so that her subjectivity, which *seems* most vulnerable to organization through ideology, is in fact the most weakly organized.

There is an odd space of optimism in the general sadness of Natalie's account. It somehow presents a view of ideology which is not imbued with power independent of people's everyday practices. We can see ideology as dependent on the very element that can change it: resistance. While at first I thought of Natalie as the perfect candidate for regulation, it soon became clear that she was no such thing. She turns regulation back on itself in the chaos of not being able to either accept or resist. Ideology in and of itself has no power.

CONCLUSION

I AM AWARE OF how a *real* conclusion should read: a final crash of the cymbals (symbols?) as prescriptions and advice are provided. But the reality is that the most meaningful conclusions are those made by readers as they connect their experiences with the information in a text. Much in the manner that it was impossible to predict the inferences that would be drawn from the accounts by Maria, Natalie and Tina, it is impossible now to provide an ending which states the "real" truth: there isn't any. But since I am a seeker, as is the reader of this book, what is perhaps valid is for me to summarize the impact that this inquiry has had on my thinking.

This book began with a description of the contradictions I experienced between feminism and mothering. The importance of the inquiry has been that I now see mothering and feminism not as fundamentally and uncomfortably opposed to each other, but as a connected site of struggle for women.

In becoming a mother I also became a Woman. That made me feel as though resisting patriarchy in some way meant resisting motherhood – yet the real experiences of my maternal body precluded such resistance. To find a way out of this apparent contradiction I had to move beyond an analysis of the social construction of mothering to an understanding of how those arrangements worked in everyday affairs to produce the concept Woman.

What made that move difficult was the blind alley of mother-infant attachment. Ever since Chodorow and Dinnerstein wrote that women's exclusive care of children produces gendered personality, preferential attachment between mothers and children has been indicted. The solution was simple: the special relationship of dependency and separation between mothers and infants had to be abolished. Equal parenting and daycare would rescue women as mothers. This solution struck me as surprisingly weak and disappointing, but I had to acknowledge that it was the only conclusion to which their work could lead.

A competing feminist discourse derived from radical feminist or gynocentric approaches. French feminists and American radical feminists urged women to regain the appropriated body of Woman; they said that women must connect to the experience of embodied womanhood, to their biological difference.

The contradictions between these two discourses are lived by mothers through conflicts which inevitably produce feelings either of failure as a mother or of failure as a feminist. The mother who attempts to experience "fully embodied womanhood" enacts that desire through such discursive practices as natural childbirth, or breastfeeding on demand; she eschews medical technology in favour of woman-centred midwifery. These very practices provide a base for preferential attachment between mothers and infants. However, in order to resist patriarchy, a mother must not lose her competitive edge by staying with her baby. Women live out such contradictory practices with the feeling of always doing something wrong; they possess no strategy which reconciles feminism and mothering.

Women live a silent despair that comes from trying to respond to contradictory statements about mothering. For instance, Chodorow concludes that equal parenting can end patriarchy – even though we know that babies are preferentially attached to their mothers. Much of the other literature from which we might have expected coherent strategies on mothering also slides over the attachment problem and arrives at equal parenting solutions – which, because they ignore preferential attachment, are therefore not real, possible, human solutions. Thus despair.

These solutions suffer from the very individualism that helps to construct the problem in the first place. For instance, if one attributes the problems of mothering to the characteristics of a particular relationship between two people, then the solution has to be seen in terms of changing the nature of the relationship. What is avoided in this formulation is an examination of the ways in which power operates to produce a Woman who is herself – in any relationship – coherent with capitalist patriarchy.

Solutions that privilege women's bodies are also individualistic, in that they ascribe an essential difference to women's experience because of sex.

I think that at the core of this dilemma is a phobic reaction to the idea of preferential attachment. Failing an analysis of the concept of Woman as organized through mothering, attachment has been scapegoated as responsible for gender relations. In and of itself, a baby's separation from its mother is not by definition oppressive, nor is it necessarily the basis for gender identity and gender divisions of labour. What implicates the experience of separation in the formation of gender identity is the construction of the concept Woman through sole caretaking. I believe that gender identity is rooted in the concepts of Man and Woman within which separation occurs – rather than in the fact of separation itself. If it were not for the existence of the category Woman, we would be able to separate from the *person* out of whose womb we emerged, rather than from a Woman.

We must be very clear that it is not the fact of children's biological dependence on and separation from women that constricts women's lives within the private sphere. It is capitalist patriarchy which requires forms of control that organize the possibilities of motherhood: forms of control that continually inscribe the category Woman. Monique Wittig (1979) is brilliantly clear on this point. She insists that we continually see our entrapment as biologically based because we cannot see ourselves as anything but Woman. Speaking of the categories of race and sex, she says,

> However, now, race, exactly like sex, is taken as an 'immediate given,' 'a sensible given,' 'physical features.' They appear as though they existed prior to reasoning, belonging to a natural order. (Wittig, 1979, p. 71)

In such a way, preferential attachment is seen to "naturally" hold *women* to the private sphere. If babies separate from women, women must be with babies; thus women's place is defined as immutable. What we fail to see here is that Woman's place is a social construction that has nothing to do with babies, but which derives from the place of Woman in capitalist patriarchy.

I am arguing for a re-focusing of attention away from *women's reproduction of mothering* and toward the practice of *mothering as it creates the gender category Woman*. Such a focus renders the polarization of biology and culture irrelevant. The object of the question becomes to discover how Woman's body is constructed through giving birth; how infant attachment rationalizes particular social arrangements; how mothering produces Woman in relationship to work structures and family structures. Framing the question in those terms demands answers which do not attribute women's oppression to single causes, but rather provide complex, concrete descriptions of how the daily experience of being human is always an experience of being organized in and through the concepts of Man or Woman.

The question itself implies that analysis must come from an examination of historical, material and discursive practices. It is a question which rejects approaches that ask "why" in any universal sense. What it aims at instead is a complex, unruly, layered and contradictory description of how, in our society, bodies with breasts and vaginas become Woman and how bodies with penises become Man.

It is such future theory that holds the promise of liberation for me as a mother. That liberation will come from severing the automatic connection between the fact of an infant attached preferentially to me as the body of birth and nourishment, and the category Woman. To break away from the polarization imposed by culturalist or biologistic explanations of the reproduction of mothering is liberating in two ways: it allows for the experienced reality of the female body, with its physical tie to infants; and it shows that the attachment born from that physical tie does not necessarily reinforce patriarchy because, as gender categories are refused, an infant's separation is not effected from a Woman.

As long as the search for a universal cause of women's subordination is at the centre of feminist interest, we will be unable to invent coherent strategies as feminist mothers. In order to break out of this fruitless search, our focus must shift to attempts to understand the everyday constitution of Man and Woman through historically located, specific accounts of power and desire.

With such a shift in focus, it at once becomes clear that feminist action on diverse and sometimes contradictory fronts makes sense. Gynocentric approaches – for example, a women's peace movement – while seemingly forged in terms of the re-creation of Woman, can in fact highlight the inadequacies of conceptualizing people as Woman or Man.

It is also possible that exploration of the personal meaning of gender categories is necessary in order to refuse the shame that is essential to the ongoing definition of people as Woman and Man. "Understanding what it means to be a woman," which takes place in various sites – consciousness-raising groups or French écriture – attempts to displace shame as a means of rejecting given reality. This is important to the long-term goal of refusing gender categories.

Furthermore, with a long-term goal of dismantling the category Woman, we are better equipped to deal with the State's attempts to handle women's issues while retaining the status quo. We know very well that when the State gives in to women's demands there is always the danger that women will be appropriated into the State's agenda. If we keep in mind the removal of Woman from motherhood, when the State gives five million dollars for daycare, as it has recently done in Canada, we can ask ourselves some hard questions about how to use this resource in a way that meets immediate needs but at the same time chips away at the concept of Woman in motherhood. How do we develop daycare in a way that helps to breach the boundaries between the public and private, rather than creating yet another ghetto / institution for children? How do we plan daycare in such a way that we confront men with their responsibility for caretaking, rather than professionalizing (while simultaneously underpaying and devaluing) caretaking by women?

We can begin to liberate our imagination with respect to what our child-raising arrangements would look like if we abolished the categories through which they are currently organized. We can begin to imagine a culture in which children are a part of life, and in which life is not divided into "play" and "work." We can begin to imagine granting children the freedom to be no more or less "special" than other people, and, therefore, to be able to participate in the world. This must be a world in which "mother" and "father" are, not concepts which exist within the categories of Woman and Man, but concepts of the category of person. We can imagine a world in which the necessity for separation does not create an interruption to real life – to be carried out under special conditions only (i.e., in private) – but rather is a part of life, no different from eating, sleeping or moving: taken for granted as part of being human. In this kind of world, the need to feed an infant would not restrict one's participation in the world, and caretaking would not be denigrated or devalued; these activities would be seen simply as necessary elements of one of the ways of being a fully grounded human being.

REFUSING "WOMAN"

If the conclusion to this inquiry is that we must resist the concept of Woman in capitalist patriarchy, then to discover how to do so we must return to the experiences of Maria, Tina, and Natalie. We must look at how power acts through the body to produce Woman, how power works through women's social space to produce Woman as caretaker.

The lesson learned from all three subjects' experiences of birth is that we must reject discourses of women's bodies as objects, and search out positions which produce a subjectivity that unifies self and body.

Maria, for example, had clear preferences for a particular kind of birth. In Maria's social space, however, few discourses exist which conceptualize women's bodies as other than passive objects of the male gaze. Thus, the only discourse available to her for explaining why she didn't get what she wanted was *disappointment in her body*. Logically enough, her disappointment in having her birth preferences ignored carried over into a view of her body as being a disappointing shape.

Tina kept an image of her active, birthing body in a "little box," which she could open from time to time for a glimpse of that image. The image of an active body simply had no field of congruent discourses which would allow her to integrate the birth into her everyday life; it therefore remained compartmentalized.

We need to expand language in order to invent discourses which acknowledge and celebrate capacities of women's bodies other than the ability to be sexually attractive in regulated ways. Such discourses imply radical social change: they are discourses which in fact subvert patriarchy by redefining power over the body. By permitting women to be persons who are valuable in their own right, they inevitably undermine a social order which defines women as valuable only in the service of men.

There are many routes toward such a re-ordering of our language and thought. For Maria, social support for the glimmers of pre-anger at her obstetrician would have helped her to conceptualize her body differently. A reframing of Tony's insistence that she lose weight – from a matter of his rights to a matter of his fear of masculine inadequacy – would have been a step toward empowering Maria. Discourses that recognize the enormous physical demands of pregnancy and lactation would have helped her respect the changes in her body, rather than mediate them through disappointment.

Tina, too, suffered from the silences which support discourses of women's bodies as objects. Tina had no discourses with which to make truth from her sense of "I did it." Tina felt that, for once in her life, her body had been just right: it had functioned for her own purpose; it hadn't needed to be different in any way. But under what conditions would "I did it" *not* have stood out as special, but felt congruent with her "normal" experience of her body?

Feminism has begun to create new discourses of women's bodies. Gynocentric feminism, which reveres the female body and encourages the conceptualization of separate female experience, ironically has been most useful in moving toward the goal of destroying gender categories: it has provided a critical strategy for experiencing feeling "for ourselves" – part of the necessary work of re-ordering our subjectivity. Gynocentric approaches reject the validity of the male gaze and push women's otherness so far that it becomes difference. While I do not share the goal of revering woman, I believe that such shifts of meaning – dislocations – within the concept of Woman are helpful moves toward the eventual abolition of the organization of culture through gender.

For me, the dislocations mean living with uncertainty and indecision. They mean constantly checking up on reactions to my body. Is it really important for me to retain my hairy legs because I want to resist my own feminization? I look at my pot belly with disgust – it's my male gaze looking in the mirror. It takes effort to remind myself that I am 40 years old, have had two babies, and won't be abandoned because of my fat.

I frequently wonder if these small sites of discomfort are really worth it: they seem so petty and so disconnected from larger social change. Natalie's account, however, reminds me of the danger of not resisting in these sites. Disembodied, split between body and self, her ability to name her own reality is disabled. Given that our liberation depends on the creation of our own names in discourse, it behooves me to remember that the petty, the ordinary, the everyday, *is* the larger social order.

REFUSING THE IDENTIFICATION OF WOMAN AS CARETAKER

Maintaining relations of domination between Man and Woman depends to a considerable extent on seeing women as caretakers. The activity of caretaking is devalued and socially denigrated; the work of power, then, is to fashion women's subjectivities so that doing caretaking is common sense, "natural and normal."

Babies' physical attachment to their mothers has been a major contributor to the ideological creation of Woman as caretaker. The fact of gestation and early infant attachment has acted as a justification for childrearing arrangements that, in reality, have been created in response to the needs of capitalist patriarchy, *not* the needs of dependent infants. Infant dependency is the foundation for claims that the separation of public and private is "natural"; once this separation has been convincingly presented as a matter of common sense, the structure of women's political, economic and social subordination is justified.

Tina, Maria, and Natalie all became totally identified as caretakers not because of the needs of their children, but because of the material, historical, and discursive factors which make sole caretaking the only possibility for women with children in our culture.

Maria's training as a "good girl" made her automatically forgo her own needs in favour of taking care of her husband and child. She lost the data from which to consider taking care of herself. She was positioned between Portuguese and Canadian culture – where both cultures, in different ways, held her solely responsible for caretaking. She was isolated, not because of her baby, but because our social arrangements preclude a baby's intrusion into public space. Maria was made aware of this prohibition every time she took public transit or tried to go out for dinner.

In Tina and Ernie's relationship, isolation structured Tina's need for predictability in daily routines. Ernie did not share this need, as he was not isolated at home with the baby. Tina's need for predictability slid into a need for control, and for sole responsibility toward the baby – producing a dynamic between Tina and Ernie in which Tina was responsible, and Ernie was irresponsible. Tina was a caretaker; Ernie was not. This dynamic had nothing to do with the baby's dependence on Tina, but was a direct result of Tina's isolation and the social devaluation of the caretaking role.

Natalie's story gives us insight into the process of her encapsulation as caretaker through discourses of mothering.

Believing mothering to be "just natural," she was devastated by the dysjuncture between her expectations and her experience. She isolated herself in order to protect herself from the harsh judgements she expected from the world – a projection of her dislike of herself – and became firmly cemented as sole caretaker by that self-imposed isolation. She, too, became sole caretaker, not because of the demands of her baby, but because of the social arrangements that produce mothering as we know it.

What these stories suggest to me is the need for a new conception of nurturing. Such a conception must start with women discovering and respecting their own boundaries: their own need and ability to take care of themselves. Ideals of mothers as selfless and passive must capitulate to the reality of mothers as persons. Women must learn to distinguish their own needs and act on them. From the position of strength gained thereby, women can begin to demand that men do their share of caretaking. The gendered division of caretaking has created men who are out of touch with needs other than their own and women who have only the haziest idea of their own needs. By beginning to take care of themselves, women can change this distorted equilibrium.

Even as I say this, I become aware of the guilt that regulates my own "needlessness" – my feminine subjectivity. I say to myself, "But what about the children – who will take care of them?" It makes me furious that I have once more fallen for the false dichotomies created to regulate me as Woman: I have been told that if I meet my own needs my children will suffer. I struggle for words to express my conviction that my children do not exist at my expense – that they are enriched and helped to gain their own personhood when they separate from a mother who has her own boundaries and an ability to take care of herself. When one of the ways of taking care of myself is to demand participation in caretaking from their father, I must work to stifle the voice that says "bitch, nag" and instead congratulate myself on my contribution to fully human fatherhood.

Three related factors in the lives of women make our claims very difficult to act on. They are: the isolation of mothers; the separation between public and private; and the values of the workplace.

Isolation is a form of oppression on a day-to-day basis, as well as being directly implicated in the production of gender identity. Isolation produces a sense of loss of self, as one's work is reduced to invisibility. It punishes children by not allowing them to participate in the world. It holds children to blame for their needs, which are in fact distorted and exaggerated through isolation. It robs women of the ability to organize collectively. It stanches both women's and children's creative potential.

It is politically important to make the work of mothering visible and to demonstrate how that work is organized in conditions of isolation. Women must have a discourse which does not blame them as bad mothers – or their children as too demanding – when the oppression of isolation is felt. A discourse which indicts isolation must become broadly known.

Capitalism has instilled us with values which force us to make paid work take priority over caring for our young; this priority is re-enforced through keeping children invisible in the workplace. This is particularly painful for fathers, whose corporate masculinity depends on never being needed by their own children.

Capitalism is afraid of children. Children don't recognize a split between work and play – they have to be taught that schismatic heresy so fundamental to capitalism. Children therefore threaten the values of the workplace; they stand as a group which needs constant regulation – provided by mothers and schools – toward capitalist values. In order to effectively ensure that such regulation takes place, women with children are prohibited from breaching the boundaries between public and private. As mothers, we are good at respecting and maintaining those boundaries, because of our guilt.

We truly live with the belief that it is not possible to work with children around. We cannot afford to maintain this belief, and must question its validity. We have to begin to invent models which show how parents can enter the public sphere *with* their children. We don't know which work really can't be done around children and which work can. We must observe mothers who are able to work effectively alongside their children, and we must understand that they can accomplish work where a differently constituted group might not be able to because they take the presence of children for granted. Interruption is normal; well, we must all share the interruptions that are imposed by the need to care for our young. We cannot go on placing the values of capitalist patriarchy before the need to reproduce the species. We must raise children in a way that abolishes in them the desire to dominate.

Because the spaces that create the possibility for change are so ordinary, so daily, it is easy to condemn efforts at change on the grounds that they are dealing merely with trivia. Our own regulation exists in such tiny ways that even refusal seems to rob us of personal power. We have to try not to lie when we have to leave a meeting in order to take the kids to a birthday party; we have to face the discomfort of breaking the public/private split by declaring what we really have to do. It is precisely the petty sites that tell us about the larger social order.

The messages sent to women telling us to stay in the private sphere are constant, and provide real barriers to occupying public space. We have to rethink how our world would be organized without a public/private split. Women must participate in public life because it is there that decisions about us are made, discourses about us are created, and images of Woman are shaped.

EDUCATION FOR
FEMINIST CRITICAL CONSCIOUSNESS

So far, I have talked about refusing the social arrangements which create the concept of Woman through mothering. We can't, however, simply declare our unwillingness to "allow" patriarchy. The problem is that patriarchy *is* us. We need a very different kind of education to be able to see past our subjectivity, past the "natural and normal," into our regulation as Woman.

In this book's three accounts, we have seen the operation of double consciousness – ideological meanings which prevail despite a contradictory experienced reality. I believe it is just these contradictions that offer us the potential for change, for two reasons: first, because experienced reality is our only resource for making discourses which describe women's reality; and second, because the ideological meaning gives us a piece of information about our regulation and therefore gives us a tool for making resistance. Thus, locating the dysjunctures between experience and meaning gives us a position from which to resist, from which to re-envision our own subjectivity.

However, as we saw in the accounts, there is a barrier set up to prevent recognition of these dysjunctures: shame. Power has already/always operated through our bodies to fashion us as Other, as Object. We *begin* from a position of shame. Consequently, when our experiences fall outside the dominant pattern of regulation, we read shame from the dysjuncture.

Education for feminist critical consciousness must insist that every moment of shame is a potential site for undoing oppression. In educating ourselves we will have to start with shame as our richest resource.

I am reminded of my daughter when she was doing a bead-work project at school. She was supposed to work from a pattern so that the project would look "right." She did not follow the pattern. She wanted to find a different way of doing it. There was no discourse or language that could support her in a different way of working, however, so when she finished the project, she hated it because it didn't look like the other kids' work. She was ashamed.

I tell this story to illustrate two critical components of feminist education. One is the need to create and propagate discourses that value different experiences: experiences that fall outside dominant meanings. The other is the need to discover connections which will enable us to support each other while claiming difference. We require connections and support because difference is our shame, *at the same time* that it is the route to a society where differences exist among people, rather than between Man and Woman.

The complex interactions that produce our social formation are precisely what give cause for optimism about such a program of feminist education. As we have seen repeatedly throughout this book, no step in the dance of being created/ creating ourselves is done independently. This means that individual and collective spaces for refusal are not as small as they feel; each has the potential to reverberate throughout subjectivity, promoting discourses which are rich in conflict and therefore rich with the promise of change.

REFERENCES

Arney, William Ray. 1980. Maternal-Infant Bonding: The Politics of Falling in Love with Your Child. *Feminist Studies,* 6 (3), 547-69.

Chesler, Phyllis. 1981. *With Child.* New York: Berkeley.

Chodorow, Nancy. 1978. *The Reproduction of Mothering.* Berkeley: University of California Press.

Coward, Rosalind. 1983. *Patriarchal Precedents: Sexuality and Social Relations.* London: Routledge & Kegan Paul.

Daly, Mary. 1978. *Gyn/Ecology: The Metaethics of Radical Feminism.* Boston: Beacon Press.

Dinnerstein, Dorothy. 1976. *The Mermaid and the Minotaur: Sexual Arrangements and Human Malaise.* New York: Harper & Row.

Foucault, Michel. 1981. Questions of Method: An Interview with Michel Foucault. *Ideology and Consciousness,* 8, 3-14.

Foucault, Michel. 1982. The Subjectt and Power. *Critical Inquiry,* 8, 777-795.

Friedan, Betty. 1963. *The Feminine Mystique.* New York: W.W. Norton & Co., Inc.

Harrison, Michelle. 1982. *A Woman in Residence: A Doctor's Personal and Professional Battles Against an Insensitive Medical System.* New York: Penguin.

Hobson, Dorothy. 1978. Housewives: Isolation as Oppression. In *Women Take Issue,* edited by the Women's Studies Group, Centre for Contemporary Cultural Studies. London: Hutchinson.

Hollway, Wendy. 1984. Gender Differentiation and the Production of Subjectivity. In *Changing the Subject,* edited by W. Henriques, W. Hollway, C. Urwin, C. Venn, and V. Walkerdine. London: Methuen.

Laing, R.D. 1960. *The Divided Self.* Harmondsworth, England: Penguin Books.

Miller, Jean Baker. 1976. *Toward a New Psychology of Women.* Boston: Beacon Press.

Oakley, Ann. 1974. *The Sociology of Housework.* London: Martin Robertson.

Oakley, Ann. 1981b. Interviewing Women: A Contradiction in Terms. In *Doing Feminist Research,* edited by H. Roberts. London: Routledge & Kegan Paul.

Olsen, Tillie. 1965. *Silences.* New York: Dell.

Rich, Adrienne. 1976. *Of Woman Born.* New York: W.W. Norton & Co., Inc.

Rowbotham, Sheila. 1973. *Woman's Consciousness, Man's World.* Harmondsworth, England: Penguin Books.

Ruddick, S. 1984. Maternal Thinking. In *Mothering: Essays in Feminist Theory,* edited by J. Trebilcot. Totowa, New Jersey: Rowman & Allanheld.

Scheman, Naomi. 1980. Anger and the Politics of Naming. In *Women and Language in Literature and Society,* edited by S. McConnell-Ginet, R. Borker, and N. Furman. New York: Praeger.

Smith, Dorothy E.. 1981. *The Experienced World as Problematic: A Feminist Method.* Sorokin Lectures, No. 12. Saskatoon: University of Saskatchewan.

Spender, Dale. 1980. *Man Made Language.* London: Routledge & Kegan Paul.